THE
POLITICS
OF
AFFLUENCE

Chandler Publications in
POLITICAL SCIENCE
Victor Jones, *Editor*

Science Research Associates, Inc., 259 East Erie Street, Chicago, Illinois 60611
Distributors   A Subsidiary of IBM

THE
POLITICS OF
AFFLUENCE

IDEOLOGY IN THE UNITED STATES
SINCE WORLD WAR II

JAMES P. YOUNG
STATE UNIVERSITY OF NEW YORK
AT BINGHAMTON

Chandler Publishing Company
124 SPEAR STREET, SAN FRANCISCO, CALIFORNIA 94105

FOR GLADYS

❧ CONTENTS ❧

IV. THE BASES OF CONSERVATISM 85

V. THE PUBLIC POLICIES OF CONSERVATISM 123

VI. THE PROBLEM OF FOREIGN POLICY 145

VII. THE PROBLEM OF EQUAL RIGHTS 173

❦ PREFACE ❦

I hope that this book speaks for itself so that no extensive preface is necessary. However, I should like to emphasize a point made in the introduction: namely, that this study is not a comprehensive treatise. Instead it is a selective and highly personal interpretation of some of the main developments of recent American political thought. Its prime purpose is to provoke discussion and I hope it will do so.

A word might be said about the documentation provided. Since there is a good deal of purely expository writing, it would be all too easy to overburden the text with footnotes. To avoid this, I have provided notes for only those passages which are crucial to either my argument or that of the author under discussion. For the rest, the citations in the supplementary bibliographies provide an additional guide to the sources. Where precise notes are not provided, I have tried to indicate the general source in the body of the text.

It remains to acknowledge the many debts I have accumulated while working on this study. Portions of four chapters are substantially revised versions of corresponding sections of my doctoral dissertation at the University of Michigan. I should like to thank my advisers on that project: George Peek, Frank Grace, John White, Roy Pierce, and Sidney Fine. I learned much from all of them. An early draft of the present manuscript was given a detailed and scrupulously fair reading by Raymond English. It was a model of the sort of prepublication critique any author would like to receive. The manuscript was also read in whole or in part by Victor Jones, Herbert Gutman, and Stewart Easton—all of whom made useful contributions. I owe a great debt to my good friends and former colleagues, Kurt Shell and James Farganis. Innumerable conversations over a period of several years are reflected in the book. They will not always agree, but our friendship would not be what it is if they did.

Scholarly convention calls upon me to absolve all the above from any responsibility for what appears here.

My wife Gladys has performed all of the traditional tasks of the traditional academic wife in the traditionally outstanding fashion.

THE
POLITICS
OF
AFFLUENCE

CHAPTER I

INTRODUCTION

In recent years American political scientists have displayed a lamentable lack of professional concern for the content of public policy. Though there are exceptions—Hans Morgenthau being perhaps the most notable—it is striking how few of the men discussed in these pages are political scientists. In their zeal to advance the scientific status of the discipline, political scientists have thus often turned their backs on the kinds of questions which have provided the impetus for a large portion of the great works in the history of political thought. All great political theory has sprung from the effort to come to grips with the critical political issues of the time. In a real sense, political scientists today are derelict in their responsibility when they abstain from the age-old functions of clarifying values and criticizing policy alternatives. It is true that no "scientific" claim to find solutions for the problems that beset society can be made; we all know that the evidence is not yet in, that science advances by eschewing engineering applications and concentrating on basic research. There are any number of similar arguments, and they are persuasive, I think—but not persuasive enough. Political scientists certainly have no monopoly of possible solutions, but it is not implausible to argue, as did Harold Lasswell,* that a coalition of social philosophers, public lawyers, historians, and behavioral scientists is particularly well qualified to criticize public policy and the intellectual assumptions on which it rests. We might do well to ask ourselves the question posed by the philosopher Walter Kaufmann in *The Faith of a Heretic:* "If I do not speak up, who will? And if not now, when?"

This book assesses from the point of view of a political scientist some of the ideas about the good society that are current today. But there is more here than a philosophical, ideological, or critical perspective. To understand scientifically what is happening in a political system, it is necessary to understand the *context* of ideas, the climate of opinion in which political action takes place. Context is particularly relevant in a political system such as ours which seems to be entering a significant transitional period. It is not essential to go into the vexed question of the role of ideas in social change; it is sufficient to underline the assumption that ideas do count significantly. It is as easy to dismiss the extreme materialist argument that ideas have no substantial role in history as it is to demolish the position of extreme idealists that ideas are all that really matter. If the intermediate view has merit, then it follows that one of the significant variables for analysis in a polity is its political thought. The emergence of new ideological trends is a factor of great importance in assessing the past, present, and future of a political system. Therefore, this book attempts not only to consider some opinions on what *ought to be* in our country, but also to examine a form of behavior that may be of genuine consequence in determining and understanding what *is*.

Before any opinions may be examined, it is necessary to examine the setting of ideological conflict in America. Ideology does not exist in a social or political vacuum. On the contrary, it is the product of a particular historical and cultural context. Patterns of ideological thought thus tend to be different from country to country and indeed may contribute much to the explanation of differences among political systems. Accordingly, it could be argued quite persuasively that many of the differences between French and American politics are related to differences in the prevailing ideological tendencies. However, in order to understand

---

* For references not cited in footnotes, see the Bibliographical Notes at the end of each chapter.

the changing patterns of ideas, it is necessary to examine the mainstream of American political thought so that we have a standard against which to judge change and continuity.

The Great Consensus

The first major theme to be considered is the lack of a feudal tradition. American scholars have often sensed that much that is unique in American history is the product of our sharp break with the European past. As Alexis de Tocqueville wrote more than a century ago, "America is a society where everyone is born equal." Seizing on this insight, Louis Hartz has elaborated it into a comprehensive interpretation of our history. In *The Liberal Tradition in America*, Hartz argues that the consequences of the absence of feudalism are immense. In a sense, Hartz suggests, we are all Lockean liberals in America. We are the captives of a sometimes irrational Lockean ideology. The meaning of this "Lockeanism" is never precisely spelled out by Hartz, but it clearly includes rationalism, constitutionalism, individualism, and laissez-faire economics. The widespread commitment to these ideals suggests reasons why America has lacked a viable socialist movement and at the same time any genuinely reactionary tradition. Reaction can have little force when there is no aristocratic, feudal Golden Age to look back on. Similarly, Hartz argues, socialism has not taken root because this ideology tends to be a response to the inequalities of a feudal regime; where there is no feudalism, there is no socialism.

Thus the spectrum of conflict in American politics is very narrow. There is a basic agreement—particularly on the institutions of government, but on the day-to-day issues of politics as well—which tends to submerge conflict in a sea of consensus. Indeed, to Hartz, the basic danger in our society is unanimity and the consequent pressure on the dissenter to conform. Since we are all liberals, we have a deep-seated distrust of those who are not—a fact which has two notable effects. First, "it hampers creative action abroad by identifying the alien with the unintelligible" and, second, "it inspires hysteria at home by generating the anxiety that unintelligible things produce."[1] As a result, the unanimity of our

---

[1] Louis Hartz, *The Liberal Tradition in America* (New York: Harcourt, 1955), p. 285.

tradition makes it especially difficult for us to understand the world around us or even to understand ourselves.

The second aspect of our ideological environment is a long-standing commitment to some form of capitalist economy. One of the most illuminating works on this theme is *The American Political Tradition*. To Hofstadter, the dominant tradition of American politics may be described as an "ideology of self-help, free enterprise, competition, and beneficent cupidity." We believe in private prosperity, individualism, competition, and the inevitability of positive results flowing from the pursuit of self-interest.[2]

In this view, the framers of the Constitution were interested in building institutions designed to leave men free to compete for property. Similarly, Jacksonian democracy is seen as a movement aimed at the separation of business and government, and its long-range impact was to facilitate the rise of liberal capitalism. Even the twentieth-century reform movements (with the possible exception of the New Deal) are seen as attempts to rescue capitalism from itself and to preserve the competitive economy celebrated in the ideology.

It should be clear that the Hartz and Hofstadter theses are complementary. Their similarity lies in the emphasis on the essential unity of American history rather than on conflict. Moreover, the emphasis on John Locke in the work of Hartz dovetails nicely with the thesis of Hofstadter. According to Hartz, the absence of a feudal tradition has made us all Lockean liberals, and for Locke the most important of the natural rights celebrated in the *Second Treatise* is the right of property. This theory is not without its ambiguities, but there is no doubt, as Robert McCloskey has pointed out, that the practical result of Locke's work was a justification not only of the British revolution of 1688 and consequently of democratic government, but also of Western capitalism.[3] Thus, by embracing Locke, we have embraced liberal capitalism as well.

The view of the American political tradition developed here emphasizes consensus. Such a view is essential to understanding

---

[2] Richard Hofstadter, *The American Political Tradition* (New York: Random House, Vintage Books, 1954), pp. vii–viii.

[3] For McCloskey's argument, see his *American Conservatism in the Age of Enterprise: 1865–1910* (New York: Harper, Torchbooks, 1964), pp. 1–21.

because it contributes to an explanation of the remarkably restrained tone of political debate in America. Our political differences are, as a rule, not deeply felt; we do not often argue about the fundamental character of our political system or economic system. However, it would be erroneous to conclude that conflict is insignificant in American politics. No society is ever completely consensual. The consensus merely provides a framework within which conflict takes place. If the consensus is not widely shared at least among the elite groups, the conflicts may get out of hand and in extreme cases may destroy the society. It was this sort of crisis in consensus which eventuated in the American Civil War. Moreover, as Robert Dahl has pointed out, the Civil War was only the most serious of the conflicts which have wracked American politics on the average of once a generation.

Any political or ideological analysis must therefore take into account both conflict and consensus. There has been a tendency in recent writing about American politics to overemphasize the consensual factors. Thus it is important to be quite clear that there has been significant conflict within the confines of our political tradition. The principal disagreements—though by no means the only ones—have been in the area of political economy. Agreement on the fundamentals of a capitalist economy does not rule out controversy over the way the benefits of such an economy are to be distributed. It is in the sphere of political economy that liberalism and conservatism enter the American political scene.

To make this point at the outset raises problems. Ideologies are notoriously hard to define or to discuss with any degree of clarity. With *liberalism* and *conservatism,* the difficulty is so acute as to render the terms very nearly meaningless. Therefore, it may be that these labels are no longer useful. Yet such is the frequency of their use and the human passion for categorization that it is virtually impossible to write about political affairs without resorting to them. As a result, it is necessary to make provisional use of these terms. In the concluding chapter, it may be possible to shed further light on their utility. In any event, since a large portion of this book is devoted to defining the position of today's liberals and conservatives, it will suffice at this point to sketch in a rough outline of the sense in which the terms will be used.

American history has been predominantly a struggle between

those forces which have been concerned with the exploitation and development of economic resources and those which have tried to "humanize" the workings of the system, to "heal its casualties," and to work for a more equitable distribution of the fruits of the system.[4] This interpretation brings us close to the heart of the conception of liberalism used in this book. The conception is by no means precise; as Andrew Hacker has suggested, this brand of liberalism expresses a mood rather than a coherent policy. Nevertheless, some general guidelines for policy may be found. To secure the general goals noted by Hofstadter, the liberal has turned more and more to government. In modern America he has characteristically adhered to the belief that private persons cannot or will not act to solve these problems, with the result that government must assume this role. Thus, health, housing, education, working conditions, wage levels, the functioning of the economy—in brief, most matters of social welfare—are causes for governmental concern.[5]

The philosophical premise on which this political stance rests is a fundamental commitment to egalitarianism. As Hacker notes, the liberal assumes that heredity is less important to individual development than is environment and that, given equal opportunity, people from all levels of the socioeconomic structure may rise to the top and achieve success in business, in the arts, and in life itself.

Here, then, is an interesting development in the history of liberalism. The earliest liberals, like Locke, placed great stress on the autonomous, even atomistic individual. This idea was later developed by the Manchesterian liberals into the rather negative

---

[4] Richard Hofstadter, *The Age of Reform* (New York: Knopf, 1955), pp. 17–18. A similar view is taken by Arthur Schlesinger, Jr., *The Age of Jackson* (Boston: Little, Brown, 1945), p. 514: "This has been the irrepressible conflict of capitalism: the struggle on the part of the rest of society, under the leadership of 'liberals' to check the political ambitions of business." It should be pointed out that this view is by no means universally accepted. See Arthur Mann, "The Progressive Tradition," in John Higham, ed., *The Reconstruction of American History* (New York: Harper, Torchbooks, 1962), pp. 177–178.

[5] For a discussion of this variety of liberalism and others, see Andrew Hacker, *Political Theory: Philosophy, Ideology, Science* (New York: Macmillan, 1961), pp. 237–244.

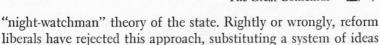

"night-watchman" theory of the state. Rightly or wrongly, reform liberals have rejected this approach, substituting a system of ideas in which government is seen as having a positive role in creating conditions under which the individual can flourish. It is with this variety of reformist liberalism that this book will be largely concerned.

Paradoxically, it is to the earlier liberal tradition that much of American conservatism is indebted. Thus both the conservative and the liberal tradition in America have common roots in a highly individualistic conception of the nature of society. They have differed largely over the means by which the individual is to be served. Conservatives have resisted egalitarian liberal measures on the grounds that they are really leveling devices designed to obliterate any real distinction by reducing all to a least common denominator and that they often represent an assault on the rights of private property, which conservatives feel to be the foundation of real freedom. As a result, much of the political conflict of American history—particularly since the Civil War—has centered around the proper role of the government in relation to the economy. On the whole, the proponents of laissez-faire have succeeded in resisting governmental expansion—except in those limited areas in which they themselves desired interventions—until quite recent times. Thus it can be argued that, in terms of policy output, the American political tradition can best be labeled conservative. On the other hand, at the level of formal political thought, American thinkers have generally been part of the liberal-reform tradition. At best, *this* group wins only occasional victories. In the sense that the term is used here, the American liberal has *normally* been in the minority. The fact that he is no longer in the minority has significant consequences which will be examined in detail later in the book.

Having isolated the central tradition and the main thrust of the liberal opposition is not sufficient. It is now necessary to distinguish between economic and noneconomic liberalism, that is, between a liberalism concerned with the distribution of economic benefits and one concerned with such problems as civil liberties, race relations, and foreign affairs. The introduction of these dimensions of political conflict greatly complicates a heretofore simple analysis. The difficulty is that not all of those who qualify as liberal on economic issues may be similarly classified on noneconomic matters. For instance, there is a clear correlation between noneconomic liberalism and high socioeconomic status, while support for liberal social-welfare measures is often coupled with low socioeconomic standing. Thus it is quite possible for these dimensions to cut across each other, so that a person may be liberal or conservative according to one measure but not according to the other. Professional politicians are almost as likely to be beset by these tensions as is the rank and file. In the 1930's, for example, many of the leading liberals on social-welfare issues were leaders of the isolationist movement. This is one reason why the two-class dichotomy posed by Marx appears too simple, at least in the context of American politics.

The best hope of finding consistency is to turn to political writers—the publicists and thinkers. These are the men whose function is to clarify policy alternatives and the philosophical foundations on which they rest. An examination of the journals of opinion reveals liberal consensus around egalitarianism, a positive role for the government (particularly with respect to the regulation of business activities), the achievement of civil rights through government action, and a commitment to international cooperation in the field of foreign affairs. American conservatives, on the other hand, are less likely to be egalitarian; they tend to resist, if not reject, a positive role for government; and they argue for a foreign policy emphasizing the independence of the United States from excessive consideration of other nations. On civil rights the pattern is mixed. Conservatives espouse the cause; but if a conflict with the values of states' rights or private-property rights arises, civil rights may give way. Needless to say, this is only a bare outline of the conservative and liberal traditions, whose substance will be filled in the course of this book.

The Dilemma of American Political Thought

American political thought is passing through a transitional period. The essence of the crisis is that the United States is faced with a set of issues unlike any it has faced before. Large segments of the population may now be classified as affluent, so that a political and economic system geared to the distribution of scarce goods no longer seems entirely appropriate. At the same time, the euphemistically labeled "pockets of poverty" which infect the economy seem strangely resistant to the same sort of economic upgrading that brought a high standard of living to the majority. Conservatives and liberals alike have become increasingly concerned with the pressures for conformity and, indeed, with the fundamental quality of life in a modern industrial society. We are in the midst of a veritable revolution in the area of civil rights. Perhaps most important of all are the new facts of international life: the rapid process of decolonization since World War II, the rise of powers fully capable of challenging America's world supremacy, and, above all, the threat of nuclear destruction inherent in "the balance of terror." Moreover, many of these problems interlock. Thus, the civil-rights issue affects our international relations—particularly with the developing nations. At the same time, the issue is closely linked to the matter of chronic poverty, since one of the forms taken by discrimination is the exclusion of Negroes from jobs and, perhaps even more critically, from the training required to hold jobs in a society increasingly dependent on highly skilled labor.

All of these dilemmas seem to call for a fundamental rethinking of traditional American responses to political problems. The natural instinct may be to retreat to solutions found helpful in the past. For some extremist groups this instinct takes the form of a headlong flight backwards to a distorted image of past values, bearing all the earmarks of a frantic paranoia. No nation can ever completely transcend its past, nor should it want to. Even Edmund Burke, the greatest conservative of all, realized that on occasion change is the means of a society's preservation. There is such an occasion today. We need to examine carefully the sources of our political tradition in order to determine what is of use in meeting new realities, and we need careful explorations of new approaches which are as much in keeping with the essence of our traditions as possible.

The Organization of This Book

There have been some rather fragmentary attempts to come to grips with the new problems outlined here. None has been wholly successful, but scattered insights of high quality abound. This book is largely concerned with an assessment of these developments as well as with some of the intellectual impediments hampering the evolution of effective new thinking and policies. A few notes about the structure and intent of the book may be helpful.

First, the organization is thematic. The material is arranged topically, and there is thus no effort to trace the thought of any particular thinker or set of thinkers through each and every one of the subjects with which the book deals. As a matter of fact, few, if any, of the writers under consideration have expressed themselves on all the topics dealt with. This fact in itself is a reflection on the state of contemporary American thought, which seems determined to shy away from comprehensive approaches to "the big problems."

Second, this book is primarily about ideologies rather than political philosophy. Provisionally, an *ideology* may be defined as a coherent, action-related set of ideas encompassing a view of the world as it is, a view of the world as it should be, and a program designed to achieve ideals in practice. The traditional problems of political philosophy (the nature of man, the source of law, the basis of obligation, and the like) will be considered only to the extent that they bear on the less abstract, policy-oriented concerns of ideology.

Because of the action-related nature of ideology, I have chosen to focus largely on thinkers whose work seems to have had some influence in policy-making or political circles. Thus, to take one example, I devote much attention to Reinhold Niebuhr, who has had a marked impact on such political practitioners as Arthur Schlesinger, Jr., and George Kennan and whose work exemplifies a mood which pervades much of American thought today.

To sum up, this book is an essay on the intellectual basis of a number of current public-policy positions. It does not pretend to be a comprehensive treatise; rather, it is an attempt to probe a number of areas in which American political thought may be undergoing significant change. Thus I have tried to avoid imposing order and system where none exists. Chapters II through V deal with some of the more traditional problems which have divided liberals from conservatives, namely, problems having to do with the economic system and the relationship of government to it, along with a consideration of the views of man and society which underlie these positions. Even here, however, the "traditional" problems are compounded by the impact of what has been called "the organizational revolution," that is, the rise of big industry, big labor, big government, and big bureaucracy. Thus, much will have to be said about the effects of mass, bureaucratized society on the "quality" of life. Chapters VI and VII deal with foreign policy and civil rights. These areas are of fundamental significance because they have produced tensions which may lead to fundamentally new ideological cleavages in American politics. Chapter VIII deals with the thesis that there has been an "end of ideology"—a view which has dominated thinking about American politics in recent years. In the light of the evidence presented in this book, this thesis appears to be of dubious validity. In the concluding chapter, an attempt is made to summarize and to speculate about the direction in which American political thought is moving.

🦅 BIBLIOGRAPHICAL NOTES 🦅

The focus of this book on emerging ideologies owes much to a suggestion in Thomas P. Jenkin, *The Study of Political Theory* (New York: Random House, 1955), pp. 87–88. The many writings of Hans J. Morgenthau have also served as models; see his three volumes of collected essays, *Politics in the Twentieth Century* (Chicago: University of Chicago Press, 1963). Morgenthau's emphasis on the need for political theory to be related to critical issues is of special importance. Harold Lasswell's remarks on policy science may be found in "The Political Science of Science," *American Political Science Review*, 50 (December 1956), 961–979.

In addition to the works of Hartz and Hofstadter, the American political tradition has been subjected to a great deal of interpretation of late. Representative works include David Potter, *People of Plenty* (Chicago: University of Chicago Press, 1954), which stresses the factor of economic abundance; David Riesman, *The Lonely Crowd* (rev. ed.; New Haven: Yale University Press, 1961), which stresses psychological change; William A. Williams, *The Contours of American History* (Cleveland: World Publishing, 1961), a semi-Marxist account; Hans J. Morgenthau, *The Purpose of American Politics* (New York: Knopf, 1960); Oscar and Mary Handlin, *The Dimensions of Liberty* (Cambridge: Harvard University Press, 1961); Hans Kohn, *American Nationalism* (New York: Macmillan, 1957). Recent historiography is summarized in John Higham, ed., *The Reconstruction of American History* (New York: Harper, Torchbooks, 1962).

Robert Dahl's reflections on the relation between conflict and consensus in American politics may be found in Dahl, ed., *Political Oppositions in Western Democracies* (New Haven: Yale University Press, 1966), pp. 34–69. In addition to his text, *Political Theory: Philosophy, Ideology, Science* (New York: Macmillan, 1961), Andrew Hacker's views on liberalism may be found in Carl J. Friedrich, ed., *Liberty* (New York: Atherton Press, 1962), pp. 308–333. The classic study of liberal thought is Guido de Ruggiero, *The History of European Liberalism* (Boston: Beacon Press, 1959). The multidimensional character of conservatism and liberalism is discussed in Seymour Martin Lipset, *Political Man* (Garden City, N.Y.: Doubleday, Anchor Books, 1963).

CHAPTER II

THE
BASES
OF
LIBERALISM

By contrast with conservatism, which is dominated by the towering figure of Edmund Burke, no single theorist in the history of political thought can serve to introduce the mainstream of liberal ideas. What follows is a mélange of ideas drawn largely from such thinkers as Locke and Mill, but by no means limited to them.

The premise from which liberalism proceeds is individualism. Classical liberal thought saw the individual as existing in a presocial state of nature. Society and government are the creation of these isolated individuals who are endowed with inalienable rights which antedate the creation of society. The government which they create is bound to respect those rights; in other words, it is subject to constitutional limitations in some form. One of these limitations is the requirement of consent of the governed either through direct participation in the decision-making process or through an electoral system for choosing representatives. A further limitation found in classical liberalism is a rather negative view of the functions of the state, best summed up in the maxim, "That government is best which governs least." In particular, this limitation was felt to be desirable in economic affairs; in other words, there was a close association between classical liberal politics and laissez-faire economics.

A few of the statements in this highly condensed survey require some elaboration. First of all, there is the rejection of the ancient idea that the state is a natural institution, that man is by nature a political animal, and that government is, if not a positive good, at least a necessary evil. The new individualists asserted the primacy of each isolated man. For classical liberals this means that the state takes on a purely instrumental value; it is a creation of man designed to fit man's needs. The primacy of the individual and the emphasis on inalienable rights further mean that man's duties to the state or to the community tend to be downgraded in importance. Thus, unless an individual acts in a manner physically harmful to another, it is hard to justify restrictions on that behavior no matter how socially unpleasant that behavior may be.

It can be argued that in the modern world this is a prescription for chaos. To an extent this statement is true, but this should not obscure the positive functions performed by this mode of thought. The "instrumental" conception of the state is vital to the growth of the Western tradition of constitutionalism. There may be some dangers in an emphasis on rights inalienable under any circumstances, but the hazards are certainly less great than those inherent in any theory of obligation which makes the individual the agent of the state.

Another important element of integral liberalism is a certain degree of faith in reason—a faith logically required by the stress on individual participation in decision making. It is possible to overemphasize this faith and thus make the thinkers of the liberal tradition appear positively simpleminded in their naïve optimism—in their faith in the "common man" and his power to understand complex problems, in the power of education, and indeed in man's ability to find solutions to all his troubles. To fall into this error is to draw a mere caricature of liberal thought. On the other hand, it must be admitted that the liberal view of democracy does rest on rationalist assumptions. The theory assumes that since men are basically rational, fundamentally good, and equally devoted to the public interest, they will carefully examine policy alternatives or candidates for office and judge them by standards reflecting these qualities. The liberal commitment to this assumption poses a fundamental intellectual dilemma, for the reason that the more information unearthed about human behavior through studies of voting and other aspects of public opinion, the clearer it becomes that men do not make decisions in any such carefully calculated way. Thus, some of the assumptions of liberal democratic theory appear weak—*perhaps* dangerously so.

The rationalism being considered here has another important aspect. As noted, the classical liberals assumed the existence of certain self-evident, inalienable rights. They further argued that a rational standard for the judgment of political acts may be based on a true understanding of these rights. Thus, part of the liberal faith has been placed in the tradition of natural law and natural right, with the assumption that there is an enduring standard of the public interest. This belief, too, has come under attack. The concerted criticism of the philosophy of natural right goes back to the days of David Hume's demonstration that it is impossible logically to derive a statement as to what ought to be from a proposition as to what is. With the notable exception of Roman Catholic thinkers, most modern philosophy has been characterized by a belief in the relativity of values to culture. Man is said to create his own values; there is thus no standard of behavior external to man. This issue poses serious problems for any modern man concerned with finding a moral base for political activity, but the problems are doubly acute for liberals because of their long-standing commitment to an enduring, and indeed immutable, standard of justice.

Enough has been said to indicate that today's liberals are in a state of philosophical disarray. The traditional assumptions of classical liberalism have been widely challenged, often by thinkers in the liberal camp. The important idea "That government is best which governs least" has long since been overturned as a result of the growing belief that meaningful equality cannot be achieved via laissez-faire. Perhaps more importantly, the faith in progress through rational action has been undermined, thus shaking the foundations of the entire liberal theory of democratic government. Even so, few liberals have turned to a fundamental, systematic reexamination of their beliefs that seems called for. One notable exception is Reinhold Niebuhr, whose work reflects, perhaps more than that of any other thinker, the profound intellectual dilemmas of the modern world. It is therefore appropriate to turn to an analysis of Niebuhr's work.

The Nature of Man and the Limits of Politics

American political thought has not been noted for its systematic or abstract character. For the most part, Americans have been content to propose solutions to concrete problems on a more or less ad hoc basis. Reinhold Niebuhr represents an exception to this general rule. Moreover, the scope and quality of his thought have earned him a place in the intellectual history of this century that far transcends our national borders.

Because Niebuhr's writing is inordinately complex, it is very difficult to assess. First, its sheer bulk is enormous; his first work appeared in 1916, and he has continued to publish regularly to this day. Second, his more technical writings are those of a professional theologian and are therefore couched in terms in which the average political scientist is generally not well versed. For this reason, insofar as it is possible, an attempt will be made to avoid purely theological issues. This is not easily done, but in Niebuhr's political writings the theological base is usually quite clearly implied or stated explicitly in nontechnical terms, so that it is possible for the layman to approach him with a minimum of theological awareness. Further, for all the importance and intellectual power of Niebuhr's work, there are certain prominent ambiguities. In fact, to a considerable extent, these very tensions in his thought are what make him such an important exemplar of liberal ideas.

The reasons for the ambiguity of his position are quite clear. First of all, a dominant theme of his writings for the past generation has been his attack on what he calls "liberalism." But it must be borne in mind that the object of his criticism is not the reform movement of twentieth-century America that is under discussion here. Rather, the bulk of Niebuhr's work is an indictment of the modern world on the ground that it is too blindly optimistic, too prone to overestimate the goodness of man, too ready to overlook man's propensity to evil and the dangers to freedom, security, and the good life that spring from this tendency. Looking on from this perspective, Niebuhr is able to state flatly that American conservatism is "nothing more than a decadent liberalism." On the other hand, it must be pointed out that Niebuhr has moved to the right on the political spectrum over the past thirty years. Having rejected the socialism of his earlier period, he now puts greater stress on the difficulties inherent in any attempt at rapid political, social, and economic change. To this extent he has even become a disciple of Burke. However, as John Bennett has noted, it is dangerous to overemphasize Niebuhr's more conservative ideas. Niebuhr does assume that there will be slow, but in the long run radical, changes in the economic system of the sort that conservatives are inclined to label "creeping socialism." He is, moreover, opposed to the intense individualism which has now become so central to American conservatism. In sum, while he has not worked out a systematic view of his conception of the good society, he nonetheless continues to apply a critical ethic to the status quo.[1]

Thus there is a tension between Niebuhr's philosophical-theological position and the everyday political stands which make him prominent in such political organizations as the Americans for Democratic Action and such liberal journals of opinion as the *New Republic* and *The New Leader*. This tension between New Deal reformism and religious conservatism makes assessment of Niebuhr very difficult indeed. As Peter Viereck has noted, liberals err when they attach too little weight to his philosophy, while those on the right misjudge him by underestimating the strength of his commitment to liberal politics.

Further difficulties arise from the fact that Niebuhr's work is

---

[1] John C. Bennett, "Reinhold Niebuhr's Social Ethics," in Charles W. Kegley and Robert W. Bretall, eds., *Reinhold Niebuhr: His Religious, Social, and Political Thought* (New York: Macmillan, 1961), p. 76.

so often polemical in character. Reading him is like reading a Platonic dialogue in which only the responses of Socrates have been printed. One must always be aware of Niebuhr's invisible opponent, whether that opponent is a weak Social Gospeler or a tough commissar. This argumentative approach occasionally leads Niebuhr to overemphasis. Moreover, his work often includes attacks on two opposite positions, so that it is necessary to examine his positions from several points of view before stating with any degree of certainty just where he stands on a given subject. It is partly for this reason that it is easy to overestimate Niebuhr's philosophical pessimism. As Bennett has pointed out, one of Niebuhr's most persistent hopes has been that if man can avoid the pitfalls of belief in progress and perfectibility, he will then be able to take a constructive approach to the solution of present dilemmas.

A final element of complexity in Niebuhr's political writings, suggested above, is that over a fairly long period of time there has been a considerable shift in his position on social, economic, and even theological issues. This evolutionary process has been described at some length by Arthur Schlesinger, Jr.[2] First of all, it must be remembered that for all of his later criticism of the movement, Niebuhr began as an adherent to the reformist Social Gospel which was so influential in both American Protestantism and liberal politics during the early part of the present century. Niebuhr may have lost the optimism of this theological school, but he still clings to the social and economic reformist tendencies which were so closely associated with it.

Allied with the Social Gospel in the history of modern American reform has been the instrumental pragmatism of John Dewey. As Schlesinger has noted, Dewey provided a secular and humanistic rationale for reform at the same time that Walter Rauschenbusch and the Social Gospelers provided a religious justification. Dewey affirmed the possibility of progress through education, experimentation, and concentrated application of the full intellec-

[2] Arthur M. Schlesinger, Jr., "Reinhold Niebuhr's Place in American Thought and Life," in Kegley and Bretall, eds., *ibid.*, pp. 126–150. The following sketch of the development of Niebuhr's work relies heavily on Schlesinger's brilliant article.

tual resources of society to a problem. Given free reign, science and education would triumph over social maladjustment. Niebuhr's early affiliation with this school is less clear than is his connection with the Social Gospel, but it is safe to conclude with Schlesinger that his political intuition, tactical sense, and practical response to political problems placed him in the pragmatist's camp.

There is a fundamental disparity between these two approaches, and Niebuhr was not long in coming to this realization. The religious approach is essentially an idealism based on another world. True, there is an attempt to realize the ideal here and now, but the spiritual base of the Social Gospel was found to conflict with the humanistic base of the Deweyans. By 1932, Niebuhr, in his first major work, launched a frontal attack on this fusion which had become the prevailing liberal ideology. The important distinction he drew is clearly pointed up by his title, *Moral Man and Immoral Society.*

In this book, Niebuhr insisted on a sharp differentiation between the behavior of individuals and that of social groups. He further argued:

this distinction justifies and necessitates political policies which a purely individualistic ethic must always find embarrassing. [As a result,] politics will, to the end of history, be an area where conscience and power meet, where the ethical and coercive factors of human life will interpenetrate and work out their tentative and uneasy compromises.[3]

It might be supposed that such a position would mean an end to any dogmatic, doctrinaire stands on contemporary issues for its author. In particular, he might be expected to have a firm commitment to the policies of the New Deal with its highly pragmatic, ad hoc character. However, such was not the case. It is interesting to note that, for all their differences, Dewey and Niebuhr were united on this issue. As Schlesinger has noted, the pragmatic philosophers abandoned pragmatism to the master pragmatist who sat in the White House and retreated to their own "crypto-utopias."

Niebuhr's lack of sympathy with the New Deal was the result

---

[3] Niebuhr, *Moral Man and Immoral Society* (New York: Scribner's, 1932), p. 4.

of indifference to the achievements of reform and of a deep feeling of despair. For one attached to the socialist ideal, the Roosevelt program was too piecemeal, too lacking in order, to lead to anything but futility. In the grip of this view of reality, Niebuhr even turned for a time to the cultivation of the "valuable illusion" that mankind can attain perfect justice. Such "sublime madness" was dangerous but necessary.

And so Niebuhr's inherent contradictions persisted through the 1930's, as he rejected the very program that most closely approximated his philosophical ideal. However, by the end of the decade, the relative success of the New Deal began to tell on Niebuhr's thinking. Even more important than the domestic program of the New Deal for Niebuhr's developing thought was Roosevelt's foreign policy with its opportunistic realism. The pacifism of the Protestant ministry and the isolationism of the socialists tended to drive Niebuhr closer and closer to the pragmatist's camp. By 1940 he had resigned from the Socialist Party. With the publication of *The Children of Light and the Children of Darkness* in 1944, the transition was complete; in his approach to practical politics, Niebuhr was now a confirmed experimentalist.

The development of Niebuhr's thought through its period of greatest trial having been sketched, it is now possible to analyze the work of his maturity, particularly his views on the nature of man. It has already been noted that the starting point for Niebuhr is his critique of what he refers to as "liberalism." It will be illuminating to see just what he means by his use of this term. To Niebuhr the essential liberal characteristic is faith in man—in man's ability to conquer nature, in his ultimate, essential goodness, and in the inevitability of his progress toward higher things. In the broadest sense this liberalism is synonymous with democracy. It offers a challenge to restraints on the individual stemming from tradition and hereditary or economic privilege and insists that the basis of political power must lie in "the consent of the governed."[4]

It can be easily seen that what Niebuhr has in mind when he talks about liberalism is the whole drift of modern civilization, a

---

[4] Harry R. Davis and Robert C. Good, eds., *Reinhold Niebuhr on Politics* (New York: Scribner's, 1960), pp. 13–15.

civilization he feels to be dominated by faith in the goodness of man, the inevitability of progress, the primacy of the individual, the importance of rationality, and in fact most of the characteristics which distinguish the modern world from medieval France, for example. It should also be noted that the attack on this huge complex of ideas is not indiscriminate. Niebuhr's work is full of sympathy for the virtues and achievements of the modern world; government by "the consent of the governed" could have no more staunch defender than Reinhold Niebuhr. And yet Niebuhr's position with respect to liberalism is not unlike that of Marx with respect to capitalism; on the one hand he praises it for what it has accomplished, and on the other he regards it inadequate as a method for the achievement of the good society.

The reason for the inadequacy of the modern faith is its overoptimism. Man's faith in his own perfectibility and in the inevitability of progress which stems from this belief is a fundamental error. What the liberal fails to realize is that the growth of freedom may have distinctly negative consequences. Those who believe in inevitable progress assume that man's freedom will be used rationally. This assumption overlooks the fact, which the history of the twentieth century has made quite clear, that reason may often be "the servant, rather than the master, of the self."

The possibility of progress is not completely denied. What Niebuhr does insist is that the possibility of progress for evil as well as for good has been increased and that, as a result of man's failure to realize this fact, he was not well prepared for the horrors of the twentieth century. In fact, Niebuhr would go even further and argue that the blind faith in progress has been partially responsible for those catastrophies.

The fundamental problem is the overly high estimate of human nature. The high estimate of the human stature implied in the concept of man as "the image of God" stands in paradoxical juxtaposition to the low estimate of human virtue in Christian thought. Man is a sinner, and his sin is defined as rebellion against God. The Christian estimate of human evil is so serious because it places evil at the very center of human personality: in the will. This evil cannot be regarded complacently as the inevitable consequence of man's finiteness or as the fruit of his involvement in the contingencies and necessities of nature. Sin is occasioned precisely by the fact that man refuses to admit his "creatureliness" and to acknowledge himself as merely a member of the total unity of life.[5]

The refusal to admit his "creatureliness" is equivalent to a refusal to admit finiteness. And yet man, being mortal, is finite, even though he persists in efforts to transcend his condition because, in addition to being finite, he is also free. It is his effort to transcend his natural state which leads man to commit the sin of pride. "All of his intellectual and cultural pursuits, therefore, become infected with the sin of pride." In this confrontation of finiteness and freedom lies man's temptation to sin. Man's great dilemma lies in the fact that he is simultaneously strong and weak, both free and bound, both blind and far-seeing. His problem is his inveterate tendency to overlook his limitations by overestimating his capacities.[6] The product of this tension is "anxiety," which is the precondition of sin. But anxiety is more than that; it is also the basis of human creativity. Man does not know his limits and keeps striving for higher and higher achievements. The same act may thus have a creative and a sinful aspect. Thus, while a statesman may be genuinely concerned with the well-being of his nation, pride drives him to anxiety over his prestige and his place in history. Similarly, the philosopher may be genuinely dedicated to truth while being motivated to establish his own particular conception of the truth.

Since man's efforts to transcend his finite character are inevitable and since these efforts are equally inevitably touched with pride, sin is also inevitable. Sin is seen as the direct consequence of the conjunction of finiteness and freedom in man. The Augustinian roots of this conception are clear. Man is a creature who inhabits two worlds, one temporal and one spiritual, the City of God and the City of Man. He is mortal; yet his every action has about it a touch of the eternal. Here, then, is the first great tragic paradox in Niebuhr's thought: the inevitability of sin even in the face of the most determined striving after good.

A second paradox in Niebuhr's thought is closely related to

---

[5] Niebuhr, *The Nature and Destiny of Man*, Vol. I: *Human Nature* (one-volume ed.; New York: Scribner's, 1951), p. 16.

[6] *Ibid.*, p. 181.

the first. As noted, Niebuhr regards sin as inevitable; man cannot escape its tentacles. At the same time, as a devout Christian, Niebuhr cannot countenance any attempt to evade moral responsibility. If man sins, he must pay. By all rules of logic there is a contradiction in these two positions, for how can man be responsible for that which he can in no way avoid? This paradox does not go unacknowledged in Niebuhr's work. He is much too acute a thinker to let such a lacuna in his argument remain unfilled.

Niebuhr starts with an open admission of the contradiction inherent in his thought. He writes:

The Christian doctrine of sin in its classical form offends both rationalists and moralists by maintaining the seemingly absurd position that man sins inevitably and by a fateful necessity but that he is nevertheless to be held responsible for actions which are prompted by an ineluctable fate.[7]

At a later point in the argument, however, this paradox is dismissed as a result of "a literalistic confusion." Unfortunately, the precise nature of the confusion is not revealed to the reader. Niebuhr does, however, attempt a resolution by a resort to the Hegelian dialectic.

We may find it necessary, argues Niebuhr, provisionally to defy logic in order not to foreclose the understanding of complex problems for the sake of "premature logical consistency." The dialectic of Hegel allows us to transcend ordinary logical limits and do justice to things which are neither "being" nor "non-being" but are rather in a state of "becoming."[8] Thus, Niebuhr seems to argue that since conditions change and since our knowledge and perceptions of conditions also change, the flux of the dialectic—the relentless alternation of thesis and antithesis leading to higher and higher levels of understanding as each new synthesis is reached—must be allowed to continue. We may be justified in holding to contradictory propositions in the hope that in the fullness of time they will be reconciled.

In rough outline this is Niebuhr's view of the nature of man. Man is a sinner of inevitable necessity. Sin as the basis of human

---

[7] *Ibid.*, p. 241.
[8] *Ibid.*, pp. 262–263.

creativity is the source of all man's greatness, of all his mightiest achievements, but because of the tension between finitude and freedom all of his efforts are tainted. Moreover, man is responsible for this taint, and no appeal to the rules of formal logic is sufficient to relieve him of his burden.

What is the application of this stern view of man to politics? To begin with, in politics, sin takes the form of injustice which stems from pride and an uncurbed will-to-power. Protection against this drive cannot be bought by mere moral force. Coercion is at the root of all political matters. The only sure protection against the power of others is the exertion of a counterforce. Justice can be achieved only by imposing an order, a balance of power, upon the anarchic conflict of self-interest which characterizes human behavior. All schemes of justice have such a balance of power at their foundation. At best, "Such a balance, once achieved, can be stabilized, embellished, and even, on occasion, perfected by more purely moral considerations."[9]

The close fit between this analysis of political reality and the pragmatic approach to political action is quite clear. Once this view is granted, there is little room for idealistic crusades. Moral suasion is reduced to a mere embellishment—at best, one weapon among many which might be adopted. The essential goals of politics lie in the sphere of power rather than morality. Such a view of domestic politics, while perhaps provocative, is hardly unique. Few close observers would argue that any other motives normally guide political leaders as they practice their trade; indeed, there are obvious similarities between this view and the reasoning which lies behind the twin constitutional principles of the separation of powers and checks and balances. However, in international politics such views run counter to long-standing American ideas.

Thus, in his works of this period, Niebuhr may be said to have provided the stimulus for the fundamental reexamination of the basic principles of American foreign policy which took place under the rubric of the "realism-idealism" controversy following World War II. Niebuhr's influence on such leading thinkers of the realist

---

[9] Niebuhr, *Christianity and Power Politics* (New York: Scribner's, 1940), p. 104.

school as George Kennan and Hans Morgenthau as well as many others is marked. Here, too, as in the domestic arena, a pragmatic approach based largely on power considerations was called for. This issue will be raised in a later chapter. At present, however, the discussion is confined to internal affairs.

What are the implications of this view of man and politics for the politics of democracy? An examination of the history of political thought shows the existence of contradictory arguments. Many theorists have tried to build undemocratic theories on the foundation of a view of man as corrupt and untrustworthy. The argument is simple: If man is so poor a beast, so misguided or even malicious in his judgments, then only the exceptional man should be allowed to rule. Democracy is dangerous, and an elite must therefore govern. Such is the argument advanced by thinkers as diverse as Plato in *The Republic* and Machiavelli in *The Prince*, as well as by any number of totalitarian leaders in the twentieth century.

On the other hand, many thinkers, particularly such figures of the Enlightenment as Rousseau and Jefferson, attempted to build democratic governments on a foundation which asserts the essential goodness of man. Again the argument is simple: If man is basically good, surely he can be trusted to govern both himself and others. Taking note of both these tendencies, Niebuhr argues that their deficiency lies in their separation of the two aspects of the Christian view of man: one emphasizing the baser aspects of man's nature; the other concerning itself with man's potential for "dignity and greatness." Only if these views are reunited can a sound theory of democracy be constructed.

The Christian idea of sin, contends Niebuhr, is vital to sound social and political theory. Only on the basis of such an understanding of man can it be recognized that even the saintliest men, even the most nobly conceived communities, are corrupted by pride and love of self. Niebuhr contends that most modern democratic theories ignore this fact. The fatal flaw of modern democracy is sentimentality about the nature of man fostered by "the children of light" who seek to bring self-interest under a universal law and who believe that this may be easily accomplished. Only a democracy based on a more pessimistic conception of the nature of man may be expected to survive.

As Niebuhr's famous formulation puts it, "Man's capacity for justice makes democracy possible; but man's inclination to injustice makes democracy necessary."[10] Healthy democracy rests on skepticism about man and all his works. It is this very skepticism which precludes dictatorship. We know, Niebuhr argues, that all men will abuse power; therefore, the way to minimize such abuse is to diffuse power widely, thereby preventing its concentration in the hands of a few. This is not to suggest that power may not be misused in a democracy; it is, however, the least dangerous of the courses open to man.

In addition, the Niebuhrian conception of man leads to the conclusion that there is no reason to expect sweeping solutions to the problem of democratic government. All the exhortations of all the ideologues will not help. We must always remember: "Nothing that is worth doing can be achieved in our lifetime; therefore we must be saved by hope. Nothing which is true or beautiful or good makes complete sense in any immediate context of history; therefore we must be saved by faith."[11] Democracy is thus not a problem-solving device, for there are no final answers; at best, it is "a method of finding proximate solutions for insoluble problems."[12] The successful, stable democracy must be constantly involved in a process of bargaining and compromise. Systematic, comprehensive blueprints designed to solve the problem of society for all time to come are the refuge of the foolish. Problems are never solved. All we may do is make adjustments. The attempt to do more is a classic instance of the sin of pride, of the attempt to achieve an earthly utopia.

Not only is this attempt foolish, it is also dangerous, for it engenders a fanaticism fatal to democracy. The man who feels possessed of final solutions to social problems is more than likely, in this view, to attempt to impose his delusions by force. This is the source of the communist and fascist dictatorships of the twentieth century, and it is this perception that leads to the strong

---

[10] Niebuhr, *The Children of Light and the Children of Darkness* (New York: Scribner's, 1944), p. xi.

[11] Niebuhr, *The Irony of American History* (New York: Scribner's, 1952), p. 63.

[12] *The Children of Light and the Children of Darkness*, p. 118.

hostility to ideological politics exhibited by Niebuhr and his numerous followers.

The Influence of Niebuhr

Niebuhr is an important figure in American thought for two reasons: first, because he is an important symbol of an intellectual mood widespread not only in the United States, but in the entire Western world; and second, because he is a significant source of that mood.

The climate of opinion illustrated by Niebuhr's work is shared by an astonishingly wide variety of thinkers ranging from Marxists to Freudians to existentialists to academic social scientists. There is a deep-seated sense of malaise, a feeling that the times are somehow profoundly out of joint, a realization that mass industrial society, for all its material achievements, is not a utopia. There are a number of sources of this mood. Perhaps the first is the long-run decline of religion in the Western world; no longer can it be said that religious belief is the center and ruler of man's life. Second, there is the increasing technological rationalization of society. As life becomes increasingly mechanized, man is separated from the products of his labor and he comes to feel that he is not a whole being, that he is rather a devitalized cog in a gigantic machine. Thus the technological achievements which have shaped the modern world and which have contributed so greatly to its achievements are paradoxically held responsible for its ills. This whole complex of ideas has been summed up by William Barrett as a sense of estrangement from others and even from our true selves.[13] We are beset by a feeling of the "fragility" of human existence. We feel isolated, alone, and unable to cope with the giant machine that is society. It is scarcely possible to rank-order our problems, but one thing is common to them all: "the radical feeling of human finitude."

Coupled with this feeling is a sense that somehow man has lost his moral bearings. Partially this feeling no doubt stems from

---

[13] William Barrett, *Irrational Man* (Garden City, N.Y.: Doubleday, 1958), pp. 31–32.

the decline of the preindustrial, "face-to-face," organic society in which tradition and social pressure provided clearly defined standards of behavior. In addition, there has been a progressive decline in the liberal belief in natural law—that is, in some absolute, enduring system of values. Contemporary American liberals are in a decidedly ambivalent position with respect to this issue. On the one hand they led a revolt against absolutes in the early part of this century in order to further political aims. Thus, pragmatists, such as philosopher John Dewey, and reform Darwinists, such as Lester Frank Ward, emphasized the relativity of cultural norms to particular societies and stressed the importance of environment as a determinant of behavior. This approach is clearly attuned to a political movement dedicated to change, but on the other hand, the question may be raised as to whether it can provide the foundation for a sound political ethic. Even liberals, Eric Goldman being a leading example, have suggested that the upshot of this intellectual movement can easily be a cynical political opportunism supported by no solid foundation of values.

All of these factors merge in a complex syndrome. Particularly during the 1950's, the intellectual mood was marked by these ideas. It can be seen, for example, in the work of such liberals as Lionel Trilling and Leslie Fiedler. Consider, as a case in point, Trilling's political novel, *The Middle of the Journey*, in which a leading character remarks, "The great danger to the progressive movement these days, as I see it, is that liberals are going to confuse their dreams with the possible realities." Or examine Fiedler's collection of essays, *The End of Innocence*, whose governing idea is indicated by his title. We in America are emerging from a state of idyllic but naïve bliss. The symbol for this condition is, of all people, Alger Hiss. To Fiedler, an entire generation was on trial with Hiss because of its substitution of "sentimentality for intelligence" and in particular for having, in its reformist zeal, overlooked the fact that the U.S.S.R. was the enemy of all the values to which they were most deeply committed. Fiedler's indictment is sweeping. Speaking of Hiss's failure to confess, he writes, "In the end he failed all liberals, all who had, in some sense and at the same time, shared his illusions (and who that calls himself a liberal is exempt?), all who demanded of him that he speak aloud a common recognition of complicity."

This analysis represents the wave of liberal self-laceration at its height, but there is still hope of redemption, for Fiedler argues that liberals can learn from the Hiss case to create a new and chastened liberalism on the ruins of the old. What we learn is that

mere liberal principle is not in itself a guarantee against evil; that the wrongdoer is not always the other—"they" and not "us"; that there is no magic in the words "left" or "progressive" or "socialist" that can prevent deceit or the abuse of power.[14]

However, the full impact of Niebuhr's work can best be seen in the work of Arthur Schlesinger, Jr.—liberal historian, intellectual, and special assistant to Presidents Kennedy and Johnson. In many ways, Schlesinger's book, *The Vital Center,* may be viewed as a manifesto for the Americans for Democratic Action. This essay is almost devoutly anticommunist and admonishes American liberals for their excessive zeal in trying to accommodate the Soviet Union. Written in 1949, the book displays the reaction to Henry Wallace's Progressive Party of 1948. In theoretical terms, Niebuhrian themes predominate. Western man is viewed as "tense, uncertain, adrift." The capitalist class has failed to be an effective agent of government because, in its zeal to pursue its own narrow ends, it has produced a plutocracy rather than an aristocracy. Even more significant is Schlesinger's emphasis on what he feels to be the failure of the left. "The defining characteristic of the progressive, as I shall use the word, is the sentimentality of his approach to politics and culture." The failure of the liberal has been the result of his excessive faith in logic and in the perfectibility of man. The solution to this problem is a more mature and therefore somewhat more pessimistic (or realistic) view of the nature of man. The defense which Schlesinger offers for democracy has a familiar ring:

The people as a whole are not perfect; but no special group of the people is more perfect: That is the moral and rationale of democracy.

---

[14] Leslie Fiedler, *The End of Innocence* (Boston: Beacon Press, 1955), p. 24.

Consistent pessimism about man, far from promoting authoritarianism, alone can innoculate the democratic faith against it.[15]

This statement, whose derivation is already quite clear, is hammered home by the passage from Niebuhr quoted earlier: "Man's capacity for justice makes democracy possible; but man's inclination to injustice makes democracy necessary."

Liberalism, Schlesinger contends, must give up its optimism about the nature of man and the possibility of progress. It must "accept the limitations and possibilities" of the real world, and return to a "tradition of a reasonable responsibility about politics and a moderate pessimism about man." Only then can there be a politically and intellectually sound noncommunist left.

The point need be belabored no longer. Niebuhr is clearly in tune with a major intellectual force in modern America, whether as cause or effect. It has been suggested that he is both. The basic position adopted by Niebuhr has become a standard starting point for much current thought on politics. As Charles Frankel puts it, what is striking is not that this dour view of man and his potential is popular in religious and conservative circles; this has always been the case. What is new is that liberal scholars, intellectuals, and publicists from a wide variety of fields have come to accept this point of view.[16]

These views of Niebuhr's are deeply rooted in the modern world. Even his terminology reflects the sources of his thought: Kierkegaard, Marx, Freud, and modern sociology are all in evidence. The approach may be called neoorthodoxy, but, as Frankel says, "the 'neo' is the operative term for Mr. Niebuhr's doctrine of original sin could only have been conceived by a contemporary mind."

It is for these reasons that so much attention has been devoted here to Niebuhr. Not all liberals would accept his analysis; most would probably deemphasize his religious roots, although many would emphasize a persistent strain of evil without reference

---

[15] Arthur Schlesinger, Jr., *The Vital Center* (Boston: Houghton Mifflin, 1949), p. 170.

[16] For a discussion of this point, see Charles Frankel, *The Case for Modern Man* (Boston: Beacon Press, 1959), pp. 23–27.

to sin; some humanist liberals would reject him outright. However, no other single writer expresses so fully the main philosophical themes of what might be called the New Liberalism: its caution, its pragmatism, its antiutopianism, and even, perhaps, its conservatism.

The Humanist Critique

Not all of contemporary liberalism has succumbed to the Niebuhrian spell, as I have already indicated. A serious attempt at rebuttal has been made by a number of thinkers who might be classified as humanists. Representative of these thinkers are Charles Frankel, Herbert Muller, and Morton White.

Niebuhr is criticized on a number of grounds. The first is the logic of his conception of original sin. It will be recalled that for Niebuhr sin is the inevitable consequence of the tension between man's finiteness and his freedom; he has free will and at the same time his actions are determined. The liberal humanists have approached this doctrine from two points of view. The first is that of Frankel, who attacks Niebuhr's conception of freedom. Frankel notes Niebuhr's admission that a paradox lies at the heart of his view of sin. However, he contends in rebuttal that Neibuhr has "been bewitched by a sentimental idea of freedom—the idea that perfect freedom means the absence of all limitations on our behavior." Not so, says Professor Frankel. The question of whether or not an action is determined has nothing to do with whether or not it is free. A causal law merely describes how things regularly happen; it does not cause them to happen. Only freedom defined in this rather distorted sense is in a paradoxical relationship with causality. But this approach does not really seem to meet the argument. When Niebuhr writes about the conflict between freedom and finiteness, he does not mean a conflict existing entirely within this world, as Frankel's critique implies. The conflict is within man who lives in two worlds—one temporal and one eternal. This problem cannot be solved by adding a little definitional clarity to Niebuhr's rather muddy style. The argument does not meet Niebuhr on his own ground, as it must in order to be successful.

Morton White's critique is more to the point. He, too, accepts Niebuhr's admission of paradox, but he does not try to redefine the terms which are in conflict. Rather he attempts to destroy the resolution of the problem offered by Niebuhr. The reader will recall that this answer is found by means of a resort to the Hegelian dialectic. White refuses to accept this bland disregard for the canons of ordinary logic. His point is well taken, although it is couched in a phraseology so biting as to border on the ad hominem.

It is difficult to argue, White points out, with someone who relies on faith, but it is even harder to argue with someone who voluntarily abandons ordinary logic. To accept willingly statements which are admittedly contradictory, in the hope that this contradiction will be resolved on some higher dialectical plane, is to abandon reason for obscurantism.[17] As White indicates, a resort to Hegel clearly does not solve Niebuhr's problem. The plausibility of Niebuhr's answer depends entirely on the acceptance of the dialectic which is in itself of dubious philosophical validity. This argument is a telling one, although in the long run it can appeal only to those, like White, who do not share Niebuhr's faith. As White admits, faith cannot be defeated by logic. However, the faith of those who are susceptible to logical argument may be seriously undermined and, when this occurs, other and less pessimistic versions of liberalism are left free to emerge.

A second major criticism of Niebuhr's approach revolves around his view of the nature and history of liberalism. Frankel contends that the idea of a liberalism based on a perfectionist theory of human nature is a parody of the facts. Even Condorcet, that favorite target of conservatives and neoorthodox liberals, is not well described by the usual stereotype. Frankel shows that all Condorcet really asserts in his theory of human progress is that we can never know when we have reached the limit of human hope—which is precisely the point Niebuhr makes in his study *Faith and History*. Frankel argues—and it would seem correctly on

---

[17] Morton White, *Social Thought in America: The Revolt Against Formalism* (Boston: Beacon Press, 1957), p. 264.

the basis of his evidence—that Niebuhr, in his critique of the doctrine of perfectibility, is hard at work on the destruction of a straw man. Even Hobbes and Locke, the first modern liberals, pictured a natural state of man which was at best beset by "inconveniences" and at worst a savage war of all against all. Even Rousseau may be interpreted as essentially pessimistic about the chances for attaining equality and freedom. To Frankel, the essential meaning of the doctrine of perfectibility is that it is a "policy of putting the *status quo* on the defensive, and of refusing to decide in advance that any given problem is beyond the power of human beings to solve." As he argues a few pages later, the word *perfectibility* might better be translated as "improvability." Few liberals, however antiutopian, would be able to deny such a usage.[18]

The humanist critics argue that Niebuhr has greatly overstated his case. No one living in the twentieth century could possibly deny that man is capable of great evil: this the humanists admit. But it is not necessary to carry the argument to Niebuhr's extreme conclusion. As Frankel writes, "to disabuse us of the belief that reason and good will have a cosmic guarantee behind them, it is not necessary to show that there is a cosmic conspiracy against these ideals. This is the same undisciplined romanticism merely turned inside out." Niebuhr has overlooked the possibility of a philosophy of history vitiated neither by a simpleminded optimism nor by the extreme pessimism which can be deduced from this doctrine. Herbert Muller has argued quite eloquently for such a tragic view of history. In fact, he contends that Niebuhr's theory has many of the elements of such a position. Eventually, however, the tension proves to be too great, and Niebuhr tries to transcend it by a Kirkegaardian leap of faith. For Niebuhr, the ultimate meaning of history lies in this faith. But as Muller

---

[18] Frankel, *The Case for Modern Man*, pp. 104–105. The passage from *Faith and History* reads, "No human achievements can annul man's subjection to human finitude. But human power is also limitless in the sense that no fixed limits can be set for the expansion of human capacities." Niebuhr, *Faith and History* (New York: Scribner's, 1949), p. 77. See also Sheldon Wolin, *Politics and Vision* (Boston: Little, Brown, 1960), Chapter 9.

contends in *The Uses of the Past*, this faith is an honorable one which it is not profitable to argue about. By definition faith exists or it does not. Certainly there is no point in discussing it.

But why, Muller asks, must history have an ultimate meaning, either immanent or transcendent? The Greeks, Romans, and Chinese produced civilizations of the highest order without such a faith. Why should contemporary man not do likewise? Man has succeeded in realizing high ideals which are real even if not eternal. History may have many meanings, and not a final meaning. Moreover, men at different times and in different cultures have agreed on many of these ideas.[19] Yet, all the great civilizations of the past have fallen. Whether based on faith, or reason, or some combination of the two, they have not been able to withstand the lashing winds of time. Surely this fact adds weight to Muller's moving peroration:

Today, I suppose, the most apparent use of the tragic view of history is the melancholy one of helping to prepare us for the worst. It gives us vast and eminent company in our misery; for if we feel that our society is damned and doomed, we can add that all the great societies were sufficiently damned and were certainly doomed. . . . Yet the tragic sense is the profoundest sense of our common humanity, and may therefore be a positive inspiration. If all the great societies have died none is really dead. Their peoples have vanished, as all men must, but first they enriched the great tradition of high, enduring values. Like Burkhardt, we might be heartened as well as sobered by the thought that we shall all vanish into the same darkness, and live on in the same tradition. We might be freed from the vanity of grandiose hopes, as of petty concerns. We might remember that "ripeness is all" and that it is enough.[20]

Conclusions

A number of conclusions clearly emerge. In the first place, Muller's work demonstrates that the alternative to a disbelief in the doctrine of original sin need not be a surrender to babbling

---

[19] Herbert J. Muller, *The Uses of the Past* (New York: Oxford University Press, 1952), p. 372.

[20] *Ibid.*, p. 374.

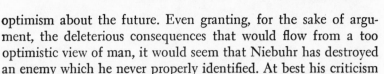

optimism about the future. Even granting, for the sake of argument, the deleterious consequences that would flow from a too optimistic view of man, it would seem that Niebuhr has destroyed an enemy which he never properly identified. At best his criticism applied only to a branch of modern thought. He is hardly justified in the sweeping attack which characterizes his work. The historical studies of Sheldon Wolin and Charles Frankel show this quite clearly. Neither in the past nor at the present time has liberalism been the sort of doctrine described by Niebuhr.

Second, it would seem that Niebuhr's theology is separable from his politics. His support for socialist positions in his early career, even while he held the same dour view of man to which he adheres today, suggests that there is no necessary connection between the two. As White contends, the liberal fascination with Niebuhr probably stems from approval of his pronouncements on contemporary political issues rather than from his theology, thus leading to the somewhat bizarre phenomenon of "atheists for Niebuhr." In the long run it may very well be that his philosophical work will give as much if not more aid and comfort to the conservatives than to the liberals.

At its best, the Niebuhrian approach can inject a properly prudential attitude into the politics of reform; at its worst, however, it can lead to a kind of intellectual stagnation, to surrender before the obstacles to a given program have been considered with a view to surmounting them. It is possible to be so pessimistic about the possibility of change that no change at all is possible. In the realm of ideas, this problem is raised in acute form by the concept of "the end of ideology." As should be abundantly clear on the basis of the preceding analysis, Niebuhr's approach to politics provides a perfect basis on which to erect such an antiideological argument. In a period which cries out for new solutions to new problems, such an approach has its dangers. The next chapter will examine some liberal answers to a few of these questions. It will also consider some of the ways in which the philosophical foundations of contemporary liberalism hamper attempts at solution.

❧ BIBLIOGRAPHICAL NOTES ❧

Perhaps the best single discussion of the liberal tradition is to be found in Guido de Ruggiero, *The History of European Liberalism* (Boston: Beacon Press, 1959). On nineteenth-century English liberalism, see Elie Halévy, *The Growth of Philosophical Radicalism* (Boston: Beacon Press, 1955), and John Plamenatz, *The English Utilitarians* (Oxford: Basil Blackwell, 1958). My interpretation of classical liberalism has been influenced in part by Leo Strauss, *Natural Right and History* (Chicago: University of Chicago Press, 1953). A notable modern statement of the classical liberal point of view is Robert MacIver, *The Web of Government* (New York: Macmillan, 1947).

Probably the best entry point into the maze of Reinhold Niebuhr's writing is Harry R. Davis and Robert C. Good, eds., *Reinhold Niebuhr on Politics* (New York: Scribner's, 1960). In this volume the editors have constructed a comprehensive theory of politics from the enormous mass of Niebuhr's writings. It is a remarkable job and it carries with it Niebuhr's endorsement. Niebuhr's views on international relations, which are not discussed here in detail, are treated most extensively in his *The Structure of Nations and Empires* (New York: Scribner's, 1959). A collection of critical studies on Niebuhr is Charles W. Kegley and Robert W. Bretall, eds., *Reinhold Niebuhr: His Religious, Social, and Political Thought* (New York: Macmillan, 1961). In addition to the essays by Bennett and Schlesinger cited in the text, the contributions by Paul Ramsey, Kenneth Thompson, Daniel Williams, William John Wolf, Karl Lowith, and Robert Fitch are especially useful. Niebuhr's own commentary on his critics is also useful and stimulating. Another volume of criticism is Harold Landon, ed.,

Reinhold Niebuhr: A Prophetic Voice in Our Time (Greenwich, Conn.: Seabury Press, 1962). This book is of use particularly for its contribution by Hans Morgenthau.

As should be clear from the text, the most telling critical commentaries on Niebuhr are Charles Frankel, *The Case for Modern Man* (Boston: Beacon Press, 1959), pp. 85–116, and Morton White, *Social Thought in America: The Revolt Against Formalism* (Boston: Beacon Press, 1957), pp. 247–264. Frankel is also very effective in his discussion of the new pessimism of contemporary liberals; see pp. 23–44 in *The Case for Modern Man*. William Barrett's *Irrational Man* (Garden City, N.Y.: Doubleday, 1958) provides a very good introduction to the existentialist mood which pervades so much of Niebuhr's thought.

The notion of "the end of ideology," which is briefly related to Niebuhr in this chapter, is discussed in detail in Chapter VIII. See the literature cited therein.

CHAPTER III

THE PUBLIC POLICIES OF LIBERALISM

To understand the condition of contemporary American liberalism, it is necessary first to understand the New Deal. This movement is vital because it represents a synthesis of older reform ideas going back to Populism and Progressivism with certain elements that were entirely new. Some historical background is thus necessary.

Populism, Progressivism, and the New Deal

Populism injected into American political life a new conception of the role of government. The prevailing dogma had been the classical liberal maxim, "That government is best which governs least." The Populists saw that if they were to win the reforms

41

they sought, they would have to forsake the traditional approach and turn to government not only for protection but also for positive assistance.

The principles pursued were Jeffersonian in their emphasis on equality and on the importance of the "common man." There was great emphasis on popular control of government, which took the form of demands for the direct election of United States Senators and for the right to recall judges. A second major theme was that of monetary reform—particularly the free coinage of silver—and a third was an all-out attack on the Populists' *bête noire*, the railroads. Populist farmers felt, and not without considerable justification, that they were subjected to real abuses of railroad power. They proposed to rectify such abuses, first by demanding severe governmental regulation of the industry and later by calling for outright government ownership. Demands were also made for the public ownership of the telephone and telegraph industries. Finally, the list of Populist demands included a graduated income tax.

One aspect of Populism which was not successful, however, was the attempt to fashion a broad base of political support. Populism began and substantially remained as a movement of poor Southern and Western farmers. Although under the leadership of William Jennings Bryan the Populists temporarily captured control of the Democratic Party in 1896, they never managed to establish any firm ties with the labor movement in the large Northern cities. As a result, the implementation of Populist principles was largely carried out under other auspices.

Much of this work was done by the Progressive movement under the leadership of Theodore Roosevelt and Woodrow Wilson. This was a movement of an entirely different sort than Populism. In particular its class base was different. Whereas Populism had been "a thrust from below," Progressivism was largely a movement of the upper and upper-middle classes. It is probably not unfair to suggest, with Richard Hofstadter, that to a considerable extent Progressivism was motivated by patrician disdain for the excesses of industrialism which were becoming clearly apparent in the early part of the century, particularly the corruption in the cities and the arrogance of the business and financial community whose leaders clearly expected to be treated as the equals, if not the superiors, of elected public officials.

As a result, part of the Progressive movement took the path of municipal reform in the form of attacks on political machines, the rise of the primary system, the initiative, the referendum, and the recall, and even going to the extent of what came to be known as "gas and water socialism." Much more important, however, was the tremendous symbolic confrontation of business and government best exemplified in the prosecution of the Northern Securities Company under the Sherman Anti-Trust Act in 1903. It seems clear that in this case, Roosevelt was primarily concerned with establishing the right and the power of government to regulate industry. Actually, Roosevelt's great reputation as a trustbuster has been considerably exaggerated. Having established his position, he was quite willing to allow the growth of considerable concentrations of economic power. Bigness in itself did not offend him; what did offend him was the abuse of power that often accompanies bigness. In fact, his position was the strikingly modern one that there were certain advantages of size inherent in large-scale industry and that the truly progressive way to proceed was to make full use of these advantages while being prepared to regulate the behavior of those concentrations of power.

It was this position which led to the major theoretical controversy of the Progressive period. Under the leadership of Woodrow Wilson, the Democratic Party urged the rejection of Roosevelt's New Nationalism and urged that the Wilsonian ideal of the New Freedom be substituted. The intellectual bellwether of the New Freedom was Louis Brandeis, whose major theme was "the curse of bigness." Bigness in itself was held to be evil, and no amount of governmental control could make palatable the large concentrations of economic power which characterized modern industrial society. In a sense, what the Wilsonian movement represented was a yearning for an earlier and simpler society. In many ways, Wilson remained true to his Southern heritage in his commitment to Jeffersonian ideals. Yet there was also a significant change in emphasis, for Wilson came to realize that bigness could be resisted only by agencies of comparable power. Hence he, too, opted for governmental assumption of a regulatory role, although he would transform this role into one committed to breaking up existing concentrations of power and to enforcing conditions of free competition. Thus, while government had a positive role, it was quite different from that laid out in the New Nationalist scheme of things; essentially, the difference was between the regulation of competition and the regulation of oligopoly or monopoly. This, of course, is something of an oversimplification; it must be emphasized that in practice the differences between the New Nationalism and the New Freedom were more apparent than real. As Arthur Schlesinger has pointed out in *The Crisis of the Old Order*, Wilson no more wanted to break up each and every large corporation than Roosevelt wanted to achieve universal monopoly. The common ingredient was the belief of both men in a positive role for the government in the economic system. Further, as Wilson's term in office progressed and particularly as the United States moved toward war, Wilson came increasingly to adopt a New Nationalist policy. Nevertheless, the *theoretical* split remained unresolved and lived on into the 1930's to plague New Deal policy makers.

The New Deal fell heir to the currents of thought described above. Franklin Roosevelt came to power faced with a crisis of gigantic magnitude which was capped by a complete breakdown of the nation's banking system coincident with his accession to office. From the earlier modern reform movements, he drew a tendency to use the power of government to right unhealthy economic conditions. Thus, among other achievements, the social-security system was established, public-works programs were instituted to provide jobs for the unemployed, new regulatory agencies such as the Securities Exchange Commission were created, minimum wage and working conditions were legislated, positive support was given to the nascent industrial union movement, and an attempt was made to regulate agricultural production.

The second Roosevelt also succeeded where the Populists had failed, by welding an urban and agricultural coalition whose rather shaky remnants still provide the single most important force in American politics today. Part of this success may well have been due to the President's willingness to work with the big-city political machines rather than attempt their destruction as had his

Progressive forbears. In any case, Roosevelt created an electoral coalition which converted the Republican Party into a minority and which still provides a basis of electoral support for his Democratic successors.

In many ways, the dominant characteristic of the New Deal was what is usually referred to as its pragmatic nature, although it might be more accurate philosophically to refer to its ad hoc qualities. The best simile is Roosevelt's own: he once likened himself to a quarterback trying one play and then, if that experiment failed, shifting to another. Perhaps, as William Leuchtenberg has suggested in *Franklin D. Roosevelt and the New Deal*, the men around Roosevelt had a vision of a Heavenly City; but when the history of the period is examined closely, it is impossible to conclude that they approached their ideal by any predetermined route. In fact, it can be argued, as does Arthur Schlesinger, Jr., that the particular glory of the Roosevelt administration was the President's willingness to eschew ideology during a period in which he was beset by extremists of the right and the left and to concentrate on the achievement of realizable gains.

This spontaneous, improvisatory approach to economic reform can best be seen by examining the response of the New Deal to the problem of industrial concentration. The first tack taken was from the New Nationalist logbook. The core of the First New Deal, as it is sometimes called, was the National Recovery Act, which involved the virtual suspension of the antitrust laws, so that industries could develop wage and production codes presumably designed to stabilize their particular segment of the economy. This tactic should not be confused with an attempt at centralized planning; at best it was a kind of interventionism and at worst an abdication of governmental responsibility to private concerns. The latter opinion was adopted by the United States Supreme Court, and before the NRA really got off the ground, it was declared unconstitutional.

In time, the NRA was replaced by a modified version of the New Freedom as the New Deal turned to a trustbusting program that was designed, as Richard Hofstadter argues, not so much to reestablish competition as to discipline the pricing policies of business. This approach, under the direction of Attorney General

Thurmond Arnold, was dictated by the destruction of the NRA, which had been designed to accomplish this end by other means. It is not necessary to evaluate here the soundness of this policy change; it is sufficient to emphasize once more the fundamentally antiideological, experimental nature of the New Deal.

Viewed in the light of the history of American reform, the New Deal represents the culmination of the reform tradition in American politics. Suddenly, American liberals found themselves in possession of most the demands which had been basic to their programs for many years—a fact illustrated by the startling triumph of Harry Truman in the election of 1948. The significance of the victory has been well analyzed by Eric Goldman. This election symbolized acceptance of the belief by most Americans that government was ultimately responsible for the welfare of the economy and, further, the acceptance of an enlarged international role for the United States. And, as Goldman notes, "In an important sense this liberal conquest came as liberalism turned into a form of conservatism."[1]

It is hard to deny the substantial force of this analysis. Certainly, no one can escape the conclusion that the fundamental conceptions which guide the formulation of American public policy today are those fixed in the national consciousness by the New Deal and World War II. This appraisal may partially explain the seeming hesitancy of our intellectual and political elites to advance any really new approaches to present difficulties. The feeling is widespread that the basic problems have been solved and that only matters of detail remain to be worked out. It is probably not too great an exaggeration to say that most thinking on the major issues of our time has been reduced to the manipulation of stereotypes. To describe the situation in nonpejorative terms, "the end of ideology" is at hand—or so it is claimed by such writers as Daniel Bell and Seymour Martin Lipset.

Actually, any assertion that our problems have been solved, even in terms of a very general framework of approach, is, to say the least, open to serious question. Certainly, a commitment to internationalism is insufficient as a guide to policy in the rapidly

---

[1] Eric Goldman, *Rendezvous with Destiny* (New York: Random House, Vintage Books, 1956), pp. 333–334.

changing world arena. Moreover, such domestic problems as administered price structures and the balancing of "countervailing powers" cannot be met by mere acceptance of the principles of governmental responsibility for the well-being of the economic system. Nor can it be said that the problems of mass society and mass culture can easily be solved by application of ideas now thirty years old. Be that as it may, there seems to be little doubt that it is within such a broad framework that Americans are attempting to confront the current dilemmas. Thus, what results is not an absence of ideology but a reliance on past and perhaps quite inadequate ideologies; the outcome is what might be called "an ideology of the status quo."

If the nature of this status quo is examined, particularly in the light cast by the recent liberal reevaluation of the reform movement, this conclusion is somewhat disquieting. The demands being made on the liberal underpinning of American policy are tremendous; in a very real sense, liberalism must be ready to support the weight of the entire noncommunist world. And yet, there is substantial opinion to the effect that the assessment made by American liberals of their society and of their world is at fault and therefore an inadequate response to the challenge. This assessment is largely the product of the ideas and policies current during the New Deal. To the extent that American liberals still rely on the New Deal as a source of ideas, this is clearly a crucial problem. Certainly, if the central American political tradition is analyzed in the terms outlined in Chapter I, it is rather hard to interpret the Roosevelt administration as being deliberately bent on any radical change. As Hartz contends, the face of the New Deal was generally turned toward the right, and among its most prominent characteristics were "a faith in property, a belief in class unity, a suspicion of too much state power, a hostility to the Utopian mood."

An important point to remember is that the New Deal came into being during a period of grave crisis. Even if the movement had been fundamentally radical in intent, it would probably have been too absorbed in recovery measures to bring about any really sweeping changes in the structure of the social or economic system. The job of halting panic and restoring order to the economy preempted the attention of most New Dealers. The pressures of the time resulted in what Hofstadter has called a "chaos of experimentation." This attribution is not necessarily to be deplored; in view of the tremendous "crisis of the old order," the situation was so novel, so unprecedented in its nature, that a period of experimentation was virtually inevitable. In fact, the New Deal probably could have been created only by a leader of the most flexible temperament. However, even while Hofstadter conceded this point, the clear implication of his analysis is that Roosevelt—and with him the whole liberal tradition—somehow failed to meet the problems posed by the crisis. Not only was the New Deal's lack of consistency a serious deficiency in its own time, but ever since a further problem has been that this same lack of coherence precludes the functioning of the movement as a source of doctrine for liberals today. Precisely because of the ad hoc, pragmatic orientation which from one point of view was the major virtue of the New Deal, the movement did not leave a residue of solid social theory. It is this, Hofstadter contends, which results in the "rudderless and demoralized state of American liberalism."[2]

There is much justice in Hofstadter's critique of the New Deal. Certainly, the New Deal did not present a clearly thought out, intellectually coherent program, nor can it be overlooked that it did collapse in 1938 with the fundamental problems of the Depression by no means solved. It must also be admitted (with the wisdom of hindsight) that Roosevelt's foreign policy, particularly with respect to the U.S.S.R., has proved to have been rather inept at times. Still, a balanced assessment of the New Deal must also consider its massive achievements. Even Hofstadter is forced to admit that they were indeed great. At the very least, there was a good deal of temporary relief, a degree of genuine recovery, a revival of American liberalism, and the passage of a number of statutes that have permanently altered the structure of the American social and economic system, such as the acts regulating banking, security sales, wages and hours, and establishing the social-security system.

---

[2] Richard Hofstadter, *The American Political Tradition* (New York: Random House, Vintage Books, 1954), p. vii.

In criticism, the first point to be made is that Hofstadter may expect too much. The social and economic system of a nation cannot be swept aside merely by willing to do so; it is just not that easy to transcend tradition. This certainly does not mean that the nation should or must always continue to do something just because it has always done so in the past. It is impossible to make a case for the position that whatever is, is right. It seems especially true that in a democratic political system even more than in others, politics is inevitably the art of the possible. Following the pragmatic rule of thumb, the New Deal did succeed in bringing about great changes in the American socioeconomic system. Given the nature of our politics, it may be unreasonable to expect more. At the least, this question remains in doubt.

The most significant theoretical problem raised by this discussion is the classical question of the limits of political action. How much can be reasonably expected of politics? If the New Deal must be called a failure, and if it is utopian to expect it to have accomplished more, then we are forced back upon the Niebuhrian dilemma of finding "proximate solutions for insoluble problems." The leaders of the liberal intellectual establishment have by and large accepted this formulation of the problem of democratic politics. In so doing, they have established a philosophical framework which, along with policy predispositions derived from the New Deal experience, structures the basic outlines of public policy in the United States today. Let us now turn to some of the problems posed by an attempt to build upon the New Deal within this framework.

Liberalism and the Economic System

How do liberals assess the basic character of the American economic system? This is a key question, for, as has been noted, most of the great ideological struggles of past generations have been fought over economic questions; therefore, it is in the economic sphere that liberal intellectuals might be expected to fulfill their roles as the professional critics of our society. Perhaps the most prominent of these critics is John Kenneth Galbraith, whose work repays careful analysis by the student of liberalism.

The starting point for Galbraith's analysis is the great American retreat from power. He notes that "the tendency to alarm over the possession of power by other people is greatly enhanced by the convention of denying that one possesses power." The solution to this problem of the refusal to admit the obvious is provided by the competitive model of the classical economic theory, since this construct very nearly excludes the exercise of economic power. As Galbraith puts it, for both businessmen and theorists, the great virtue of the competitive model is that it does away with power, thus serving what is essentially a political rather than an economic function.[3] Here is an explanation of one of the most persistent myths of American life: the idea that this nation has a free-enterprise, competitive economy such as that described in the theoretical writings of Adam Smith. If the economy is indeed controlled by a benevolent but unseen hand, then certainly there is no need for control by the clearly seen and not necessarily benevolent hand of government. At the same time, a justification for big industry is provided, in that fear of a large industrial combination is scarcely possible if, almost by definition, the combine cannot wield any real power because of the very nature of the competitive system.

Yet, an unmodified classical conception of the economic system is held by few economists indeed. The idea was dealt two fatal blows during the decade of the 1930's. The first was that it became more and more obvious that under conditions of imperfect competition the individual producer could control price changes rather than be controlled by them, as the classical theory demanded. The second and far more devastating blow was the realization that the Smithian economy did not work—a fact brought home with terrible force by the Depression.

If it is no longer possible to believe in the classical theory of economic competition, what can be substituted for it? Galbraith has provided what is probably the most general answer. The exercise of power is not precluded by the impersonal forces of the market, he argues. Power exists but it is held in check by what he

---

[3] John Kenneth Galbraith, *American Capitalism: The Concept of Countervailing Power* (Boston: Houghton Mifflin, 1956), p. 24.

calls countervailing power—that is, by the counterpressures that can be brought to bear by those who are subject to economic power. Moreover, "The first begets the second," writes Galbraith.[4]

The typical competitive picture is thus no longer one of competition between sellers, although there are some markets where this sort of competition still plays a role. More often than not, the restraints on economic power are provided "not by competition but from the other side of the market by strong buyers." The classic example of this phenomenon in operation is the rise of the large industrial labor union, which acts as a check on the power wielded from the management side of the market. Management can no longer unilaterally impose its will on its employees. At one time this may have been possible. Jobs were controlled solely by industry, and labor had no alternative but to accept management's dictates because failure to do so could mean severe sanctions, including even the loss of a job, since unorganized persons had no power with which to oppose gigantic industrial concentrations. The rise of the industrial unions changed this situation: collective bargaining redressed the balance of power by creating a position of strength which could aid the traditional underdog in the industrial power struggle.

The role of government in such a system is clear. Although, as Galbraith notes, the phenomenon may not be fully recognized as yet, the creation of countervailing-power situations has become a major—perhaps *the* major—domestic function of the state. Much of the legislation passed by Congress in the years since 1933 may be fully understood only from this point of view.

Thus the national government gave tremendous impetus to the rise of the trade union by the passage of the Wagner Act of 1935, and farmers have received support for their market power by means of the subsidy program; examples of government intervention in economics can be easily multiplied. The fact of governmen-

---

[4] *Ibid.*, p. 111. Galbraith implies here, and asserts flatly on page 113, that countervailing power is self-generating. The argument of C. Wright Mills to the contrary should be noted. Mills contends that the theory is less an attempt to describe the actual structure of the economic system than a guide to policy, "a moral proposal for strategic action." See Mills, *The Power Elite* (New York: Oxford University Press, 1956), p. 126.

tal assistance in the development of countervailing power tends to bear out C. Wright Mills' claim that the concept is more a normative imperative than a scientific theory. It is hard to exaggerate the extent to which weak groups are reliant on government for support and protection. Indeed, some argue that the creation of countervailing power has become the special task of the liberal in our politico-economic system. As Galbraith says, "Liberalism will be identified with the buttressing of weak bargaining positions in the economy; conservatism—and this may well be its proper function—will be identified with the protection of positions of original power."[5]

This distinction between original and countervailing power is important to Galbraith's analysis. Original power is that power which derives from a firm's control over prices, which in turn derives from the production, processing, or distribution of a particular product. Galbraith's rule of thumb is that positions of original power may be justifiably attacked by means of antitrust action if they are not subject to a countervailing power. This assessment of the liberal role is very much to the point. Certainly, it provides an accurate interpretation of much of the underlying purpose of the New Deal legislative program; moreover, it falls easily into the pattern of liberal egalitarianism. The theory rejects any notion that in our economic system, only the strong should survive. For this, it substitutes a belief in the importance of creating conditions in which the weak will be able to survive. Thus, what Galbraith offers is a very clear rationalization, phrased in the terms of economic theory, for the positive role increasingly assumed by government in this century.

The implication of the analysis is clear. No longer does the liberal live in fear of bigness in the economic system. The answer to bigness is not the destruction of large concentrations of economic power, but rather the creation of new concentrations to act as counterweights to them. To the extent that this view is accepted, the long internecine struggle between liberals over the merits of the New Nationalism and the New Freedom has been ended by the triumph of the former. Galbraith himself, in his

---

[5] Galbraith, *American Capitalism*, p. 151.

collection of essays *The Liberal Hour,* has urged liberals to give up regretting bigness and to learn to live with it in order that they may devote themselves to more pressing questions. A similarly optimistic view of large industrial combines has been presented by A. A. Berle, Jr., who, over a long period of years, has established himself as perhaps the leading liberal theoretician on this problem. Berle, too, rejects any belief that the classical laws of economics are still applicable to the present scene. It does not even make sense, he argues, to view the great concentrations of corporate power as private, except in the formalist sense that they are not state-owned. Moreover, even the classical market mechanism which is supposed to regulate these concerns is no longer fully operative, as attested by such industries as oil and sugar which are often able to create a "planned equation of supply to demand."[6]

Again and again Berle returns to the theme of the growth of corporate concentration—a theme which has dominated his entire career since the publication (with Gardiner Means) of *The Modern Corporation and Private Property* in 1937. In agreement with Galbraith, he shows that the United States has an oligopolistic economy in which one half of American industry is owned by concentrates and in which 135 corporations own 45 per cent of the industrial assets of the nation. He also continues to emphasize the separation of ownership and control. This development takes on a new significance in view of the fact that more and more funds for capital investment now come from sources internal to the corporation itself, thus removing one of the checks on management provided in classical theory—the need to go to the public for such resources. More and more it is true that major corporations need not submit themselves to the judgment of the market.

But Berle is not so unhappy about this trend as he once was. He writes:

in broadest outline we are plotting the course by which the twentieth century in America is expected to produce an evolving economic utopia, and, apparently, the potential actually exists, bringing that dangerous and thrilling adventure within reach for the first time in recorded history.

---

[6] Adolph A. Berle, Jr., *The 20th Century Capitalist Revolution* (New York: Harcourt, Harvest Books, 1960), p. 12.

At the same time, he sounds an important warning note, being not quite so unreserved in his praise of our economic structure as his critics believe. The great problem of the system, he bluntly asserts, is that it is guided by "self-perpetuating oligarchies," so that "the only real control which guides or limits their [the large corporations'] economic and social actions is the real, though undefined and tacit, philosophy of the men who compose them." The difficulty is that the community has not created any referent of responsibility from which the corporation may take its mandate. Left to its own devices, the corporation has become the "conscience" of this century in the United States by virtue of its key position. In Berle's picturesque terms, "Our ancestors feared that corporations had no conscience. We are treated to the colder, more modern fear that, perhaps, they do."[7]

Thus, according to Berle, we have created something like Frankenstein's monster: a creature blessed with an enormous capacity to do good, but burdened with an equally great capacity to do evil. Moreover, the problem raised is essentially political rather than economic. Originally, corporations were viewed as a legal problem; thirty years ago they began to be treated as economic institutions; while today they must be viewed as at least quasi-political. This is true, Berle notes, because where there is a question of power, there is also a question of legitimacy—which is, after all, one of the classical problems of political theory. And yet, for all of his occasional qualms, Berle is not pessimistic about the future; he does foresee developments that will provide the needed standard of legitimacy. However, before the matter of legitimacy is discussed, two other themes remain to be analyzed.

The first is the role of the trade union. Ignored by Berle, the union is at least suggested in Galbraith's analysis of the structure of American capitalism. Perhaps because of the long-time commitment of liberals to the cause of organized labor, there seems to be some reluctance to assess the current place of labor in the economic power structure. Few liberal leaders (Reinhold Niebuhr being a leading exception) have emphasized the essential parallelism between Big Labor and Big Business. What has developed,

---

[7] *Ibid.*, p. 184.

Niebuhr asserts, is a kind of "new feudalism," with the place of the old feudalities taken by the new economic leviathans.[8] This same theme is elaborated at some length by Hans Morgenthau, whose analysis brings out some significant points. We are faced with what Morgenthau calls the paradox of thwarted government; in our time we have seen a tremendous increase in the power of government in relation to the people, accompanied by a decrease in the over-all power that is exercised. As Morgenthau puts it, "This paradox is the result of the decomposition of governmental power from within and without; through the feudalism of semi-autonomous executive departments and through the feudalism of the concentrations of private power."[9]

In other words, there exists a political and economic stalemate partially brought about by the conflict of the countervailing powers hailed by Galbraith. It is important to emphasize that this situation is political as well as economic; it could hardly be otherwise since the government has taken on the buttressing of countervailing power as one of its primary tasks. The economic sphere is no longer autonomous, if indeed it ever was. More and more it is subject to political control, and it in turn tries to influence political decisions. Thus, as Morgenthau has pointed out, we have seen the revival of a truly political economy.[10]

This mixing of politics and economics is no doubt inevitable under our present system. An excellent case study of the sort of problems involved may be seen in Vice President Nixon's intervention in the steel dispute of 1959–1960. The intransigence of the steel negotiators led to a political and economic situation which was intolerable for the administration, causing it to force a solution more favorable to labor than either it or the steel companies thought desirable and which was undesirable from a purely economic point of view. The important point is that a Democratic administration would no doubt have done the same thing, al-

---

[8] W. H. Ferry, *The Corporation and the Economy: Notes Followed by a Discussion* (Santa Barbara, Calif.: Center for the Study of Democratic Institutions, 1959), pp. 28ff.

[9] Hans J. Morgenthau, *The Purpose of American Politics* (New York: Knopf, 1960), p. 275.

[10] *Ibid.*, p. 281.

though it might have been more difficult for it to make a settlement so favorable to labor. President Kennedy's later intervention in another steel crisis exemplifies the same phenomenon, as do the still later conflicts of President Johnson with the same industry.

No matter how difficult it may be to accept such a method of achieving economic order, it is clearly impossible to repudiate the present system and return to anything approximating a classical, free-market economy. The situation has been ably summed up by the economist J. M. Clark, who points out that between the individual and the government there now stands a plethora of organized groups. In a simpler economy the pursuit of self-interest is an almost viable mode of economic organization. However, in a complex modern economy, in which interests are represented by organized groups, the conflict of interests can lead to corruption and may lead to social chaos.[11]

In addition to the organizational problem, there is another aspect of the current economic situation which is of interest to the liberal ideologist. Simply put, the economy does not work very smoothly. On the one hand, there are periodic bouts with inflation, and on the other, there has been until recently a good deal of chronic unemployment. These probelms must also be assessed before examining liberal prescriptions in the economic area.

Galbraith has treated the question of inflation quite extensively, asserting that it is the endemic problem of an affluent society. This admission reveals a great weakness in the theory of countervailing power, since, as Galbraith points out in *American Capitalism*, the system described does not act as a brake on market power when there is inflation or even inflationary pressure. What then is to be done? Here Galbraith is somewhat at a loss. The traditional remedies, such as monetary or fiscal policy, are both rejected: the former because it is economically unsound; and the latter because, while theoretically defensible in purely economic terms, it raises serious political difficulties for liberals. To wit, liberals are called upon by their egalitarian ideology to oppose any taxation which does not follow the rule calling for an equalization

---

[11] John M. Clark, *Alternative to Serfdom* (New York: Random House, Vintage Books, 1956), pp. 5–6.

of income differentials or which sacrifices production to price stability. The most logical way out of the dilemma is through fiscal policy accompanied by wage and price controls. But here, too, a feasible solution must be rejected because the idea of controls is rejected by the conventional wisdom.

Chronic inflation is not the only problem with which the economy is faced. Perhaps even more serious is the threat posed by an equally chronic unemployment which seemingly cannot be combated within the confines of a system based on the clash of countervailing powers. What must be emphasized is that pockets of economic distress are not merely the result of temporary fluctuations which will right themselves if left alone; rather they may well be the product of a deeper malaise which is structural in nature. As the distinguished economist Alvin Hansen has written, the changes we are witnessing are fundamental in character. They involve more than the decline of some industries or geographic areas. Rather, they reflect a "basic, perhaps revolutionary" decline in the number of workers engaged in the production of material goods in comparison with those occupied in service industries.[12] We have reached a point where one and a quarter million workers may be discharged every year *without engendering any decline in production.*

It is hardly too much to suggest that we are faced with a second Industrial Revolution—this one sparked by the rise of automation. The extent and significance of this revolution are matters of great controversy among economists and industrial sociologists. Some fear that major dislocations will result, particularly in the form of high unemployment among the unskilled. Others are much more cautious and argue that automation need have no repercussions greater than those induced by the technological advances of earlier periods.[13] A representative of the latter

---

[12] Alvin Hansen, "Automation and the Welfare State," *New Republic,* CXLIV (June 18, 1961), 10–11. See also Victor Fuchs, "The First Service Economy," *The Public Interest* (Winter 1966), pp. 7–17.

[13] For examples from the vast literature, see Ben Seligman, "Automation and the State," *Commentary* (June 1964), pp. 49–54; Seligman, "On Theories of Automation," *Dissent* (May–June 1966), pp. 243–264; Robert Heilbroner, "Where Do We Go From Here?" *New York Review of Books* (March

group points out, for example, that it is possible to have full employment with technical progress that is either fast or slow. In political terms, what is significant is the assertion that full employment under these conditions will not come about automatically and thus that government must consciously manage demand. Referring to the celebrated case of West Germany, Robert Solow points out that although the Germans talk a good game of laissez-faire, "at the same time [West Germany] does dozens of things each one of which would be instantly denounced in the United States as creeping socialism."[14] If this analysis is correct, the prospects are that there will be an intensified ideological conflict over the long-submerged issue of economic planning. This would appear to be the minimum consequence of recent technological change.

Other observers raise the possibility of even more significant developments. For instance, Organski argues that "automation will bring about significant changes in the power structure that underlies government, even in a democracy."[15] These will include a greater concentration of economic and political power, a new class system brought about by the changing job structure, and an "increasingly close identification between government and industry." Under these conditions the masses would be more and more dependent upon government, and welfare measures would be greatly expanded in order to cushion the adjustment to an automated society. The great problem will be to make government democratically responsible. With the concentration of power and the likely emergence of a technological-administrative elite with a high potential for dominating the new system, popular control may be very hard to maintain. While Organski's analysis is admittedly speculative, it is not implausible, and it should be clear that the development of a society even closely resembling the one he

---

17, 1966), pp. 12–16; Robert Solow, "Technology and Unemployment," *The Public Interest* (Fall 1965), pp. 17–26; Daniel Bell, "The Bogey of Automation," *New York Review of Books* (August 26, 1965), pp. 23–25. The materials cited contain further bibliographic information.

[14] Solow, "Technology and Unemployment," p. 23.

[15] A. F. K. Organski, *The Stages of Political Development* (New York: Knopf, 1965), p. 193.

projects would prove a formidable challenge to democratic theory. Even under present conditions, social theorists have provided only the most fragmentary answers to the dilemmas of advanced industrialism. So far, little more has been done beyond the identification of the problems of inflation, automation, poverty, and the myriad opportunities for irresponsible behavior on the part of the economic elites.

One of the most interesting responses to this complex of problems has been the idea of the guaranteed income. Although this concept was mentioned as early as 1962 by—interestingly enough—the conservative economist Milton Friedman, it first achieved widespread attention in 1963, when it was advocated by Robert Theobald in his book *Free Men and Free Markets*. It was then picked up in 1964 by the Ad Hoc Committee on the Triple Revolution, a group of liberal social scientists and political activists concerned with the overlapping problems of cybernation, modern weapons systems, and civil rights. By 1966 the basic idea of the guaranteed income had something like an official seal of approval when it was endorsed in the Report of the National Commission on Technology, Automation, and Economic Progress, a group appointed by President Johnson and including distinguished academic figures such as Daniel Bell and Robert Solow, businessmen such as Thomas Watson, Jr., and labor leaders such as Walter Reuther. The wide range of support which the guaranteed income finds—at least in theory—is illustrated by the continuing support of Professor Friedman. This range amounts to something like a Popular Front in support of this potentially revolutionary concept.

The motives underlying this wide base of support are extremely varied. Thus, Theobald's position stems from his extreme views on the likely impact of automation. He seems to believe that full employment is a goal impossible of attainment and that we must therefore accept a really fundamental change in our attitude toward work and leisure. Direct payments must be made to the poor, not only in order to maintain the level of demand in the economy, but also in order to make it possible for all men to achieve the ancient goal of full development of their capacities *regardless* of their ability to compete in a market economy.

Others, like Leon Keyserling, a former chairman of the Council of Economic Advisors under President Truman, are less pessimistic about the impact of cybernation on employment. Keyserling notes that, contrary to the apocalyptic predictions of Theobald, unemployment has been declining since 1963. A good deal of poverty, he argues, is suffered by those who should not be in the labor force at all—the aged, the chronically ill, the disabled, the handicapped, and many women. These people include about 40 per cent of the poverty-stricken, and direct payments should be made to those who fall in these categories. Keyserling believes that it should be possible for the economy to generate meaningful work for the remainder of those living in poverty. Still other approaches can be found in the writings of conservative advocates like Milton Friedman; these will be discussed in Chapter V.

An analysis of the spectrum of opinion running from Theobald to Friedman uncovers numerous other areas of disagreement, notably over such questions as the precise level of income to be guaranteed and the ends to which the proposal is said to be a means. Analysis is often inchoate and fragmentary—a fact which is not too surprising if indeed we are experiencing a revolution in the basic modes of production. The sociopolitical theory of modern corporate society, as opposed to the economic theory, is still decidedly underdeveloped.

This point is particularly clear with respect to the problems inherent in exercising control over the giant corporations. Several possible lines of argument have been advanced. One is Berle's faith in the conscience of the corporation. Little need be said about this chimerical and ultimately rather naïve argument beyond pointing to the price-fixing scandals in the electrical industry, recent revelations about pricing policy in the drug industry, and the cavalier attitude toward safety displayed by the leading automobile manufacturers. It would probably be incorrect to cite these examples as typical behavior, but they do suffice to indicate the need for some institutionalized system of control which is not merely a matter of conscience.

Second, Berle indicates, in his *Economic Power and the Free Society* (a pamphlet published by the Fund for the Republic), that we may be moving toward a new constitutional doctrine. The idea is that in view of the tremendous scope and power of the new corporations, they should be subject to the same sort of restraints which regulate the federal and state governments. In other words, such provisions as the Bill of Rights and the Fourteenth Amendment would apply to the activities of corporations. An example may perhaps be found in the pressure civil-rights groups have applied to corporations in an effort to induce them to employ more Negroes, particularly in management positions. It may be that these pressures will succeed. However, the evidence that the modern corporation has as yet assumed its responsibilities in this area is scant.[16]

Thus it must be said that Berle's idea remains an interesting possibility; unfortunately, he does not elaborate the theme and it remains at best an interesting suggestion. A somewhat more likely development is an increasing tendency toward more comprehensive economic planning than has been done in the past, at least since the collapse of the NRA. This suggestion is made, again in somewhat underdeveloped form, by Berle. As noted above, Organski has also pointed out the enormous pressures for an increasing level of government planning which current technological developments create. This trend may have increasing significance in liberal thought in the future. "Planning" is not a popular word in the context of the American political culture, and its use could easily precipitate a renewal of ideological conflicts which have seemingly been buried. In any case, such liberal intellectuals as Schlesinger and Galbraith have laid an appropriate groundwork in their attempted historical rehabilitation of the NRA. As both writers admit, the stereotyped view that this experiment was a total failure is firmly fixed in American history books, and it is likely to remain so. However, the best recent historical works, such as Schlesinger's, have done much to undermine this view. Galbraith sums up these findings when he argues that the NRA may have reflected a much more sophisticated understanding of the market processes of an

---

[16] Andrew Hacker, "Imperium in Imperio Revisited," in Gottfried Dietze, ed., *Essays on the American Constitution* (Englewood Cliffs, N.J.: Prentice-Hall, 1964), p. 57. Hacker goes so far as to add that ". . . a corporation is by construction and temperament, unfitted to represent the fundamental values of a free society." *Ibid.*

industrial society than did the views of its opponents.[17] Unfortunately, the failure to recognize this fact has deleterious consequences. As Galbraith remarks earlier in his book:

The misapprehension of the nature of modern industrial society by most of the historians of the New Deal, especially in the treatment of NRA, continues to delay the development of a price stabilization policy that would be relevant to an economy of vast corporations and strong unions.[18]

However, all of this retrospective analysis merely lays a possible foundation for liberals who are interested in exploring the potential of systematic economic planning. Even the NRA cannot be classified as a planned effort; to do so is to confuse planning with interventionism, as Hofstadter has so aptly pointed out. Genuine planning implies a measure of centralization, and the key feature of the NRA was the decentralization of economic power into the hands of industrial trade associations. Coordination of these efforts was missing. As a result, even a rehabilitation of the NRA's reputation might well lead liberals in a direction which they do not intend. Aside from this hazard, the American political and economic tradition militates against any such "revolutionary" approach. To be effective, the ideas of theorists must be converted into political action, and there is a natural reluctance to predict a mass movement behind a program easily labeled with the dreaded tag of "socialism." At the same time, there are powerful forces in the economy which tend to push liberals in this direction, and it must be said that one of the more interesting features in American politics in the next few years should be the struggle between the forces of tradition and those of economic rationalization.

So far, the argument for planning has been considered largely in terms of the economic pressures which might bring it about. The conservative response to the argument will be assessed in a later chapter. However, more than economics is involved, and liberals must face the possibility that in the context of general

---

[17] Galbraith, The Liberal Hour (Boston: Houghton Mifflin, 1960), p. 84. For Schlesinger's view, see The Coming of the New Deal (Boston: Houghton Mifflin, 1959), pp. 170–176.

[18] Galbraith, The Liberal Hour, p. 4.

social thought the planning approach might come into conflict with other key values. In order to evaluate this possibility, it will be necessary to consider another major line of contemporary thought.

The Trend toward "Qualitative" Liberalism

One of the most interesting recent developments in American liberalism has been the movement toward a new kind of thought, an approach less concerned with economic or "quantitative" questions and more concerned with the "quality" of American life and culture. This movement has grown out of the general intellectual ferment of the 1950's. As Schlesinger points out, those years witnessed a sense of "anxiety and frustration" about the state of our culture, a feeling that somehow things were not right, boredom with materialistic complacency, and in general a questioning of the purposes of our society.[19] The signs of this ferment were many: the rise of the Beat Generation, the revival of satire, the growth of religion, the popularity of such a book as *Doctor Zhivago* with its spiritual message, and lastly and most importantly here the great attention received by such books as David Riesman's *The Lonely Crowd*, William Whyte's *The Organization Man*, and Galbraith's *The Affluent Society*. All of these signs, which Schlesinger feels parallel the intellectual stirrings of the 1920's, led him to expect a new period of political liberalism.

Perhaps the earliest document of qualitative liberalism was *The Lonely Crowd*. The work is an outgrowth of Riesman's attempt to determine how a society manages to produce in its members "the social character" that it must have in order to remain a going concern. The analysis begins with a description of the pattern of population growth in Western nations. This pattern may be represented by an S curve, the three segments of which are called high growth potential, transitional growth, and incipient population decline. Riesman's major theme is then announced: "My thesis is, in fact, that each of these three different phases on

---

[19] Schlesinger, *The Politics of Hope* (Boston: Houghton Mifflin, 1963), pp. 81–82.

the population curve appears to be occupied by a society that enforces conformity and molds social character in a definably different way." The first stage has a typical character whose conformity derives from an adherence to tradition (tradition direction); in the second stage, an internalized set of goals acquired early in life is the determining factor (inner direction); while in the third stage, pressures from the social environment produce the required character structure (other direction).[20] The key to the present American social character is to be found in the shift from the stage of high growth potential to the period of incipient population decline. Individuality, which was once the keynote of the American character, has suffered great setbacks. Our ideology may remain competitive, Riesman contends, but there has been at the same time a marked shift toward ideological justification for submission to the group, so that one's peers become the "measure of all things."[21] We have become an other-directed society.

Riesman's criticism of the other-directed should not be over-emphasized. He admits that in the comparison between inner-directedness and other-directedness the latter comes off a poor second. Indeed, it is difficult to be fair since the very term suggests shallowness and superficiality, "even though direction in *both* cases comes from the outside and is simply internalized at an early point in the life of the cycle of the inner-directed."[22] However, when he extends his thesis to the analysis of politics, the other-directed appear in a favorable light when compared with their predecessors. In politics the inner-directed tend to be "moralizers," while the other-directed tend to be "inside-dopesters." This shift in characterological style is marked by a shift from indignation to tolerance in political psychology and by a shift in the structure of

---

[20] David Riesman, *The Lonely Crowd* (rev. ed.; New Haven: Yale University Press, 1961), pp. 3–36. It should be noted that in the extended preface to this new edition, pp. xxx–xxxii, Riesman admits that the reliance on the population-growth curve is very dubious indeed. However, from the point of view of Riesman's analysis, it makes little difference whether the postulated linkage with the population curve is valid or not. The important thing is still the discussion of the character types.

[21] *Ibid.*, p. 82.

[22] *Ibid.*, p. 159.

decision making from a pattern of ruling-class dominance to a system in which power is dispersed among a variety of conflicting interest groups, or "veto groups." This transformation, Riesman contends, indicates a growing political sophistication. The nineteenth-century moralizers tended to view politics "not only in a confused and ethically limited but also in a slightly paranoid and autistic way," which resulted in the projection of their fears into politics in such a way as to make subtlety or even tolerance difficult.[23] Psychological factors of this sort may account for the recurrent xenophobia which besets American politics as well as for such closely related phenomena as the radical right. By contrast, the other-directed inside-dopester may be inclined to view politics rather cynically—as at best a kind of spectator sport—but at least he is not likely to turn political activity into a fanatical moralistic crusade.[24] Thus, while Riesman does not hope for a return to inner direction, it is equally clear that he does not applaud the ascendency of the other-directed either.

A roughly similar picture of American society is painted by William Whyte. Whyte's approach to the problem is an analysis of the dominant social myth of our culture. What he describes is the decline of the Protestant ethic and the rise of what he calls a social ethic as a substitute. The major beliefs of this new ethic are "scientism, belongingness, and togetherness." Whyte sums up the major propositions of the social ethic as "a belief in the group as the source of creativity; a belief in 'belongingness' as the ultimate need of the individual; and a belief in the application of science to achieve the belongingness."[25]

What makes Whyte's work of interest is that while it advances a thesis similar to Riesman's, its popularity indicates that it presents a view which large numbers of Americans find congenial. It should also be noted that Whyte has forsaken the more or less neutral tone adopted by Riesman in his discussion of recent characterological changes. He is openly critical of these developments, a fact which makes his popularity (especially among the organiza-

---

[23] *Ibid.*, p. 177.

[24] *Ibid.*, pp. 182–187.

[25] William H. Whyte, Jr., *The Organization Man* (Garden City, N.Y.: Doubleday, Anchor Books, 1957), p. 7.

tion men themselves) even more noteworthy. Moreover, there is a good deal of empirical evidence to be found in support of that thesis. In an exhaustive study on shifting values in American society, Clyde Kluckhohn has found support for the following propositions:

1. Decline of the Puritan ethic as the core of the dominant middle-class value system.

2. Increase in other-directedness.

3. Emergence of explicit value placed on psychological health.

4. More prizing of some kinds of tolerance and of some kinds of diversity.

5. Drift toward equalization of the roles of the sexes.[26]

As Kluckhohn has emphasized, a certain amount of caution must be used in interpreting these data. It must be borne in mind that this work is the product of intellectuals who are a specialized, highly articulate group with definite biases and who, because of their functional roles as social critics, tend to speak as nonconformists. There is also the possibility that an older generation may be attempting to judge the younger set by values which are no longer quite applicable. It should also be noted that there has been considerable debate among students of national character as to the extent and even the existence of major characterological change.

Thus, in a symposium on the work of Riesman, Seymour Martin Lipset argues that American character has been essentially *unchanging* and adduces the writings of such nineteenth-century observers as Harriet Martineau and Alexis de Tocqueville as evidence. These students, while using different terminology, describe American life in much the same way as does Riesman. Since their findings date back to the 1830's, they call Riesman's conclusions into question although the evidence is not sufficient to invalidate the thesis of a basic characterological change.[27] Nevertheless, the

---

[26] Clyde Kluckhohn, "Have There Been Discernible Shifts in Values in the Past Generation?" in Elting Morrison, ed., *The American Style* (New York: Harper, 1958), p. 207.

[27] See Seymour Martin Lipset, "A Changing American Character?" in Lipset and Leo Lowenthal, eds., *Culture and Social Character* (New York: The Free Press, 1961), pp. 136–171.

data that can be marshaled in behalf of the Riesman-Whyte position are impressive and must be taken quite seriously. Moreover, the question of whether or not there has been change is perhaps less important than the accuracy of the description of the present. Here Riesman has not been seriously challenged, and even Lipset admits that contemporary "bureaucratization and mechanization *reinforce* those social mechanisms which breed other-directedness."[28]

What is the import of these findings for normative theory? In the title essay of his book *Individualism Reconsidered*, Riesman makes it quite clear that he is not calling for a return to nineteenth-century values. He writes, "To the degree that capitalist individualism has fostered an ethic of callousness, the result has been to undermine all forms of individualism, good and bad." This point may be buttressed by his highly critical remarks on the inner-directed in politics. What he is attempting to do goes beyond an effort to score empty triumphs over the vulgar excesses of American mass culture. Rather, he is looking for ways in which it is possible to build on the present social base in order to achieve the goal posited by all classical social thought: the fullest development of the individual personality.

The goal, then, is the production of social conditions conducive to the rise of the "autonomous man." By an autonomous man Riesman means the man who is psychologically able to choose whether or not to conform to the pressures of his society. Moreover, this man is consciously aware of his choice. Autonomy thus connotes a rational condition in which the free individual chooses to live his life as he wishes, not necessarily without regard for community norms, but certainly without slavish, unquestioning obedience to them. In brief, the autonomous man is the masterless man who is the protagonist of classical liberalism—hopefully, devoid of any sense of anomic rootlessness stemming from his sense of detachment from his community.

It must be clear that Riesman's cultural criticism is very much in line with the main thrust of "qualitative" liberalism. The approach is not primarily economic or political; instead, it is essen-

---

[28] *Ibid.*, p. 168; emphasis in the original.

tially a cultural critique of the society produced by a modern industrial economy and its accompanying bureaucratic structure. This nonpolitical variety of liberalism is a new and significant development. The spokesmen for this new intellectual movement feel that the major domestic problem of our time is the preservation of individuality and excellence in a modern, bureaucratic social system. The crisis of individuality forecast by de Tocqueville more than one hundred years ago seems to be at hand. Few would argue that liberal concern with this problem is not laudable; the difficulty is that the problem has such deeply rooted causes that it is easier to identify than to solve. Moreover, the concern with individuality may well be in considerable tension with the rest of the liberal program. However, before this point can be discussed, it is necessary to weave one more major strand into the argument.

That strand is the economic variant of qualitative liberalism. Here again, Galbraith is a significant liberal ideologist. The keynote is sounded in *The Affluent Society*, in which Galbraith argues that the "classical program" of American liberalism is now obsolete. Until the 1930's, the key to liberal thought had been the achievement of economic security through the redistribution of existing income, the strengthening of previously weak groups such as trade unions, the regulation of industry, the development of governmental services, and so forth.[29] An important shift occurred in the 1930's with the coming of the Keynesian revolution in economic theory. Today the liberal program still bears the marks of this intellectual revolt. The new emphasis is now on production. The question of *how* the product is to be distributed has become a secondary matter, argues Galbraith. "There is almost no concern at all over the *kinds* of private goods and services that are produced. *All* are important and the *total* counts."[30]

What the conventional wisdom of the liberals fails to take into account, Galbraith contends, is that we live in an economy of abundance. There is a difference in kind, a *qualitative* difference, between production increases that ease unemployment and those that merely increase affluence. "In continuing to emphasize pro-

---

[29] Galbraith, *The Affluent Society* (Boston: Houghton Mifflin, 1958), pp. 187–188.

[30] *Ibid.*, p. 190; emphasis added.

duction, liberals, who once had a great issue, have without realizing it come to possess no issue at all." Again and again Galbraith
returns to this theme. The refusal to distinguish between different
kinds of production is "curiously unreasonable"; the idea that
wants do not become less urgent as they are better met is "repug-
nant to common sense." To be sure, in his later works—perhaps
due to the pressure of the 1960 political campaign—Galbraith does
place a slightly more conventional emphasis on productivity. In
The Liberal Hour he asserts that the rate of economic growth has
not been satisfactory, but even here he continues to argue that "we
must ask ourselves *why* we want more." Clearly, Galbraith associates himself with the qualitative liberals, and to them he presents a
program for action.

What must be done, he writes, is to make a major effort to
redress the social balance of American society. Here he lays down a
witty and sarcastic barrage in the form of a scathing analysis of the
grossness and mediocrity of American life today. The well-known
problems of the large metropolitan areas, such as underdeveloped
housing, polluted air, and juvenile deliquency, are described at
some length and with biting sarcasm. The social balance which he
wishes to redress is defined as the "relationship between the supply
of privately produced goods and services and those of the state."[31]
What we must do is to increase spending in the public sector of
the economy, even when this means (as it almost necessarily does)
the violation of some of the central canons of the contemporary
liberal's stock of conventional wisdom. The reason that a violation
of the sacred texts will be necessary is that the redress of social
balance requires expenditures which come from an increase in
taxation. This reasoning does not run against the liberal grain at
all; what does hurt is the next point. Since Galbraith operates on
the assumption that we live in an affluent society in which very
nearly everyone has the basic essentials of life, it follows that taxes
need no longer be levied so as to redistribute the national income.
This is clearly a frontal assault on liberal egalitarianism. On this
point he is quite frank: "The only hope—and in the nature of
things it rests primarily with liberals—is to separate the issue of

---

[31] *Ibid.*, p. 255.

equality from that of social balance." Further, "The rational liberal, in the future, will resist tax reduction, even that which ostensibly favors the poor, if it is at the price of social balance."[32] Galbraith's major concerns having been established, it is now possible to attempt an evaluation of the whole thrust of American liberalism's response to contemporary socioeconomic conditions in the United States.

Summary and Comment

The key idea which informs most of the liberal thought discussed here is that of affluence. Just as certainly as Galbraith is the economist of the affluent society, Schlesinger is its political theorist and Riesman its sociologist. Schlesinger's work presumes the essential success of the New Deal in its mission of achieving a "quantitatively" sound base for society while avoiding messianic ideological commitments; at the same time Riesman's fundamental assumption is that we have moved into a stage of high consumption. Indeed, one of the major problems which dominates Riesman's *Abundance for What?* is the matter of determining the uses to which our newfound abundance should be put.

It must be mentioned, however, that a fundamental challenge has been hurled at this basic premise. Gabriel Kolko, for example, charges that Galbraith "does not fulfill the minimum function of social analysis, which is to describe the basic form and outline of society *as it is.*" We still have poverty, Kolko argues, along with gross inequalities in income, which in turn lead to inequalities in consumption patterns. As a result, "nearly one-half of the population is financially able to meet only its immediate physical needs," while a large part of this group, amounting to one-third of the total population, is "in want of even basic necessities."[33] Thus, "the basic economic fact of life for a majority of the population is insecurity." Poverty has not disappeared, Kolko contends; social scientists like Galbraith only *think* it has.

A less technical but much more widely read study than Kol-

---

[32] *Ibid.*, pp. 313–314.

[33] Gabriel Kolko, *Wealth and Power in America* (New York: Praeger, 1962), p. 128.

ko's is the analysis by Michael Harrington in his influential little volume *The Other America*.[34] In effect, Harrington contends that there are not one but two Americas: the one described by Galbraith (and Riesman, it might be added), and the other by himself. The "other America" consists of 40–50 million people who, ironically enough, are seldom noticed for the simple reason that, as Galbraith suggests, the poor are a distinct minority for the first time in history. As Harrington points out, if one is poor and hopes to receive aid, it is much better to be poor in a country in which the large majority fall into the same category. The poor today, however, find it very hard to adjust to the ways of the affluent society which surrounds them. Typically, they lack education, or they live in isolated parts of the country such as the West Virginia coalfields, or they have been replaced by machines in the automation revolution and lack the skill to find new jobs, or they are Negroes, or perhaps they suffer from several of these handicaps at once. In any case the poor tend to be isolated psychologically, educationally, geographically, and often even physically, so that residents of the "familiar America" are hardly aware of their existence.

The precise dimensions of poverty and the developmental trend are still matters of controversy. That there is significant poverty in America is not in dispute. Even Galbraith does not deny this, contrary to the implications of his critics. The best available studies by economists such as Herman Miller and Robert Lampman indicate that in fact poverty has declined, *even taking into account the steadily rising "poverty line"*—that is, the income level chosen to distinguish poverty from nonpoverty. Thus, there has been a gain in absolute terms, brought about largely by a steadily rising Gross National Product. On the other hand, income distribution is not becoming more egalitarian. As Lampman has shown, there was substantial income redistribution in the period from 1938 to 1948; since 1948 there has been no clear trend. The lessening of inequality is confined, Lampman contends, to the top half of the income distribution; the bottom half shows no change

---

[34] Michael Harrington, *The Other America* (New York: Macmillan, 1962).

in inequality. In fact, a few straws in the wind suggest that 1949–1950 may have been a "turning point toward more economic inequality among persons." The tentative nature of this conclusion must be emphasized; nonetheless, it is disconcerting.[35]

In any case, the poor do exist and their presence provides a standing challenge to the theory of affluence. It might be noted in passing that it is these contradictions within the affluent society that give the New Left much of what interest it has. The "movement" has failed to produce any social theory of real import— indeed, it seems self-consciously to avoid theorizing—but it has pointed up the disparities between ideals and reality, not only with respect to affluence and poverty, but also with respect to civil rights.

A second major flaw of the new liberalism is its political weakness. Qualitative liberalism has not yet succeeded in winning a mass following, partly because its aims are so ill-defined, but also because in the nature of things a movement heavily committed to cultural reform is always likely to find it difficult to achieve such support. A higher standard of culture is not the banner to wave if one wishes to found a mass movement. The further away one gets from bread-and-butter issues, the harder it is to build a mass base. Thus urban blight is an aspect of our culture that may be attacked politically, but the "wasteland" of commercial television probably is not. "Art by act of Congress," to borrow Jacques Barzun's phrase, is unlikely to succeed. There is little evidence that very many people are genuinely unhappy with the wasteland or with the other manifestations of mass culture. It might also be noted that problems like urban blight appear to be as much "quantitative" as they are "qualitative"; hence the distinction drawn by Schlesinger between the liberalism of the 1930's and that of the 1950's tends to break down. Some of the *new* liberalism consists of fundamentally apolitical cultural criticism, while much of the politically viable remainder is really an extension of the old liberal-

---

[35] The basic information on poverty is drawn from two articles: Herman P. Miller, "Changes in the Number and Composition of the Poor," and Robert Lampman, "Income Distribution and Poverty," both in Margaret Gordon, ed., *Poverty in America* (San Francisco: Chandler, 1965), pp. 81–101 and 102–114 respectively.

ism. To the extent that this is true, the ultimate value of qualitative liberalism is that it may force us to look at our problems in a new way; unfortunately, the programs it breeds have not yet been brought into line with the new point of view.

Even if the premise of an affluent society denied by such writers as Kolko and Harrington is accepted, certain problems may be seen in contemporary liberal thought. Let us consider the tension which exists between two lines of development described here: the slowly building pressures for more economic planning, and the rise of qualitative liberalism. Perhaps the conflict stems from an insufficient recognition of some of the fundamental social forces in a modern industrial economy. A classic description of these forces is provided in Max Weber's famous essay, "Bureaucracy." In Weber's analysis, bureaucracy is based on fixed jurisdictional areas ordered by laws or administrative regulations. The system of order which results is stable, methodical, carefully defined, based on written records, and hierarchical. This sort of institutional structure is fully developed only in the modern state and in the "most advanced institutions of modern capitalism." Moreover, the fundamental dynamic of modern society moves it inexorably in the direction of bureaucratic growth, if for no other reason than that this form of organization is technically superior to any other. Even so, there are inherent dangers; as Weber points out, democracy as such is opposed to bureaucratic rule in spite of the fact that it tends to promote bureaucracy. In fact, as Gerth and Mills point out, the whole process of rationalization is to be identified with "mechanism, depersonalization, and oppressive routine."

Building on the works of Weber, Seymour Martin Lipset has developed an interesting paradigm which explains in very broad terms some of the tensions of our society while avoiding some of the pitfalls of Weber's somewhat simplified interpretation. It will be useful to speak in terms of an input-output model of our democratic system. The inputs into the system include an open class structure, economic wealth, an egalitarian value system, a capitalist economy, a high literacy rate, and high participation in voluntary associations. These are viewed by Lipset as conditions favoring democracy. Some of the positive consequences of these conditions are a reinforcement of the open class system, high literacy rate, and egalitarian value system with the additional, but negative, consequences of promoting political apathy, bureaucracy, and mass society. The last three factors tend to feed back into the democratic system in a fashion detrimental to its healthy functioning. The failure to come to grips with these tremendous forces is a significant flaw in the work of Riesman, Galbraith, and the other leaders of the movement toward qualitative liberalism as well as of the exponents of increased economic planning.

Let us look at the problems raised by planning. As has already been shown, it is possible to make a very good case for such a policy, particularly in purely economic terms. In an economic system where classical market forces no longer operate and where the economy is in the control of the monolithic leviathans of both labor and business, some sort of rationalization imposed from a higher level is very attractive and quite possibly very necessary. At the same time, this process of rationalization in the economy would almost inevitably lead to an expansion of already highly developed bureaucratic tendencies in both the public and the private sector of the social system. As Weber correctly foresaw, this trend is one of the most significant dynamic forces of a modern industrial society. However, the trend alone does not lead to the deterministic conclusion that the battle against bureaucracy must inevitably be lost. For instance, Lipset suggests that the development of bureaucratic systems may provide new sources of freedom deriving from a decline in the arbitrary authority of power holders because of the bureaucrat's emphasis on action through regularized channels. Further, as Charles Frankel has suggested, it is conceivable that the multiplication of bureaucratic agencies might well be halted by a more systematic approach to planning than has been employed in America to date. Finally, planning for a degree of decentralization, as suggested by writers like Paul Goodman, is not beyond the realm of the possible.

These points all have a certain force. After all, the factors making for group conformity in American life were noted by de Tocqueville a number of years before the emergence of the modern United States as a major industrial power. Thus, the tendency toward conformity cannot be attributed entirely to the growth of bureaucracy under modern capitalism. However, this later development does increase the pressure, which cannot be ignored, particularly given current concern over the quality of life and the problem of bureaucratic conformity. The liberal who wishes to use the agencies of government either to lessen the carnage resulting from the conflict of countervailing powers or to insure a more rational distribution of Gross National Product between the private and the public sector of the economy must recognize this fact. Galbraith and Riesman have tended to ignore this issue: Galbraith because he does not unite the analysis of the economics of affluence with the analysis of the realities of countervailing power; and Riesman perhaps because, being fundamentally apolitical, he has not seriously considered the means of achieving his goal of a society of autonomous men. As a result, Riesman must finally be considered a utopian—a classification with a noble heritage and one from which he would not shrink, but one nonetheless likely to be doomed to limited success at best.

Another major problem of the contemporary liberal is suggested by an examination of *The Affluent Society*. As Ernest Van Den Haag has pointed out, a significant flaw in Galbraith's analysis is the failure to provide a standard against which the prevailing distribution of Gross National Product between public and private concerns may be measured. It is all very well to suggest that an imbalance exists. It is easily agreed that the proposition is correct; even many conservatives might well be inclined to desist from their attacks on Galbraith long enough to add their assent. But if a guide for public policy is sought, a more precise statement of the public-private mixture is required. Thus, perhaps the greatest difficulty of *The Affluent Society* is its social philosophy rather than its economics. Galbraith is much more sure and much more precise about his means than about his ends. Exactly where should society be going? What sort of a person should the ideal society produce? How are the various approaches to the ideal to be integrated? These are all questions left unanswered by Galbraith.

It is unfair to single out Galbraith for special criticism on this score. In this defect his work is merely representative of most contemporary liberal thought, and indeed of nearly all social thought of our time. There is a tendency to shy away from answers to these really vital questions. The roots of this situation are complex. Perhaps first in importance is the long decline of belief in natural-law concepts, such as the doctrine of the public interest. When men no longer believe in absolutes, it is more difficult to argue that any particular course of action constitutes the public interest to the exclusion of other possible approaches. At least so runs the claim of many of the critics of modern relativism. At a somewhat lower level of abstraction lies the pragmatic, antiideological temper of American politics. As I have argued in Chapter II, it is possible for change to be so piecemeal, so unplanned, that little or no *controlled* change is possible and policy making consists largely of a process of groping in the dark without vision and without a real sense of direction. Thus the premises of our thinking preclude coming to grips in a systematic, comprehensive way with the basic problems of advanced industrial society.

In a sense, what is required is a reevaluation of what constitutes the political in the modern world. There has been a marked tendency to view politics as merely a congeries of subissues which can easily be broken down into separate, discrete compartments—economic, sociological, and the like. Thus it is possible to ignore the political implications of social and economic activities. The idea of politics as a comprehensive, architectonic, Aristotelian master science has been lost. None of the liberal ideologists considered in this chapter has entirely escaped this trap, although Galbraith has made a valiant try. All of them are involved to some extent in a depoliticization of politics—an easily understood phenomenon. As Lipset has noted, the functional role of the intellectual is that of the critic. Since liberal intellectuals won so large a part of their program during the period of the New Deal, this function is now seen by many as best performed by turning to other areas which seem to demand critical treatment. Thus:

many intellectuals have turned from a basic concern with the political and economic systems to criticisms of other sections of the basic culture of American society, particularly of elements which cannot be dealt with politically.[36]

---

[36] Lipset, *Political Man* (Garden City, N.Y.: Doubleday, Anchor Books, 1963), p. 445.

At the same time, there is a tendency to find politics every-where—in schools, in business, in churches, in fact anywhere there is contact between two or more people. Perhaps this is in part a reaction to the fragmentation of American society, but it seems to lead to a debasement of the genuinely political, in other words, of those aspects of the social system which deal with society-wide questions in an authoritative manner. Sheldon Wolin has summed up the argument thus:

> political theory must once again be viewed as that form of knowledge which deals with what is general and integrative to men, a life of common involvements. The urgency of those tasks is obvious, for human existence is not going to be decided at the lesser level of small associations; it is the political order that is making fateful decisions about man's survival in an age haunted by the possibility of unlimited destruction.[37]

The problem which analysis along these lines raises for the American liberal is clear. The task of American liberalism must be to find ways to integrate a high degree of respect for the dignity of the individual with the complexities of a highly industrialized economy. The only possible way to ease the tension among the various components of liberal ideology is to approach the problem in terms of a higher level of generality than is usually attempted. A renewed attempt to define the content of the public interest is called for. Some of the attempts assessed in this chapter may prove promising, but contradictions remain to be resolved. In particular I have tried to show that the liberal must try to clarify the relation of political action to the goals which he seeks.

Galbraith on the New Industrial State: An Appendix

Just as this study was about to go to press, John Kenneth Galbraith published his first major work in ten years: *The New Industrial State*. This section is a brief and by no means comprehensive attempt to relate this book to matters discussed in this chapter.

---

[37] Sheldon Wolin, *Politics and Vision* (Boston: Little, Brown, 1960), p. 434.

Galbraith himself notes that the analysis of *The New Industrial State* is closely related to that of *The Affluent Society*: As he puts it, the relation is that of a house to a window. "This is the structure," he writes; "the earlier book allowed the first glimpse inside."

Several major themes stand out. The first is the emphasis on planning. Substantial use of heavy capital and advanced technology cannot be subject to the vagaries of the market; the risks are simply too great. The market must somehow be brought under control. The techniques by which the market may be controlled, suspended, or superseded need not be discussed here.[38] What is important is Galbraith's incisive discussion of the relation of government to the economy. In the new industrial system, the economy has won extensive influence over the polity. Indeed, for many purposes the state is reduced to providing services for industry. For example, it regulates aggregate economic demand, maintains the public sector of the economy on which this regulation depends, underwrites technology, and provides an increasing volume of skilled manpower.[39] In consequence, what has emerged is a close union of state and economy which leads Galbraith to write: "Men will look back in amusement at the pretense that once caused people to refer to General Dynamics and North American Aviation and A.T.&T. as *private* businesses."[40]

Thus, in Galbraith's view, the mixed economy is a planned economy in which the planning is the result of an informal but nonetheless firm alliance between government and the industrial system. Needless to say, this development represents a major departure from the semiautomatic balance achieved by the countervailing-power mechanism discussed earlier in this chapter. At the very least, it may be said that automaticity becomes unimportant and that such balancing of economic forces as exists must be the result of conscious action. As a corollary, the logical implication of Galbraith's analysis is that the already large governmental role in the economy will increase.

Galbraith continues to believe that concentration of eco-

---

[38] For a discussion, see Galbraith, *The New Industrial State* (Boston: Houghton Mifflin, 1967), pp. 27ff.

[39] *Ibid.*, p. 320.

[40] *Ibid.*, p. 393.

nomic power is socially useful; he remains in the New Nationalist tradition. However, he continues to be highly critical of many aspects of the new industrial system. The semiprivate planning arrangements developed in this nation display several major lacunae. Urban and interurban transportation, urban and suburban housing, real-property development, and in general the aesthetic dimension of life tend to be ignored. Such concerns must be strongly championed, Galbraith argues, even though they do not satisfy demands of the industrial system as such. If these goals are asserted with sufficient vigor, "the industrial system will fall into its place as a detached and autonomous arm of the state, but responsive to the large purposes of the society."[41]

Thus, even more firmly than ever, Galbraith challenges what he sees as the myth of the free, competitive market. At the same time, his argument for an expanded governmental involvement in planning is advanced much more forcefully. Planning is a reality which cannot be evaded; the main concern is whether the public sector of the economy will receive its fair share. It is the function of the "educational and scientific estate," Galbraith argues, "to see to it that it does." And this estate is said to be in a good position to do so because of the dependence on trained manpower. Indeed, Galbraith suggests, this new elite is in a power position analogous to that of the banker in the great period of entrepreneurial expansion. Using its leverage, the intellectual stratum could thus do much to improve the quality of American life.

In this analysis there are two major problems. The first is that it can be argued that the "educational and scientific estate" may not be as deeply committed to humane cultural values as Galbraith believes. Instead, it may well be that an increasingly technological society will produce an elite which will at best pay mere lip service to such values. Moreover, a reorientation of effort toward housing, transportation, aesthetic concerns, and the like would very possibly weaken the power position of this elite; paradoxically its members might well become technologically unemployed. Therefore, while it may be hoped that Galbraith is correct, the chances are that he errs on the side of optimism.

Second, an old problem emerges. Once again, Galbraith's

---

[41] *Ibid.*, p. 399.

analysis of contemporary society is sharp and insightful, but his discussion of what is to be done is less so. At one point he explicitly states that questions as to where the industrial system is taking us and how it should be guided are secondary to an understanding of the present. But to take this position is very nearly to accept the status quo which Galbraith has so painstakingly dissected in his writings. Once again, as in his earlier books, his hints about future possibilities are tantalizing, but they are not systematically worked out. There remains only a hazy picture of what Galbraith would like our society to be like.

🦅 BIBLIOGRAPHICAL NOTES 🦅

The literature on the reform movement in America is immense. Eric Goldman's *Rendezvous with Destiny* (New York: Random House, Vintage Books, 1956) is a perceptive and stimulating general historical account. For a very influential but rather harsh interpretation of Populism, see Richard Hofstadter, *The Age of Reform* (New York: Knopf, 1955), pp. 23–130. Hofstadter's interpretation is challenged by Norman Pollack, *The Populist Response to Industrial America* (New York: Norton Library, 1966); Walter R. K. Nugent, *The Tolerant Populists* (Chicago: University of Chicago Press, 1963); and C. Vann Woodward, *The Burden of Southern History* (New York: Random House, Vintage Books, 1961), pp. 141–166. On Progressivism, see Hofstadter, *The Age of Reform*, pp. 131–269. See also John Morton Blum, *The Republican Roosevelt* (Cambridge: Harvard University Press, 1954); Blum, *Woodrow Wilson and the Politics of Morality* (Boston: Little, Brown, 1956); Arthur S. Link, *Woodrow Wilson and the Progressive Era: 1910–1917* (New York: Harper, 1954); George E. Mowry, *The Era of Theodore Roosevelt and the Birth of Modern America, 1900–1912* (New York: Harper, 1958); and Russel B. Nye, *Midwestern Progressive Politics* (New York: Harper, 1965). A revisionist interpretation of the Progressive movement is offered by Gabriel Kolko in *The Triumph of Conservatism* (New York: The Free Press, 1963). The philosophy of the reform movement is dissected in Morton White, *Social Thought in America: The Revolt Against Formalism* (Boston: Beacon Press, 1957). On the New Deal, see the three great volumes of *Age of Roosevelt* (Boston: Houghton Mifflin) by Arthur Schlesinger, Jr.: Vol. 1, *The Crisis of the Old Order* (1957); Vol. 2, *The Coming of the*

81

New Deal (1959); and Vol. 3, *The Politics of Upheaval* (1960). The early chapters of *The Crisis of the Old Order* constitute a very useful, brief summary of the reform movement prior to the New Deal. Hofstadter provides, as usual, a provocative and controversial treatment of the New Deal in *The Age of Reform*, pp. 300–328. He argues that the New Deal represents a departure from the earlier reform movements rather than a continuation of them. He assesses other aspects of the New Deal in *The American Political Tradition* (New York: Random House, Vintage Books, 1954), pp. 315–352, in which the emphasis is on the basic incoherence and opportunism of the New Deal. Hofstadter's work should be read in conjunction with Goldman's *Rendezvous with Destiny*, which offers a rather different interpretation. See also William E. Leuchtenberg, *Franklin D. Roosevelt and the New Deal* (New York: Harper, 1963), and Louis Hartz, *The Liberal Tradition in America* (New York: Harcourt, 1955), pp. 259–283.

In addition to *American Capitalism: The Concept of Countervailing Power* (Boston: Houghton Mifflin, 1956), *The Affluent Society* (Boston: Houghton Mifflin, 1958), and *The Liberal Hour* (Boston: Houghton Mifflin, 1959), the student of John Kenneth Galbraith's work should also consult *Economics and the Art of Controversy* (New York: Random House, Vintage Books, 1959). Galbraith's work is analyzed in Allen M. Sievers, *Revolution, Evolution, and the Economic Order* (Englewood Cliffs, N.J.: Prentice-Hall, 1962), pp. 59–96, and Ernest Van Den Haag, "Affluence, Galbraith and the Democrats," *Commentary* (September 1960), pp. 206–214. In addition to *The 20th Century Capitalist Revolution* (New York: Harcourt, Harvest Books, 1960), Berle's *Power Without Property* (New York: Harcourt, Harvest Books, 1959) should also be read. Much of the work on the corporation sponsored by the Center for the Study of Democratic Institutions has been collected in two volumes: Andrew Hacker, ed., *The Corporation Takeover* (Garden City, N.Y.: Doubleday, Anchor Books, 1965), and Edward S. Mason, ed., *The Corporation in Modern Society* (Cambridge: Harvard University Press, 1959).

The literature on automation grows almost daily. In addition to the materials cited in the text, the following are also useful. For provocative reviews of the Report of the National Commission on

Technology, Automation, and Economic Progress, see Robert Lekachman, "The Automation Report," *Commentary* (May 1966), pp. 65–71, and Wassily Leontief, "Primer for the Great Society," *New York Review of Books* (December 15, 1966), pp. 20–24. The works of Robert Theobald should be consulted both for their discussion of the impact of automation and for their argument on behalf of the guaranteed income: *Free Men and Free Markets* (New York: Clarkson Potter, 1963); "Should Men Compete with Machines?" *The Nation* (May 9, 1966), pp. 544–550; and "The Goal of Full Unemployment," *New Republic* (March 11, 1967), pp. 15–18. Theobald has edited a collection of essays which are of interest to the student of ideology, *The Guaranteed Income* (Garden City, N.Y.: Doubleday, Anchor Books, 1967). The article by Leon Keyserling referred to in the text is "Guaranteed Annual Income," *New Republic* (March 18, 1967), pp. 20–23. Donald Michael, *Cybernation: The Silent Conquest* (Santa Barbara, Calif.: Center for the Study of Democratic Institutions, 1962), has attracted a great deal of attention. The Triple Revolution Statement may be found in a variety of places. I have used it in the form of a pamphlet published by the magazine *Liberation*. It may also be found in Erich Fromm, ed., *Socialist Humanism* (Garden City, N.Y.: Doubleday, Anchor Books, 1966). Some of the members of the ad hoc committee which produced the manifesto are (in addition to Robert Theobald) W. H. Ferry of the Center for the Study of Democratic Institutions, Michael Harrington, Todd Gitlin, Roger Hogan, Robert Heilbroner, Alice Mary Hilton, Irving Howe, A. J. Muste, Gunnar Myrdal, Bayard Rustin, and such academic figures as Everett C. Hughes, H. Stuart Hughes, and John William Ward. The coalition of the peace, socialist, and civil-rights movements is notable.

An unusually provocative, if often extreme, analysis of the nature of advanced industrial society may be found in Herbert Marcuse, *One Dimensional Man* (Boston: Beacon Press, 1964).

David Riesman's work has been extensively criticized in a volume of essays edited by Seymour Martin Lipset and Leo Lowenthal, *Culture and Social Character* (New York: The Free Press, 1961); see especially the contributions by Lipset, Lowenthal, Ralf Dahrendorf, Norman Birnbaum, William Kornhauser, Eric Larrabee, and the reply to the critics by Riesman and Nathan Glazer. To understand Riesman's concerns fully, consult his two volumes of collected essays: *Individualism Reconsidered* (New York: The Free Press, 1954); and *Abundance for What?* (Garden City, N.Y.: Doubleday, 1964). See also Riesman's *Faces in the Crowd* (abridged ed.; New Haven: Yale University Press, 1965) for an elaborate analysis of some of the interview materials on which *The Lonely Crowd* is based.

Arthur Schlesinger's most recent comments on qualitative liberalism are in *A Thousand Days* (Boston: Houghton Mifflin, 1965), especially pp. 739–758. In general the book reflects Schlesinger's position very well. See also his article "The New Liberal Coalition," *The Progressive* (April 1967), pp. 15–19. For links between Schlesinger and Senator Robert Kennedy that may prove politically significant, see Andrew Kopkind, "Waiting for Lefty," *New York Review of Books* (June 1, 1967), pp. 3–5.

A rich source of information on poverty is Margaret Gordon, ed., *Poverty in America* (San Francisco: Chandler, 1965).

For Max Weber's analysis of bureaucracy, see Hans Gerth and C. Wright Mills, eds., *From Max Weber* (New York: Oxford University Press, 1946), pp. 196–244. For Lipset's paradigm of the impact of modern society on democracy, see *Political Man* (Garden City, N.Y.: Doubleday, Anchor Books, 1963), pp. 58–62. Charles Frankel's views on industrial society in modern America are developed in *The Democratic Prospect* (New York, Harper, 1962). For Paul Goodman's ideas on decentralization, see "Notes on Decentralization" in Irving Howe, ed., *The Radical Papers* (Garden City, N.Y.: Doubleday, 1966), pp. 183–201. A more comprehensive statement of Lipset's views on the politics of the intellectual is to be found in *Political Man*, pp. 332–371.

Finally, the interested reader should take note of William J. Newman, *Liberalism and the Retreat From Politics* (New York: Braziller, 1964). Newman's approach to liberalism through its philosophy of history is quite different from the one taken in this book, and some of the writers he considers are also different. However, he arrives at a number of conclusions similar to mine.

CHAPTER IV

THE
BASES
OF
CONSERVATISM

It may seem somewhat strange to begin a discussion of contemporary American conservatism with an analysis of a thinker whose greatest work was published in 1790. However, there is little alternative; Edmund Burke was not only the founder of modern conservatism, but his writings are accepted as authority by so many contemporary conservatives that it is tempting to end as well as begin with him. Indeed, Burke is a formidable figure—a brilliant polemicist, a superior stylist whose prose is among the glories of the language, and the creator of a body of thought which, while not systematic, is nevertheless profound and influential.

The Legacy of Burke

The fact that Burke was not a system builder raises a question as to the appropriate starting place for a consideration of his work.

Perhaps the most commonly accepted conception of conservatism holds that it is a doctrine dedicated to the preservation of the status quo, that it is, in other words, a doctrine opposed to social change. This seemingly plausible notion is clearly, *in and of itself*, deficient, because it empties conservatism of all substantive content. If preservation of the status quo is *all* that is meant by the term, then the leaders of the Soviet Union must a fortiori be classified with the conservatives. To press the point further, the Soviets may be considered conservatives with respect to internal politics and radical—at least from an American viewpoint—in the context of international affairs. Surely this is not a fruitful use of the term; while ideological labels are highly relative, this approach leads ultimately to absurdity.

Yet, if the emphasis is shifted just a little, it is quite clear that the Burkean conservative is, to say the least, not an enthusiastic devotee of change. Any given status quo creates certain barriers to change, certain limitations on political action, which the conservative feels the prudent politician will do well to consider. The existence of limitations is the major theme of Burke's *Reflections on the Revolution in France*, which is fundamentally an attack on the revolutionary leadership for what Burke considered its wholesale disregard of the limitations imposed by the French past. The error of the revolutionary was to "consider his country as nothing but *carte blanche*, upon which he may scribble whatever he pleases."[1] The problem lies in the attempt to fashion society after some model built upon a foundation of abstract principle bearing no relation to the history, tradition, culture, and social structure of a people.

The science of politics is experimental rather than deductive, argues Burke. Schemes for social reconstruction which appear plausible in theory may fail badly when put to the test of practice. Therefore, social change must be approached with great caution.

---

[1] I have used the following editions of Burke's writings: Peter Stanlis, ed., *Edmund Burke: Selected Writings and Speeches* (Garden City, N.Y.: Doubleday, Anchor Books, 1963); *Reflections on the Revolution in France*, bound with Paine, *The Rights of Man* (Garden City, N.Y.: Doubleday, Dolphin Books, 1961). I have taken the liberty of modernizing some of Burke's spelling.

Thus, the most important justification for a particular policy or institutional structure is prescription and immemorial usage. The very fact that an institution has survived lends weight to the judgment that it ought to be preserved, for presumably survival would be impossible in the absence of real virtue. Burke is reluctant to count on even the best of men to behave with complete rationality or even with minimal decency:

History consists, for the greater part, of the miseries brought upon the world by pride, ambition, avarice, revenge, lust, sedition, hypocrisy, ungoverned zeal, and all the train of disorderly appetites. . . .

The best way to minimize these natural tendencies of man is to cling to roots buried deep in the soil of tradition. The virtue of Britain and the source of her stability is that "instead of casting away all our old prejudices, we cherish them to a very considerable degree." Indeed, Burke contends, prejudice is a thing to be valued for it "renders a man's virtue his habit."

On these grounds the social-contract theories of the early liberals must be abandoned. It is a rationalistic conceit compounded with a false individualism to imagine the absence or destruction of society and its reconstruction anew. And yet, to Burke, society is, in a much more profound sense, the product of a contract, in that society represents an organic partnership between "those who are living, those who are dead, and those who are to be born." Society is an organic unity linking past, present, and future. It was the merit of British political leadership in contrast with that of France that it acted in accordance with this principle. Thus Burke opposes two alternatives to each other: the order and stability of British politics against the disorder and chaos of France.

But Burke must not be read as opposed to any and all change. Indeed, the mark of a statesman is "a disposition to preserve and an ability to improve taken together." There are times when change is necessary, for "a state without the means of some change is without the means of its conservation." Even for Burke, conservatism is not to be equated with standpattism. Somewhere between complete quiescence and revolutionary disorder there is room for beneficent social change. This position suggests that Burke believed in some set of principles over and above tradition which would guide political leaders in making decisions. These principles merit careful consideration, for they tell much about the traditional conservative's image of the good society.

First of all, it is necessary to emphasize that Burke was in open revolt against the fashionable doctrine of natural right, with its individualist insistence on inalienable liberties predating the social state. To Burke, a right was not an abstract thing; rather, rights were rooted in a definite social context. All talk of rights independent of the social order was nonsense—and rather dangerous nonsense at that. It is impossible to make universal affirmations on any moral or political subjects. The principles of morality "admit of exceptions; they demand modification."

On this point, Burke has been frequently misinterpreted. A long tradition of scholarship contends that in the light of his criticism of natural right, Burke must be read as an opponent of the earlier tradition of natural law, which starts with Plato and runs through Aristotle to Thomas Aquinas to Richard Hooker. This is not so, as shown by a wealth of recent scholarship, notably by Peter Stanlis. What Burke fought against was the liberal version of this doctrine which abstracted man from his social setting and emphasized his rights to the exclusion of his reciprocal duties. It is this redirection of the history of political thought which was reflected, as Burke saw it, in the tumultuous events of the French Revolution. Actually, Burke did believe in a body of more or less absolute moral standards which he thought were to be found in the teachings of Christianity and in the writings of the classical philosophers. It was the duty of the philosopher to determine the ends of government in the light of these principles, and it was the duty of the politicians to achieve these ends in practical affairs. Thus, as Stanlis argues, prudence becomes the key political virtue, "because it supplies the practical means by which Natural Law Principles are fulfilled in the various concrete circumstances of man's social life." Needless to say, there is some question as to the utility of natural-law principles which cannot be universally affirmed and which demand modification; but this nonetheless is Burke's view.

The first of these principles is that society is natural, that it is not an artificial creation but rather an organic growth. This belief, deeply rooted in the teachings of Aristotle, appears time and time again in the works of Burke, although nowhere so eloquently as in the famous passage on the true nature of the social contract quoted above. No abstract right, no spurious claim to some ill-conceived liberty, must be allowed to disrupt the natural order of this organic unity. A belief in right does not compel the release of a madman from confinement, for example. We must always ask ourselves, Burke argues, what use will be made of liberty once granted. If the purposes to which liberty is put are prejudicial to order, society is quite right to curtail liberty.

Liberty, then, is not an unmixed blessing. Its purchase at the cost of order must always be avoided. Order is best kept if there is a well-defined class structure which minimizes the participation of the masses in political decisions. Burke views few men as really fit to be free; in many, if not in most, he sees tendencies toward "an oppressive degrading servitude." The passions of these people must be restrained for their own good. Men have no claim at all to anything which is unreasonable or not for their own benefit. While men ought not to be oppressed, neither should the state be allowed to fall under the domination of the masses. Burke was no democrat; he did not shrink from saying that "the road to eminence and power, from obscure condition, ought not to be made too easy, nor a thing too much of course." In common with many eighteenth-century thinkers, including many of the framers of the United States Constitution, Burke felt that democracy was a dangerous form of government easily capable of degenerating into mob rule. Although a commoner himself, Burke was at heart an aristocrat who saw nobility as "the Corinthian capital of polished society."

Burke's attitude toward equality might be anticipated from the view outlined above. Under the great contract of society, men are entitled to equal rights, *"but not to equal things."* Men are most certainly entitled to fair and equal treatment under the law, but it does not follow that social or property distinctions should be leveled. This emphasis on property is important. Burke argued that the characteristic essense of property was to be unequal. The possession of property—particularly hereditary possession—is one of the great bastions of ordered liberty, since property provides a suitable base for the security required by wise and benevolent leadership. Thus, a system of private property makes an important contribution to the social stability so much desired by Burke.

Finally, a word must be said about the role of the church. Large portions of the *Reflections* are devoted to this question, but the basic point is simple. Religion and the churches are seen as fundamentally conservative forces. Indeed, Burke claims, "we know, and what is better we feel inwardly, that religion is the basis of civil society, and the source of all good and of all comfort." As Peter Viereck has pointed out, Burke would have agreed with Marx that religion was "the opiate of the people." The only real difference is the evaluation made of this contention.

Many of Burke's pronouncements fall rather harshly on the ears of the modern American reader. America, at least in its ideals, is an egalitarian, democratic society. It is committed to the principles of popular sovereignty and majority rule. As a result, to many Americans, the principles of Burke seem a shameless defense of entrenched privilege. But they are not simply that; rather they must be interpreted in the context of Burke's own time. In his day, Burke was a supporter of many popular causes, most notably those of American independence and improved colonial administration in India. In these instances he argued with all of the considerable force at his disposal that deeply rooted prescriptive rights were being violated by the Crown. There is no discontinuity between these positions and the position outlined in his attack on the French Revolution. Here, too, the problem was defiance of the established tradition and inherited order of things, except that in the Revolution it was the rights of the nobility which Burke felt to have been abrogated. Burke was not a standpatter. His emphasis on the need for slow, ordered change was a great deal more than mere lip service.

The essence of the Burkean position can be summed up thus: Real liberty can only be obtained under conditions of order, and the alternative to liberty-*cum*-order is not truly liberty but license in the context of a murderous Hobbesian anarchy. As a logical consequence, Burke was antiegalitarian and against popular control. It is primarily these characteristics which set him apart not only from present-day liberals, but also from such predecessors as Locke.

If politics is conceived as "the art of the possible," then, as I have already remarked, Burke must be singled out for his acute sense of political reality. His emphasis on the context of political action and on the limits placed on the rational politician by this context is admirably sound. Only a political know-nothing attempts to do that which is manifestly impossible in the light of existing conditions. But prudence can be carried to excess almost as easily as can the a priori rationalism against which Burke fought. Excessive prudence can lead to quietism, which in turn can put off badly needed reforms, so that a situation is created which only a major upheaval can remedy. In fact, it is probably not unfair to suggest with John Plamenatz that this is what happened in prerevolutionary France. As Plamenatz argues, "A well ordered and peaceful France could not have been disturbed so profoundly by nothing but arrogance and ill will." Only in a situation where gradual, piecemeal reform can be counted on can it be argued that more dramatic social change is never desirable. It is clear that the Burkean model of social change is preferable, but it may not always be possible to achieve.

The logic of Burke's theory, if strictly followed, seems to run the risk of leading to an avoidance of *all* change rather than mere abstention from revolutionary upheaval.[2] Burke suggests that progress comes from the remedy of "proved abuses." But, for Burke, a proved abuse is a violation of a prescriptive right. Therefore, the remedy for an abuse is the restoration of the status quo ante, with the result that, as Plamenatz points out, "the more successfully abuses are remedied, the less society changes." To allow for truly progressive change, it must be recognized that practices not now considered abuses may become so in the future.

Plamenatz also has significant things to say about Burke's position on abstract ideals. First, the real objection from Burke's point of view was not the excessive abstraction of the Revolution-

---

[2] For the following argument, I am indebted to John P. Plamenatz, *Man and Society*, Vol. I: *Machiavelli to Rousseau* (New York: McGraw-Hill, 1963), p. 359.

aries, but just the reverse. Many of the ideals advocated in the Revolution had been bandied about for centuries, but the Revolution converted these ideals into concrete demands for social changes of the most specific sort. If these demands had been made and met earlier in French history, there is at least a chance that the excesses of the Revolution could have been avoided. This very point adds support to Burke's own contention that a stagnant society, blindly clinging to its status quo, is doomed to disorder, although Burke himself certainly did not draw this inference from French history.

Second, ideals may have positive social functions. Indeed, this contention is a major assumption of this book. As Plamenatz says, the key question to be asked of a social theory is the essentially pragmatic one of determining the likely consequences of its acceptance. This is the central endeavor of any prudent political leader. Even Burke had a vision of the good society which he strove to implement. If carefully guided reform is the means of a society's conservation, then surely the architect of change should have some blueprint in mind. To make complete sense of Burke, it is necessary to interpret him rather narrowly. What I think he really means is that some blueprints, some plans, some ideals are better than others as policy recommendations for a particular situation. Read in this way, he is hard to disagree with, and in fact he may be contributing little more than a truism.

A major portion of the conservative critique of liberalism is the argument of excessive rationalism. This charge is sometimes justified, particularly when versions of liberal thought preceding the twentieth century are under consideration. The liberal answer to this charge holds that conservatism is a philosophy of heart and emotion which can easily degenerate into a celebration of the value of irrationalism. In its most extreme form, as stated here, this contention is clearly unfair. When Burke insists on the value of the traditional, inherited institutions, he is not urging unquestioning acceptance of received values. What he does argue is that the traditions of the past are the products of the great minds and thoughts of the past and that they should be treated with full respect. Individuals may make gross mistakes, but if the individual is sometimes foolish, the species is wise. True rationality consists in heeding the collective wisdom of the past. Once again it is hard to disagree with Burke, but once again it must also be noted that there is a fine line between adherence to the riches of past thought and institutions and an irrational refusal to face new situations and to make necessary changes. Much of Burke's greatness lies in the extent to which he avoided this trap; it remains to be seen whether his contemporary advocates succeed as well.

Finally, a few comments about Burke's conception of the aristocratic society are in order. That Burke feared the common man both politically and culturally is indisputable. He lived and wrote at a time when only a tiny fraction of British subjects were allowed to vote, and he wanted to keep it that way. British society in the eighteenth century was strikingly different from the mass democracy of twentieth-century America. A real question is thus raised as to whether Burke's conception of a society under the control of a benevolent aristocracy has any applicability to the United States today. On the surface the answer might appear to be a clear negative, but below the surface this answer appears less tenable. Conservative writers, as well as many liberals, have attempted to apply the Burkean scheme to life and politics in America today. An evaluation of the New Conservatism of the past fifteen years depends to a great extent on the applicability of Burke to the present. Interpretations of the available empirical data related to the problems raised by Burke are highly controversial. It is sufficient to say at this point in the analysis that these questions remain open and that Burkean arguments may not be dismissed as irrelevant. These questions will be raised again later in this chapter. First, however, it is necessary to examine briefly another aspect of conservatism in America.

Conservatism and Business

The relationship between American business and American conservatism is both complex and important. Business in America has traditionally been to the right on the political spectrum. As Clinton Rossiter points out, business leaders have been opposed to many forms of change; they have viewed reformist liberals as a menace to order; and they have claimed to be the defenders of a political, social, and economic system based on the inherited wisdom of the Founding Fathers. The one major exception to this basically conservative viewpoint has been in business and industrial development; in this context no group has been more dedicated to change than the group usually viewed as the conservatives of American politics. This fact is particularly true of the nineteenth century, and in this period lie the roots of many paradoxes of modern American thought and politics.

As Richard Hofstadter has noted:

from Alexander Hamilton through Nicholas Biddle to Carnegie, Rockefeller, Morgan, and their fellow tycoons, the men who held aristocratic or even plutocratic views in matters political were also men who took the lead in introducing new economic forms, new types of organizations, new techniques.[3]

These men and others like them rushed headlong away from the old agrarian society of Jefferson's America toward a new industrial order. Oddly enough, as Hofstadter notes, it was the left, the side of popular causes, that tried to resist this process. Jeffersonians, Jacksonians, Populists, and Progressives alike were concerned to restore America, insofar as possible, to the pristine condition of years gone by. Only with the coming of the New Deal did liberals or progressives side unhesitatingly with the new and the untried in social and economic affairs.

As a result, conservatism in America took on a unique character. More than any other group, those men who in American parlance have come to be identified as conservatives brought about the sweeping changes in economic structure so vital to the history of modern America. In fact, these leaders laid the basis—often by somewhat questionable means—for the affluent society of today.

The basis of late nineteenth-century conservatism was a materialism as thoroughgoing as that of Marxism. In particular, the profit motive came to be seen as especially important. An industrial capitalist economy unhindered by the hand of government was heralded as almost the sole source of American virtues. In defense of this system, a many-layered complex of thought was

[3] Richard Hofstadter, *Social Darwinism in American Thought* (Boston: Beacon Press, 1955), p. 9.

erected. The key features of this system were laissez-faire economics and Social Darwinism.[4]

With the acceptance of Adam Smith's laissez-faire theory,
conservatism in America took a decisive turn, for Smith's theory
and its assumptions were profoundly liberal. The basic principles
of this classical economic theory are simple, although they may be
elaborated to great complexity. The economic system was said to
be governed by certain immutable natural laws which would allocate economic resources fairly *if there was no interference with
the market*, particularly by the state. The most important of these
laws was the principle of supply and demand, which held that the
supply of any particular product would never exceed demand, and
vice versa; that the price of goods and services (wages included)
would automatically adjust to a fair and equitable level; and that,
as a result, there would be a just and proper distribution of wealth.

This principle was built on a psychological foundation which
held self-interest to be a universal motivating force. However, the
pursuit of self-interest was not felt to be disruptive of social order.
On the contrary, it was argued that this pursuit unconsciously
promotes general well-being, since the public interest is really
nothing more than the total of all the particular interests of the
individual members of society. Thus, in this Panglossian world, the
most rapacious economic buccaneer was really acting for the good
of all, no matter how antisocial the uninitiated might feel his
actions to be. As a result, competition in the Smithian sense
frequently went into a marked decline.

Since it was improper under the rules of the game to intervene
in the economy, even in order to preserve the conditions of free
competition, government was viewed with considerable distrust, as
at best highly inefficient and at worst hopelessly corrupt. (In the
latter part of the nineteenth century, these criticisms were not
without merit.) In addition, the public official could not be ex-

---

[4] In the following discussion, I have drawn heavily on three important
works. The first is Hofstadter's *Social Darwinism in American Thought*, which
I have already cited. The other two are Clinton Rossiter, *Conservatism in
America* (New York: Random House, Vintage Books, 1962), pp. 128–162,
and Sidney Fine, *Laissez Faire and the General-Welfare State* (Ann Arbor:
University of Michigan Press, 1956), pp. 32–95.

pected to make sound economic decisions, for the simple reason that he had no real motivation. Only the businessman directly affected in profit-and-loss terms by his course of action could really be trusted with economic power. This fear of upsetting the delicate mechanism of the market led to the virtual abdication of government from significant participation in the economy—except, paradoxically, in the grant of subsidies to such industries as the railroads. Hence arose the "night-watchman state," which may be described as a state solely devoted to protecting public order, particularly against the increasing popular discontent with the policies of the leaders of American industry.

The second major aspect of the intellectual justification of late nineteenth-century American capitalism was Social Darwinism. This body of thought reached America in the wake of Herbert Spencer, the greatest British popularizer of Charles Darwin, who enjoyed a tremendous vogue in this country during the latter part of the nineteenth century. Spencer saw the same sort of struggle for existence going on among human beings that Darwin saw among lower animals. His attitude toward this struggle was much like the attitude of laissez-faire economists toward competition. If the species is to be preserved, argued Spencer, there must be no interference between "conduct and consequence." Each person must reap the benefits and suffer the disadvantages due him as the result of his own actions. If this is done, then the individuals best adapted to their environment will survive and flourish. Those who do not adapt will perish. If the fit who survive are required to look out for the inferior, then their evolution will be retarded and the progress of the whole society will be checked.

Spencer felt progress to be inevitable. Society was governed by natural laws which could not be altered. Legislation could in no way halt the inexorable march of the human race. Thus, most governmental activities were of no use, and Spencer was led to a contempt for the state bordering on a belief in anarchy. Even public education, postal services, the coinage of money, and other such activities should, in his view, be discontinued. (The logical incompatibility between the insistence on the ineffectiveness of government action and on the deleterious consequences of interference between conduct and consequence seems to have escaped Spencer: If progress were truly inevitable, government intervention could not stop it.)

This stern ideology won widespread support in our country, its main advocate being the prominent sociologist William Graham Sumner. Sumner's thought owes a great deal to Spencer. His whole attitude was summed up in *What Social Classes Owe to Each Other*. The answer was simple—nothing. As he put it, "It is not at all the function of the state to make men happy. They must make themselves happy in their own way, and at their own risk."

This is pure individualism cast in a form which would have been abhorrent to Burke. The same may be said of the basic assumptions of the doctrine of laissez-faire. In attempting to adopt these two social theories to their own purposes, American conservatives took a fateful step. There is a large gap between "laissez-faire conservatism," as Clinton Rossiter calls it, and "traditional" Burkean conservatism. Classical liberalism—the liberalism of Hobbes, Locke, Adam Smith, and the Social Darwinists—rests on a fundamental contradiction.[5] On the one hand, there is an assumption that an "unseen hand" guides the economic system, so that there exists a natural harmony in this sphere of action. In this view, government control of the economy is not only unnecessary but fundamentally unsound; it is this side of liberalism which was emphasized by Smith, Spencer, Sumner, and the laissez-faire conservatives not only of the last century but of this as well. On the other hand, there is an assumption that, in noneconomic affairs, natural harmony is lacking—hence the need for the night watchman. This side of early liberalism is best seen in Hobbes, but it is also exhibited by the Smithians and Darwinists as well.

The difficulty with this view of man is that it splits him into two parts: social and political on one side, and economic on the other. But man must be viewed as a whole being. To divide him thus is profoundly contradictory. Both aspects of laissez-faire conservatism are part of the folklore of our culture and in addition have behind them, as Hofstadter notes, the not inconsiderable intellectual force of three major traditions of the Western world:

---

[5] In the following discussion, I draw on Elie Halévy, *The Rise of European Liberalism* (Boston: Beacon Press, 1955), pp. 486–514.

the Protestant ethic, the ideas of classical economics, and the concept of natural selection. It is thus hard to reject these traditions. Nevertheless, the evidence of recent history clearly supports contemporary liberals in having done so. Whatever deficiencies they may have, today's liberals clearly have a more coherent view of man than did their counterparts in the past. The dilemma of most American conservatives is their failure to face up to the problem and admit the contradictory nature of these premises. Moreover, this seemingly abstruse intellectual problem is not without political consequences. As Hofstadter has pointed out, one of the keys to contemporary controversies over the welfare state is that the very idea offends the sensibilities of the large number of Americans in whom the Social Darwinist ideology, or the moral presuppositions upon which it rests, still may be found.

These moral imperatives make more difficult the task of meeting the problems of advanced industrialization. The confusion is compounded for American conservatives by the recent revival of interest in Burke. While Burke might not have endorsed modern American liberalism, he most assuredly would have rejected laissez-faire conservatism. Thus, much contemporary conservatism involves a tension between laissez-faire, libertarian ideas and the organic, traditionalist concepts of Burke. The future of conservatism—both intellectual and political—in the United States will be determined by the balance between traditionalism and libertarianism in the movement. The remainder of this chapter is devoted to that subject.

Contemporary Forms of Traditional Conservatism

In many ways the most important of modern American Burkeans is Russell Kirk—publicist, professor, historian of ideas, and one of the most biting of today's social critics. Kirk's view of America is one of contempt bordering on revulsion. He believes the United States is in an advanced state of decay, likening our society to a battered, neglected old house, full of dry rot in which a "rat, creeping down the stair at midnight, gnaws his dirty way from the desolate kitchen to the mildewed satins of the parlor." Less metaphorically, he writes that Americans live in an egalitarian world, "smudged by industrialization," devoted to change, dominated by the masses, and victimized by an overcentralized government.[6]

There are many sources of this decay, although for the most part they may be boiled down to an abandonment of the principles of Edmund Burke. Tradition and hierarchy have declined before the onslaught of egalitarianism, and with them has gone the foundation of civil order. In their place, Kirk finds mass-produced mediocrity. The mass man is in the saddle, and he is typified by automobile workers in Flint, Michigan—newly recruited from the hills, placed in a "grim and hideous" town, given large sums of money for their labors, and yet unable to spend it intelligently because they lack the guidelines of a traditional society and indeed the minimal decencies of cultivated civilization.[7]

The picture is one of men without community, whose ties with an organic society have been broken. The source of Kirk's discontent is industrialism. He realizes that we cannot escape this force "without starving half of the world's population"; but at the same time he devoutly wishes that we could, and he cannot resist quoting with approval a passage from laissez-faire economist Wilhelm Röpke citing the ability of the Swiss worker to find lunch in his garden and supper in the lake while earning his potatoes by helping clear his brother's land. This back-to-the-farm psychology is reinforced by Kirk's belief that our cities are increasingly cut off from the "old rural verities" which are the source of most American virtues. With these attitudes, Kirk can feel nothing but dismay in our increasingly urbanized society.

Kirk's critique is not directed only at industrial laborers. He fully endorses the descriptive portions of David Riesman's *The Lonely Crowd*. In fact, large parts of *A Program for Conservatives* can be read as a running commentary, often favorable, on Riesman's work. Kirk, too, feels that the middle classes are milling around in a crowd, cut off from traditional values, and taking their political and cultural cues from peers no more qualified to lead than they are. Kirk differs from Riesman not in his description of

---

[6] Russell Kirk, *The Conservative Mind* (Chicago: Regnery, Gateway Editions, 1960), pp. 2–3.

[7] Kirk, *A Program for Conservatives* (Chicago: Regnery, 1954), p. 148.

the phenomenon, but in his prescription for it. Whereas Riesman tends to feel that the tradition-directed man is a relic from a more primitive time, Kirk calls for a return to a more traditional orientation. And whereas Riesman calls for the cultivation of the autonomous man, Kirk argues that autonomy really means individualistic atomization—the very force that destroyed true community in the first place.[8] An evaluation of Kirk's position must await further discussion of his views, but there can be no doubt that he has precisely pinned down his differences with Riesman and, in so doing, considerably illuminated the conflicting conservative and liberal critiques of mass society.

Another major focus of Kirk is his vitriolic assault on American education. There is a dual enemy: on the one hand, progressive education (which is undeniably a liberal product); and on the other, what Kirk feels to be the increasing control by the egalitarian mass mind over the whole educational process. The essence of Kirk's argument is that education has nothing to do with "life adjustment" or other social skills; that it has everything to do with the production of trained intellects by means of exposure to a rigorous program of study in the traditional arts and sciences; and that educators are guilty of pandering to the most debased tastes of their constituents in matters educational when, properly, educational decisions should be the province of an elite. (Kirk quotes the president of a large state university as saying, "There is no program of study to which we will not stoop if the public seems to desire it.") To Kirk the difficulty lies in the uniquely American delusion that everyone can and should be educated to an equal degree. It is probable that Kirk thinks education—like political power—should be confined to the few.

Finally, Kirk feels that another consequence of modern egalitarianism is the leveling of property distinctions by means of an increasingly centralized, collectivized economy in which liberty must eventually perish. "There is," he writes, "such a thing as 'creeping socialism'; and the worst of it is that socialism never

---

[8] It is clear that Riesman and Kirk do not mean precisely the same thing when they write of *tradition*; but it is also clear that for Riesman it is a pejorative term, whereas for Kirk it is not.

ceases to creep until it becomes totalitarian, nor can it, in its nature." Here, too, the decay is already well advanced.

Thus, Kirk offers a twofold critique of modern America. On the one hand, he launches a cultural attack on the vagaries of an affluent mass society and its attendant waste, corruption, miseducation, and materialism. On the other hand is his sociopolitical critique, which is essentially a vigorous attack on the economic reforms of the Populist-Progressive-New Deal tradition. This attack is coupled with a deep-seated discontent with a political system seen to be increasingly under the control of the large cities and proceeding rapidly along the path to a plebiscitarian, collectivist democracy.

Kirk's solution to these problems is also twofold. First, he argues for the restoration of the traditional values of Burkean conservatism. These values have been so well summarized by Kirk that his presentation provides perhaps the most important single formulation of the beliefs of the New Conservatism to date; indeed, they are cited as authority with almost monotonous regularity. These principles hold that "a divine intent rules society" and that all political problems are fundamentally "religious and moral"; that the conservative society feels "affection for the proliferating variety and mystery of traditional life"; that there must be a "conviction that civilized society requires order and classes"; that a belief in the close connection between freedom and property and a disbelief in the equation of "economic levelling and progress" is necessary; that a "faith in prescription" is required; and, finally, that it must be recognized not only that "change and reform are not identical," but that innovation carries with it great dangers.[9] It is by an adherence to these principles that the great problems of our time can be solved: spiritual regeneration, the rebirth of leadership under a system of order and class, education, economic stability, and the need for "status and hope" in our society. If these questions are successfully faced, "the problem of war and peace are likely to fall into some manner of settlement."

But these answers are on the level of general principle. Kirk is

---

[9] Kirk, *The Conservative Mind*, pp. 7–8.

also very much interested in specific policy problems, particularly of the economic variety. It is in this second aspect of his solution that his antiegalitarianism becomes even more pronounced. Poverty, Kirk insists, is not an evil, nor are ignorance and stupidity. These things are "either indifferent, or else are occasions for positive virtue, if accepted with a contrite heart."[10] What really matters to Kirk is that one accept one's station in life with the proper humility. Coupled with his attitude toward governmental intervention in the economy, Kirk's opposition to virtually all major economic legislation of the past thirty-odd years follows logically. He believes it is a fallacy to hold that "justice is identical with equality." This much may well be true. However, acceptance of the position does not require the adoption of Kirk's heartfelt opposition to redistributive economic reform. Society can be made more egalitarian without "leveling" all economic distinctions. Such leveling is probably a chimerical goal in any case, but fostering equality may be required in order to provide that basis of economic security which is so necessary for the attainment of the level of civilized behavior urgently sought by Kirk.

What does he propose as an alternative? Unfortunately for the logic of Kirk's argument, the answer is a barely modified laissez-faire. He endorses the arguments of such economists as Ludwig von Mises and Friedrich Hayek, who hold that the classical economic theory of Adam Smith is the only reasonable standard for an economy. Why, then, asks Kirk, have these theories not prevailed? The answer, he claims, lies in the individualistic, liberal, community-destroying assumptions of the whole classical school. These theories, therefore, are on the right track because they recognize the dangers of collectivism, but they do not retreat far enough from the twentieth century to suit Kirk. Another neoliberal economist, Wilhelm Röpke, comes closer to the mark. Röpke does not believe in a managed economy; still less does he believe in a large-scale, centralized economy. The market must be made to work: industries must be decentralized, factories must be smaller, individual self-sufficiency must be substituted for modern welfare policies. (Later, in *A Program for Conservatives*, Kirk

---

[10] Kirk, *A Program for Conservatives*, p. 177.

attacks the social-security system as collectivist and nonvoluntary, and he argues that the school lunch program represents an invasion of states' rights.) Thus, for all his protestations to the contrary, Kirk comes very close to asking for the dismantling of the industrial economy. How this miracle is to be achieved without resort to the governmental power Kirk abhors is not explained. Neither is there an explanation of the apparent contradiction between Kirk's basic organicism on the one hand and his endorsement of the antiorganic laissez-faire theory on the other. Kirk's hope—which is open to doubt—is that in a simpler life in which the rural verities prevail, decency and order may once more be found.

It has been obvious since the outset of the discussion that Kirk is a man profoundly ill at ease in this country at this time. It now becomes clear that what he longs for is a return to the days of his master, Edmund Burke. As Rossiter points out, Kirk is a man "who has lost all patience with the course of American development in almost every field from art to politics. . . ." He has, as Rossiter says, the sound of "a man born one hundred and fifty years late and in the wrong country."

Peter Viereck is a traditional conservative who provides an entirely different outlook. If Russell Kirk is a prophet of doom writing in the style of Burke, Viereck is a jaunty gadfly whose style owes more to Nietzsche and *Time* magazine than to Burke. Not that Viereck does not revere Burke; however, he sees in him something rather different from what Kirk sees.

Viereck may be said to have started the conservative boom following World War II with a tiny volume entitled *Conservatism Revisited*.[11] In later works he continued his efforts and established himself a firm place near Arthur Schlesinger's *The Vital Center*, first in *The Shame and Glory of the Intellectuals* by a sharp attack on those left-wing intellectuals who he felt were deluded by the false lures of communism, and later in *The Unadjusted Man* by a scathing attack on the excesses of right-wing conservatism.

For all its importance, little need be said of Viereck's first

[11] Peter Viereck, *Conservatism Revisited* (rev. ed.; New York: Macmillan, Collier Books, 1962; orig. pub. 1949). Note the use of the important revised edition, which contains thirty-five pages of new material evaluating the recent development of American conservatism.

major work. The argument is essentially orthodox Burkeanism although, interestingly enough, the hero of the piece is Prince Metternich. One or two slightly new emphases should be noted, however. First, there is perhaps a little more stress than in Burke on the need for ordered change and a little less on the virtues of the status quo. As Viereck put it, "The conservative conserves discriminately, the reactionary, indiscriminately." Second, there is less emphasis on an aristocratic *class* and more on the aristocratic *spirit*, which is open to all classes. There is also an insistence on the need for discussion among people of differing ideological persuasions. Thus, to Viereck, the liberal, because of his articulate conscience, fills an indispensable role as a critic of social abuses. "Thoughtful conservatives should welcome his opposition, for it saves society from stodginess." Finally, there is a greater insistence than in most earlier conservative writing on the importance of moral absolutes as a guide to behavior. In fact, Viereck argues, it is the decay of such values that has created many of the problems of this century up to and including the death camps of the Nazis and Soviets. Thus, he takes as a motto for his book a passage from Gaetano Salvemini: "Our civilization will break down if the school fails to teach the incoming generation that there are some things that are not done." Curiously, in the light of the preceding point, Viereck's ultimate argument is a pragmatic one which turns the Deweyan argument on itself. "Pragmatism," Viereck writes while looking at the disarray of the modern world, "is unpragmatic; it won't work."

Like Kirk, Viereck is discontented with much of modern industrialism, but at the same time he is quite clear that we cannot turn our backs on it. He urges us to reject the "rootless nostalgia for roots" which characterizes so much of the new conservatism and which threatens to convert it into a mere intellectual fad. Romanticism must not be confused with conservatism, he argues. We must accept American traditions for what they are. "What is really rootless and abstract," he writes, "is not the increasingly conservatized New Deal liberalism," but the romantic dream of an "aristocratic agrarian restoration."[12] The true conservative must

---

[12] Viereck, *The Unadjusted Man* (Boston: Beacon Press, 1956), p. 99.

build on the existing historical base, which, in Viereck's mind, clearly includes the New Deal as well as the British constitutional liberalism of the 1680's. To Viereck, the New Deal was only "pseudo-radical." In its impact on American history it was really a conservative force, in that it directed the economically underprivileged away from the revolutionary extremes of either right or left which loomed so ominously in the 1930's. Thus, the New Deal met the Burkean challenge of conservation through change. The conservatives who forget this are moving along a dangerous route, Viereck contends. In their zeal to obliterate the New Deal and all its works, many conservatives have aligned themselves with political leaders and movements fundamentally opposed to constitutional guarantees for civil liberties and hence fundamentally non-conservative.

This point raises Viereck's important interpretation of the radical right in America. According to Viereck, the radical right is the conservative counterpart to the leftist activities of the 1930's and 1940's which so agitated liberal circles. Only when the conservatives win their fight, as the liberals won theirs, can there be a responsible movement of the right in this country.

The key to the radical right, argues Viereck, is rooted in the role that social class plays in American politics. Many labels could be attached to the source of the problem—majority rule, Populism, direct democracy—but the essence of Viereck's analysis is quite simple. Democracy can be safe only if it is strictly limited, so that mass passions do not control the decision-making processes. The message is explicitly Burkean. The poison in the wellsprings of mass behavior is everywhere waiting to be tapped—sometimes by a McCarthy, roaring that he would take his case to the people; sometimes by political candidates eager to exploit racial prejudices—the forms of mob politics are many. It is not the masses who protect the great tradition of civil liberties. On this point the data of any number of careful studies of public opinion are quite clear. As Viereck points out, the classic work in this field, by S. A. Stouffer, shows that

the American masses are overwhelmingly more hostile to civil liberties than their supposed exploiters and corrupters, the powers-that-be. What saves civil liberties from the intolerant majority is not universal suffrage, not equality, not universal rational Rights of Man, but an educated, self-restrained elite, the Constitution, the Supreme Court, and an organic, historical continuity of the unwritten, concrete habits of free men ("prescriptive right").[13]

American limited government thus depends on the preservation of certain traditions, among the most important of which is the complex, convoluted, often exasperating system of indirect government, checks and balances, separation of powers, and all the rest. The Senate's censure of McCarthy and the Supreme Court's attack on segregation are seen by Viereck as "magnificent defeats" of the people which vindicate the aristocratic overtones of our political institutions.

Although this point of view is somewhat oversimplified, there is considerable evidence to support it. Clearly, the system of segregation was protected for altogether too long a time by other parts of our governmental structure before the Supreme Court mounted its attack. At the same time, there is no escaping the fact that this "aristocratic" institution did finally make the first halting steps toward the redress of centuries of Negro grievances. The great outcry on the part of extremist groups against the Court merely serves to buttress Viereck's conclusions, as do more recent public-opinion studies of attitudes toward civil liberties. Still more support is to be found in the passage of Proposition 14 repealing the California fair-housing act during the 1964 election—a decision which even at the time of writing is a potent issue in California politics. Still later evidence is to be seen in the "white backlash" in recent summers.

The extremist tradition which leads to such ridiculous demands as the impeachment of Earl Warren has deep roots in American politics. At various times it has infected both the right and the left. Thus while Viereck endorses much of the New Deal program, he is severely critical of many of its methods— particularly the attempt to pack the Supreme Court and the Rooseveltian tendency toward a plebiscitarian approach to his

---

[13] *Ibid.*, p. 136. See also Samuel A. Stouffer, *Communism, Conformity, and Civil Liberties* (New York: Peter Smith, 1955), and Seymour Martin Lipset, *Political Man* (Garden City, N.Y.: Doubleday, Anchor Books, 1963), pp. 87–126.

office. Further to the left and back in time there are startling similarities between Populism and today's radical right. The same themes are there: a distrust of an Eastern "Establishment" and the press which it is said to dominate, an attack on international cosmopolitanism, a yearning for a return to the simple life and simple virtues of a bygone day, a conspiracy theory of politics. The point is that radical movements of both left and right have been frequent occurrences in American political life and *that they have received substantial popular support.*

However, great care must be exercised in interpreting the available data. First, caution is necessary in suggesting on the basis of evidence adduced by writers such as Stouffer and Lipset that the "working class" is particularly prone to adopt authoritarian attitudes. It is true that the survey data upon which such analysts rely indicate this distribution of attitudes. However, recent studies call these findings into serious question. The possibility is raised that the syndrome of working-class authoritarianism may be a product of the methodological quirks of the surveys which made the original findings and that entirely different results would have been obtained if the interview schedules had been reworded.[14]

Second, from historical evidence, it is quite clear that the American upper class has functioned as a defender of civil liberties only sporadically at best. For every Boston Brahmin intellectual turned abolitionist there is a rabidly anti-Semitic Henry Adams. The idealized aristocratic behavior celebrated by traditionalist conservatives from Burke to Viereck is certainly not unknown, but it may be said with some certainty that it is not the norm—at least not for American society.[15]

Third, there is room for doubt about Viereck's assertions as to the role of Populism as a source for the radical right. There may well be justification for his position if *populism* is defined rather broadly, but if it is defined as the Populist Party of the late nineteenth century or even more generally as the agrarian reform movement of the same period, Viereck's argument is questionable.

[14] V. O. Key, Jr., *Public Opinion and American Democracy* (New York: Knopf, 1961), pp. 135–138.

[15] E. Digby Baltzell, *The Protestant Establishment* (New York: Random House, 1964).

In fact, some recent evidence suggests that the Populists were among the more tolerant groups of the period in question.[16]

Insofar as much of American conservatism is concerned, Viereck is a maverick. He rejects the close ties with business and industry which have so often characterized the American right, he endorses much of the New Deal, and he takes the position that most of what there is to conserve in American life is liberal. To some extent this résumé merely involves the manipulation of words which have a variety of confused meanings, as we have abundantly seen. Yet Viereck's writings illustrate an important point—the relative narrowness of the ideological spectrum in our politics. Most Americans, whether liberal or conservative, have more in common than they hold in disagreement. Politically speaking, Viereck shares the "vital center" with such men as Schlesinger and Niebuhr. Such differences as exist are mainly of emphasis. Viereck certainly would place more stress on the necessity for a hierarchical class structure than would Schlesinger, and he is no doubt more pessimistic about human nature than most liberals—although certainly no more so than Niebuhr. Further, like so many liberals, Viereck is deeply concerned with the quality of American life. The most truly conservative aspects of his work are revealed when he discusses that quality. The conservatism that Viereck calls for is primarily an ethical and cultural one. The new conservative, contends Viereck, can best begin by being nonpolitical. In the end it is this humanistic approach to American life and thought that may prove to be the modern conservative's most important contribution. It also may prove to be his Waterloo for, as the "qualitative liberals" have found out, it is not easy to maintain high cultural standards in a mass industrial society—with or without the use of governmental influence. To overcome this fact is one of the great challenges facing the "vital center."

A third and strikingly different form of traditional conservatism may be found in the work of the political scientist Willmoore Kendall. Kendall begins his analysis of *The Conservative Affirmation* with a series of disclaimers. He claims that he has no axe to

---

[16] See Walter R. K. Nugent, *The Tolerant Populists* (Chicago: University of Chicago Press, 1963), and C. Vann Woodward, *The Burden of Southern History* (New York: Random House, Vintage Books, 1961), pp. 141–166.

grind for aristocracy—he is not primarily beholden to Burke. He is not preoccupied with preventing change as such; it is only change "in certain directions" that he opposes. He insists that American conservatism is not doctrinaire and that it swears no allegiance to free enterprise, to a particular set of rights, to "a certain holy trinity of government functions," or even to a fundamental distrust of government authority. What, then, is the essence of conservatism? "Its highest political loyalty is to the institutions and ways of life 'bequeathed' to us by the Philadelphia Convention."[17] Kendall is firm in his insistence that there is a sharp, clear line to be drawn between conservatives and liberals on this point. The liberals, he asserts, have substituted "novel principles for inherited principles." More precisely, liberals have substituted relativism of values for absolutism, "government-imposed egalitarianism" for the Founding Fathers' equality principle which held merely that everyone should have an equal right to compete with his fellows, an "open society" for a society embodying a "public truth," and a plebiscitarian democracy for the "*purely* representative" institutions of the Framers.

We are faced with two major problems, says Kendall. The first is the danger of perversion of our political institutions. The starting point for his analysis is the recurrent tension between the executive and the legislative branch of government. This tension is illustrated by reference to a number of specific issues. The legislature is more concerned about problems of internal security than is the executive. It tends to be more protectionist with respect to foreign trade. It tends, unlike the executive, to be opposed to foreign-aid programs unless they have a clear *military* advantage. It is more critical than the executive of the civil-rights movement. It tends, again in contrast to the executive, to favor a continuation of our restrictive immigration policies. It is, unlike the executive, deeply concerned with increased government spending. It tends to be more nationalist and more prone to increase the size of the military establishment. Finally, the legislative branch tends to be opposed to executive-supported plans for increasing the chances of

[17] Willmoore Kendall, *The Conservative Affirmation* (Chicago: Regnery, 1963), pp. ix–xi.

carrying out popular policy mandates by such means as the realignment of the political parties or the abolition of the filibuster. In all these cases, Kendall's sympathies lie with Congress.

The root of the tension is said to lie between the two "majorities" in American politics: one Congressional, and the other Presidential. As an analytical proposition, this position is easy to accept, at least with a change in terminology. There are not two majorities, but rather two constituencies. The President is obviously required to appeal to different groups for popular support than are Congressmen. His is the only *national* constituency. In Kendall's context, however, it makes little sense to refer to two majorities; *there is only one.* What Congress represents is not a different majority but a different set of constituencies—constituencies which underrepresent the urban areas on which the President must rely for support and to which he must increasingly appeal. This does not in itself weaken Kendall's case for the Congressional position, nor does it mean that the dual constituency system must be abandoned. It does clarify the issues, however. Kendall is happy to note that the Congressional "majority" has prevailed in a large proportion of cases. His goal is to maintain that particular status quo, and his fear is that conservatives will not be able to do so. (This fear is probably well taken, as the recent Supreme Court decisions attacking rural overrepresentation indicate. However, Kendall's concern may be less with constitutional principles than it is with preserving the kind of system which maximizes the chance to produce the policy decisions he prefers.)

The second major problem which Kendall sees in our politics today is that of the "open society." It is Kendall's belief that the Framers did not contemplate the establishment of such a society. The ultimate issue between liberals and conservatives revolves around this point. The villains of the piece are Hobbes, Locke, and Rousseau. These thinkers are normally lumped together in the history of political thought as originators of the modern version of social-contract theory. But their real significance lies, Kendall argues, in their repudiation of the classical tradition of natural law. Following the work of Leo Strauss, Kendall contends that after all the talk about "society, justice, right and wrong, obligation" and everything that can be explained in terms of consent has been "peeled off" from the writings of the contractarians, all that remains is a natural right to self-preservation. In other words, the social-contract thinkers upon whose work so much of modern democratic theory is based created a system in which the ultimate right is the pursuit of self-interest in the absence of any meaningful sense of duty to society as the natural concomitant of rights.[18]

To Kendall, this is a pernicious doctrine. It denies that there is a higher law independent of the actions of men. American liberals are Lockeans; therefore, Kendall concludes, American conservatives must become anti-Lockeans. There is, he argues, a public truth in America. Not all questions are open; some are permanently settled. There exists a consensus—a shared body of belief. Such a consensus is incomprehensible unless it "excludes ideas and opinions contradictory to itself." Some questions "involve matters so basic to the consensus that society would, in declaring them open, abolish itself, commit suicide, terminate its existence as the kind of society it has hitherto understood itself to be."[19] America, then, can proscribe certain doctrines; in fact, it must do so in order to survive. Such a doctrine, for example, is communism. Internal communism need not even pose a real danger; America may *"persecute"* it (the word is Kendall's) simply because it is there and because, "from the standpoint of the consensus," it is "wrong and immoral."

But here Kendall has drifted far from the intellectual moorings discussed above. It is one thing to talk about the existence of a higher law independent of the will of man. This tradition has one of the oldest intellectual pedigrees in Western thought; and while it is subject to debate, Western civilization as we know it would have been inconceivable without it, at least during the formative years. However, any resemblance between a national consensus and an enduring body of natural law is purely coincidental. At the crucial moment, Kendall subtly shifts the basis of his argument. It is not the higher law but the prevailing beliefs of American citizens which permit him to argue for the "persecution" of Communists. He turns, in fact, to Stouffer's *Communism, Conformity, and Civil Liberties* to show that the American people have not contracted among themselves for an open society. In doing so, he

---

[18] *Ibid.*, p. 98.
[19] *Ibid.*, pp. 74–75.

undercuts his whole argument, for his appeal is to public opinion and comes perilously close to an endorsement of the contractarian point of view against which he inveighs at great length.

In taking this position, Kendall adopts a stance which from a Burkean point of view is profoundly nonconservative. Nothing more clearly illustrates the deep divisions which separate American conservatives from one another than the obvious contrast between Kendall and Viereck. As noted earlier, it is precisely the same body of data to which Kendall appeals that leads Viereck to support the censure of Senator McCarthy and the segregation decisions—both of which Kendall opposed. In the end, Kendall has abandoned the external standard of truth for which he pleads and substituted for it the highly mutable standard of opinion. But without such an external standard, how is he to know that the consensus on which he relies does in fact embody truth? This is the fatal flaw in the argument. Contrary to Kendall's analysis, the liberal argument for an open society does not reject the existence of truth. It does not require that all values be called into question. It merely raises the logical possibility, as Charles Frankel suggests, that some things we firmly believe to be true may conceivably not be true, and it holds that a truly strong nation can withstand the stresses of free inquiry into these matters. This is no blank check for subversion; a constitution, as Mr. Justice Jackson reminded us, is not a suicide pact. But surely there is sufficient allowance for tolerance without the "persecution" of dissidents. To deny this proposition is virtually to deny the possibility of a free society. In a real sense Viereck is right when he argues that civil liberties are an aristocratic ideal even if the elites do not always live up to this ideal in practice. Kendall's approach is a betrayal of this ideal to the tender mercies of mob psychology.

Romantic Conservatism

Romantic conservatism[20] is a blend of a number of ideas which hang together loosely at best and sometimes not at all. It is

---

[20] This term is used with some hesitation. Like comparisons, all classifications are invidious. The writers I wish to touch on in this section are a disparate lot; moreover, they have tried to weave together a number of contradictory arguments. Still, labels have their uses, and I think it is possible to show a pervasive romanticism among these analysts.

more a political movement than a political theory and hence deserves more extended treatment in later chapters dealing with specific public policies. It is a form of rebellion against the prevailing tendencies of American life and politics in favor of a return to a far simpler Golden Age. Its great significance lies less in its intellectual vigor than in the fact that it has captured at least temporary control of the Republican Party. The ideological center of this movement is William Buckley and his staff on the *National Review*, and its political hero is Barry Goldwater.

Several streams of thought are joined rather uneasily together. The first can best be called libertarianism. The roots of this tradition are to be found in Social Darwinism and laissez-faire. The great danger to liberty is seen as the march of modern "collectivism." The classical liberal economics which constitutes such a vital part of conservative ideology in the age of enterprise is seen as a powerful bastion against these encroachments. "Without their mighty intellectual endeavors," writes Frank Meyer of the classical economists, "we should be disarmed before the collectivist economics of Marx, Keynes, and Galbraith."[21] To these conservatives the prime value is a highly individualized liberty. Moreover, as in the early ideology, freedom is conceived in negative terms as the absence of restraint rather than in positive terms as the ability to perform some desired action. It is no accident that Barry Goldwater is accepted by these writers as a hero. Goldwater, too, proposes to extend freedom by removing external restrictions. "My aim is not to pass laws, but to repeal them," he has written. The key question for every conservative, he continues, is, "are we maximizing freedom?"

The argument outlined above makes certain assumptions about the nature of liberty that are questionable at best. Is it really true that freedom consists merely in the absence of restraint? And what constitutes "restraint"? The problem is well illustrated by the frequently quoted remark that the rich are as free as the poor to sleep under bridges at night. It does not constitute free choice for a man to decide between starvation and a particular form of behavior in which he would prefer not to engage. The pangs of hunger

---

[21] Frank Meyer, "Freedom, Tradition, Conservatism," in Meyer, ed., *What Is Conservatism?* (New York: Holt, 1964), p. 18.

may be as great a restraint as those imposed by government action. True freedom requires a measure of genuine choice and an opportunity for positive action. In this view—a view which has guided reform liberalism and much of contemporary conservatism as well—freedom is a good deal more than the mere absence of restraint. This is not to say that there are not serious arguments against economic planning and other extensions of political power; these will be considered in the next chapter. All that must be conveyed here is an understanding of the relative simplicity and naïveté of the libertarian view of freedom.

A second major aspect of romantic conservatism is its attitude toward the authority of tradition. Little needs to be said on this score because the most important of the tradition-oriented romantic conservatives is Russell Kirk, who has already been considered in some detail. Willmoore Kendall also fits into this category, although for him the fountainhead of American conservatism is *The Federalist* rather than Burke's *Reflections*. In any case, where the libertarians lament the loss of freedom which they see in contemporary America, the traditionalists bemoan the decline of our national heritage which is clearly apparent to them.

Third, the romantics are characterized by an intense nationalism coupled with an equally intense anticommunism. Communism *in and of itself* is seen as a fundamental threat to the whole tradition of Western civilization. It is a messianic religion whose danger stems only in part from its support by major world powers whose aims are contrary to those of the United States; it is evil per se and must be combated as such. In this combat the United States is felt to have a special role. This task is the large one of preserving not only traditional American values, but also the entire Western heritage. To accomplish this end, the United States has, Mr. Goldwater notes, the values which the world most admires—"Strength, courage, and ingenuity!" With these attributes America can win victory in the Cold War and destroy the communist enemy. Only the bungling, or perhaps the treachery, of those who have failed to exploit these great resources has prevented this goal from being won.

There are certain obvious difficulties in this mélange of ideas, some of which have already been hinted at. To begin with, there is a tension which is hard to resolve between the demands of Kirk's organic traditionalism and the fervent individualism of a Buckley or a Goldwater. As a reading of Burke makes clear, an organic society cannot long endure the disruptive effects of laissez-faire and the view of man and society on which this doctrine is founded. An additional level of contradiction is found in the clash between the libertarian plea for a reduction in the size and role of government with the demand for total victory in the Cold War. The two points of view—as has often been pointed out—are simply incompatible with each other.

These contradictions are so great that romantic conservatism hardly repays analysis if considered purely as a system of ideas. This does not mean that it is without significance, however. It is of considerable value to consider the sociological and psychological roots of this conception of American politics, as well as the consequences of accepting the policy proposals which the romantics advocate. These questions will be reopened in later chapters.

Summary and Conclusions

On the basis of the analysis presented in this chapter, the problems inherent in creating a viable American conservatism are virtually self-evident. On the one hand, there are the romantics (whether libertarian or traditionalist) whose great hope seems to be the return of an earlier and simpler era—one which is spared, depending on the observer, either industrialism or the growth of government which industrialism seems to bring. But this is not all; the romantics want to have a world in which the United States is once again the supreme and unchallenged power.

Compared to this goal, the aristocratic yearnings of a Peter Viereck seem easy to achieve. Moreover, there is real although controversial evidence to support his analysis of the aristocratic foundation of civil rights and civil liberties. In addition, his indictment of the excesses of mass industrial society which he shares with numerous critics ranging from socialists to romantic conservatives has a considerable measure of truth. The thought of Viereck and others like him therefore concerns "the real world," not some romanticized image.

But it takes more than a measure of sound analysis to build a political movement, and as a result several problems face Viereck. His argument that the New Deal has become part of the heritage that must be preserved often leads conservatives of other schools to brand him as a thinly disguised liberal. They claim that Viereck empties conservatism of all meaningful content and reduces it to a mere defense of the status quo regardless of what that may be. There is some truth in this criticism but not quite enough to stand up. Viereck offers more than a defense of the status quo; built into his analysis is the ideal of a Burkean, aristocratic, hierarchical society hopefully modified enough to meet modern industrial conditions. Here Viereck encounters a major difficulty. Louis Hartz has pointed out (as did de Tocqueville one hundred years earlier), the facts simply are that America has never passed through a feudal stage. Hence it has had no true aristocracy, and no society on the Burkean model really fits in with the American tradition. Thus, Viereck's ideal is almost as much a retreat from reality as is Russell Kirk's. It might even be conceded that America needs some aristocratic values, but the fact remains that this country has precious few to fall back on. As Schlesinger has written, "For better or worse, our upper classes base their position not on land or tradition or a sense of social responsibility but on the folding stuff. They constitute not an aristocracy but a plutocracy."[22] So, Schlesinger's charge that the new conservatism is "the politics of nostalgia" is close to the mark. The frequent assaults throughout American history on some of the "aristocratic" institutions, like the Supreme Court, which have somehow managed to endure merely buttress the point.

Burkean conservatives thus have no permanent political home in the United States. The aristocrats of American politics—the Adamses, the Roosevelts, and the rest—have been few and seem to be getting fewer. In their place have risen "the new men of power," as Andrew Hacker calls them—talented, intelligent, highly skilled manipulators—technicians who are almost totally devoid of the marks of tradition. These are not the men to provide

---

[22] Arthur Schlesinger, Jr., *The Politics of Hope* (Boston: Houghton Mifflin, 1963), p. 75.

the *noblesse oblige* for which Viereck longs. It is the conservatism of business and industry and sometimes the romantic yearnings of a Barry Goldwater that win support as a political movement in the United States. For good or ill these have been the most successful varieties of American conservatism. To the Vierecks of our time this situation can only be viewed as a calamity; it means the triumph of "tradesmen" or even of the abstract libertarianism which Burke deplored. As a result, the left wing of the new conservatism tends to be increasingly devoted to nonpolitical cultural criticism of the quality of American life. Like their liberal counterparts, they have no place to go and so they, too, have become stranded on the "vital center."

❧ BIBLIOGRAPHICAL NOTES ❧

Several general works on conservatism are important. Perhaps the best is Clinton Rossiter, *Conservatism in America* (2nd ed. rev.; New York: Random House, Vintage Books, 1962); this study is particularly valuable for its massive bibliography. M. Morton Auerbach's *The Conservative Illusion* (New York: Columbia University Press, 1959) is rather hostile to the New Conservatism but is nonetheless a good scholarly effort. More problematical is William J. Newman's *The Futilitarian Society* (New York: Braziller, 1961), which is strongly biased against conservatism and is marred by an excessively flippant tone, although it does contain some genuine critical insights. Russell Kirk's *The Conservative Mind* (Chicago: Regnery, Gateway Editions, 1960) is strongly proconservative; its range is from Burke to Eliot. I disagree with much of his interpretation, but this is still a useful book.

There are two very good collections of Burke's writings. One is Peter Stanlis, ed., *Edmund Burke: Selected Writings and Speeches* (Garden City, N.Y.: Doubleday, Anchor Books, 1963), which has been used fairly extensively in this study. Stanlis' introduction is very good. The other useful collection is Louis I. Bredvold and Ralph Ross, *The Philosophy of Edmund Burke* (Ann Arbor: University of Michigan Press, 1961). This volume is arranged by topic and thus provides a fairly systematic overview of Burke's thought. A thorough study of *Reflections on the Revolution in France* is essential to an understanding of Burke; it is available in several editions.

The secondary literature on Burke is large, and only a few items can be listed here. Peter Stanlis, *Edmund Burke and the Natural Law* (Ann Arbor: University of Michigan Press, 1958),

118

places Burke in the tradition of political theory. Kirk's *The Conservative Mind* contains a good discussion of Burke, pp. 11–79. In *Natural Right and History* (Chicago: University of Chicago Press, 1953), Leo Strauss provides an analysis which juxtaposes Burke with Rousseau; see pp. 294–323. Finally, the student of Burke should consult the brilliant critique by John P. Plamenatz in *Man and Society*, Vol. I: *Machiavelli to Rousseau* (New York: McGraw-Hill, 1963), pp. 332–363. My interpretation of Burke has been influenced by Andrew Hacker, *Political Theory: Philosophy, Ideology, Science* (New York: Macmillan, 1961), pp. 341–383.

The basic studies on which I have relied in the discussion of the relation of conservatism to American business are those by Hofstadter, Fine, and Rossiter cited in the text. Two other valuable studies which also deal with the late nineteenth century are Sigmund Diamond, *The Reputation of American Businessmen* (Cambridge: Harvard University Press, 1955), and Robert McCloskey, *American Conservatism in the Age of Enterprise: 1865–1910* (Cambridge: Harvard University Press, 1951). Contemporary thinking in the business community is analyzed in Francis X. Sutton *et al.*, *The American Business Creed* (New York: Schocken Books, 1962), and Earl F. Cheit, ed., *The Business Establishment* (New York: Wiley, 1964). The essays by Robert Heilbroner, John William Ward, and Richard Hofstadter are particularly important. It should be noted that the dogma of laissez-faire was advanced mainly as a defense against government regulation of business. Business leaders had no such scruples if the intervention was on their side, as it often was. Indeed, in the earlier period of American history, conservative businessmen often viewed government as a natural ally. See Louis Hartz, *Economic Policy and Democratic Thought: Pennsylvania, 1776–1860* (Cambridge: Harvard University Press, 1948).

Russell Kirk has been a very prolific writer, but the basic themes of his work are stated in two books: *The Conservative Mind* and *A Program for Conservatives* (Chicago: Regnery, 1954). For other samples of his writing, see *Academic Freedom* (Chicago: Regnery, 1955), *Beyond the Dreams of Avarice* (Chicago: Regnery, 1956), and *The Intelligent Woman's Guide to Conservatism* (New York: Devin-Adair, 1957). The revised edition of Viereck's *Conservatism Revisited* (New York: Macmillan, Collier Books, 1962; orig. pub. 1949), referred to in the text, is notable for its sharp critical commentary on Russell Kirk and on Goldwaterite conservatism in general. In addition to this book and *The Unadjusted Man* (Boston: Beacon Press, 1956), the student of Viereck should also consult *The Shame and Glory of the Intellectuals* (2nd ed.; New York: Putnam, Capricorn Books, 1965); "The Revolt Against the Elite" and "The Philosophical 'New Conservatism,'" both in Daniel Bell, ed., *The Radical Right* (Garden City, N.Y.: Doubleday, 1963), pp. 135–174; and *Conservatism: From John Adams to Churchill* (Princeton: Van Nostrand, Anvil Books, 1956).

The question of the relation of the Populist movement in particular and of the masses in general to civil liberties and civil rights is very complex and highly controversial. The works by Key, Stouffer, Lipset, Woodward, and Nugent cited in the text offer a good beginning for an exploration of the problem. Two important articles which shed light on the popular base (or lack thereof) for civil liberties are James Prothro and Charles Grigg, "Fundamental Principles of Democracy: Bases of Agreement and Disagreement," *Journal of Politics* (May 1960), pp. 276–294, and Herbert McClosky, "Consensus and Ideology in American Politics," *American Political Science Review* (June 1964), pp. 361–383. Robert E. Lane, *Political Ideology: Why the American Common Man Believes What He Does* (New York: The Free Press, 1962), presents much material based on depth interviews with fifteen middle-class and lower-middle-class respondents.

E. Digby Baltzell, *The Protestant Establishment* (New York: Random House, 1964), is a rich source of information on the politics and intellectual history of the upper class in America. It also propounds an interesting theory as to the role of this class.

Willmoore Kendall's book *The Conservative Affirmation* (Chicago: Regnery, 1963) is a stimulating collection of essays and reviews. His discussion of the two majorities is one of the best available on legislative-executive relations. An article by Kendall and George W. Carey, "Towards a Definition of 'Conservatism,'" *Journal of Politics* (May 1964), pp. 406–422, also develops Kendall's rather unusual viewpoint. Kendall is clearly under the influ-

ence of Leo Strauss' *Natural Right and History.* The liberal position on the relativity of values may be found in Charles Frankel,
The Case for Modern Man (Boston: Beacon Press, 1959), pp.
45–84. The conservative case for a stronger Congress is also argued
in James Burnham, *Congress and the American Tradition* (Chicago: Regnery, 1959).

The variety of conservatism I have somewhat reluctantly labeled "romantic" finds a major outlet in William Buckley's period-
cal, *National Review.* For more theoretical aspects of the work of
this school of thought, see the essays in Frank Meyer, ed., *What Is
Conservatism?* (New York: Holt, 1964). This volume illustrates
full well the uneasy compromise between libertarianism and traditionalism. Much of the literature cited in the Bibliographical
Notes to Chapter V is also relevant to this topic.

Schlesinger's remarks on the American upper classes are to be
found in his discussion of the New Conservatism in his article
"The Politics of Nostalgia," pp. 12–80 of *The Politics of Hope*
(Boston: Houghton Mifflin, 1963). For Andrew Hacker's
thoughts on the "new men of power," see "Liberal Democracy and
Social Control," *American Political Science Review* (December
1957), pp. 1009–1026.

CHAPTER V

🦅🦅🦅🦅🦅🦅🦅🦅🦅🦅🦅🦅🦅🦅🦅🦅

THE
PUBLIC POLICIES
OF
CONSERVATISM

The basic outlines of conservative policies have already been suggested by the intellectual foundations sketched in the previous chapter. The dominant characteristic of conservative policy has been its close relationship to the business world, stemming from the twin doctrines of laissez-faire and Social Darwinism. For most of his history, the American conservative has been primarily interested in protecting business interests, at least on concrete policy questions. From this fact flow a number of basic commitments. Roger Freeman has posed a series of alternatives which can provide the basis for a discussion. These are more government or less, more *centralized* government or less, and more redistribution of income or less.[1] From each set of alternatives, Freeman chooses

---

[1] Roger A. Freeman, "Economic Priorities: Needs *v.* Expediency" in *The Conservative Papers* (Garden City, N.Y.: Doubleday, Anchor Books, 1964),

123

the second. The major themes of much of American conservatism are here: the rejection of egalitarianism (especially in its economic form) and a determined resistance to the further growth or centralization of the national government.

It must be noted at once that within these guidelines there is still considerable room for disagreement as to what they imply in terms of economic policy. One need only consider the gulf between two such eminent economists as Milton Friedman and Henry Wallich. One of the nation's outstanding economic theorists and a leading member of Senator Goldwater's campaign brain trust, Friedman, although embraced by today's conservatives, classifies himself unashamedly as a liberal in the nineteenth-century sense of the word; that is to say, he is a believer in a virtually absolute system of laissez-faire.

As noted earlier, Senator Goldwater is more interested in repealing laws than in passing new ones. A glance at the programs Friedman would like to abolish shows clearly the affinity between the two men: the agricultural price-support program, government control of output as in the farm program, rent control, minimum wage rates, most detailed regulation of industry, regulation of radio and television, present social-security programs, licensing of professional people, public housing, national parks, toll roads, and the government monopoly on the carrying of mail. Friedman would also abolish tariff and export restrictions—a course which might displease many of the most thoroughgoing conservative businessmen.[2] Friedman is thus a completely, even rigidly, consistent advocate of a barely modified Smithian doctrine. Government has a role at all only "because absolute freedom is impossible." Anarchy is thus impractical, and a few tasks remain for the state—

---

p. 111. There is no editor listed for this volume, but it may be taken as an authoritative presentation of one school of conservative doctrine. The introduction is by Representative Melvin R. Laird, of Wisconsin, who served as chairman of the Platform Committee at the 1964 Republican National Convention. The copyright is held by Ralph de Toledano of the *National Review* and Karl Hess, a leading aide in the Presidential campaign of Senator Goldwater.

[2] Milton Friedman, *Capitalism and Freedom* (Chicago: Phoenix Books, 1963), pp. 35–36.

maintenance of law and order, enforcement of contracts, definition of property rights, and the provision of a monetary system.[3]

The one apparent exception in Friedman's argument is in fact
not an exception: the "negative income tax." Like such liberal
writers as Robert Theobald, Friedman proposes a system of direct
payments to the poor. Thus, if someone received no income, he
would receive a "negative tax" which would allow him a subsistence living. But Friedman's motivation is quite different from
Theobald's. Theobald would place the subsidy well *above* the
subsistence level because he hopes to provide the material base for
the full development of the individual personality. Friedman, on
the other hand, hopes that his approach would permit the abolition of the whole "ragbag" of antipoverty measures which interfere
with the operation of the free market. Thus, equality of opportunity would be achieved, and all could then compete within the
market framework. It is clear that Friedman's seeming concession
to the welfare state is actually a step toward the resurrection of the
"night-watchman state."

Not all conservatives would agree with Friedman's rather
extreme position. Henry Wallich, another distinguished economist
and a member of the Council of Economic Advisors under President Eisenhower, views a certain amount of government intervention in the economy as not only legitimate, but essential.
Involvement is particularly necessary in two government activities:
stabilization of the business cycle and maintenance of competition.
In addition, Wallich would allow a substantial role for government
in a number of other areas: social security, conservation of natural
resources, development which exceeds the capacities of private
industry (as in the field of atomic energy), and protection of bank
depositors and homeowners against certain risks.[4]

How, then, do conservatives draw the line between the private
and the public sector of the economy? The laissez-faire advocated
by Friedman is rejected out of hand by Wallich on the ground
that "It is so much at odds with contemporary reality that to

---

[3] *Ibid.*, p. 27.
[4] Henry C. Wallich, *The Cost of Freedom* (New York: Macmillan,
Collier Books, 1962), pp. 69–70.

support it would be tantamount to joining a suicide club, even if its claim to provide a natural dividing line could be upheld." It is similarly impossible to develop some mechanical formula such as a certain per cent of national income beyond which the public share of national income should not rise. "A formula is no substitute for judgment," writes Wallich. Nor is it sufficient merely to list "legitimate" activities, as in the passage quoted above, for the reason that no activities are inherently excluded by such a practice. Thus, Wallich is thrown back on the Lincolnian maxim which holds that government should do for people only what they cannot do or cannot do well themselves. To this statement, Wallich would add that the difference between private and public performance would have to be substantial in order to warrant government intervention.

Although the differences between these two writers is great, they share some common assumptions which reveal a good deal about the conservative view of the proper relationship of government to the economy. In brief, they have a similar conception of freedom. As Wallich puts it, "The ultimate value of a free economy is not production, but freedom, and freedom comes not at a profit, but at a cost." Both men view freedom as the absence of restraint. Regulation of the economic system by government is absolutely inimical to freedom in Friedman's view; and in Wallich's, it is highly dangerous, though sometimes necessary. However, even to Wallich, there has been a progressive "seeping away of individualism."

The views of both men reflect the now famous argument of Friedrich Hayek in *The Road to Serfdom*. Friedman endorses Hayek's position in full, and while Wallich rejects some of Hayek's conclusions, he nevertheless also finds himself in substantial agreement. A close look at *The Road to Serfdom* therefore sheds much light on contemporary conservative thought.

The Road to Serfdom?

In recent years one of the great conflicts in both political theory and practical politics has raged over the question of economic planning. The most important point at issue is the compatibility of democracy with economic planning. To what degree is it safe to manage the economy by means other than the free operation of the market postulated by classical economics? The violence of the argument is a phenomenon rare in academic literature. Hayek attacks planning as an inevitable step toward dictatorship and labels attempts to manage the economy as "the road to serfdom." His book of that title is answered in vigorous counterattack by Herman Finer, in which Hayek's work is blasted as "the reactionaries' manifesto" and a sinister offensive against democracy, while the policies which it advocates are dubbed "the road to reaction" (the title of Finer's book).

First, let us examine some definitions of the concept of economic planning. Hayek claims:

What our planners demand is central direction of all economic activity according to a single plan, laying down how the resources of a society should be "consciously directed" to serve particular ends in a definite way.[5]

The key phrases "*all* economic activity" and "a *single* plan" indicate Hayek's belief that planning is an all-or-nothing proposition. In other words, because of the inherent logic of a planned system, it cannot go just so far and then be stopped. A somewhat less restrictive definition is given by Barbara Wootton: "Planning, in the sense that is relevant here, may be defined as the conscious and deliberate choice of economic priorities by some public authority."[6] Clearly, this definition is more flexible; its virtue is that it allows the possibility of a wide variety of plans, ranging from complete socialization of the means of production to any number of less comprehensive arrangements. Perhaps the best definition of planning is Herman Finer's:

a series of well concerted laws, separate as to substance, but integrated and then carried into further detail by a series of rules and orders, made

---

[5] Friedrich Hayek, *The Road to Serfdom* (Chicago: Phoenix Books, 1957; orig. pub. 1944), p. 35.

[6] Barbara Wootton, *Freedom Under Planning* (Chapel Hill: University of North Carolina Press, 1945), p. 6.

by officials deputed thereto, and controlled by the standards enacted in the statutes and subject to parliamentary or judicial revision or both.[7]

The excellence of this definition stems from the fact that it combines the flexibility of Miss Wootton's definition with a recognition of the type of administrative procedure needed to carry out such a plan.

The necessity for some sort of plan seems to be recognized by both parties to the controversy. However, the plan endorsed by Hayek as an alternative to the now defunct laissez-faire theory is rather different from that advocated by such thinkers as Finer. Certain types of regulation are definitely precluded. Among the forbidden activities would be any rules designed to control such factors of the market equation as prices or the quantities of particular commodities. Thus *methods* of production might be restricted, but only so long as the restrictions were not designed as an indirect scheme for control of commodity prices or quantities. The ultimate test is whether a proposed regulation will impose social costs greater than any advantages gained. However, even by this test, such legislation must be very limited, for Hayek also argues that "Although competition can stand some admixture of regulation, it cannot be combined with planning to any extent we like without ceasing to operate as an effective guide to production." Competition or planning are both held to be inefficient if they are incomplete. A mixture is very likely to be worse than either one consistently applied. Therefore, planning for competition rather than against it is the only possible combination.

To Hayek any other form of planning is an unmitigated evil and is responsible for many of our present discontents. As he puts it, "We have progressively abandoned the freedom in economic affairs without which personal and political freedom have never existed in the past." There has been a subtle perversion of the meaning of the term *freedom*. In his view, it no longer means freedom from coercion and arbitrary power. Instead, it means "freedom from necessity, release from the compulsion of the cir-

[7] Herman Finer, *The Road to Reaction* (Boston: Little, Brown, 1945), p. 26.

cumstances which inevitably limit the range of choice of all of us, although for some very much more than for others."[8]

Hayek further contends that it is impossible to limit planning once it has begun:

> That planning creates a situation in which it is necessary for us to agree on a much larger number of topics than we have been used to, and that in a planned system we cannot confine collective action to the tasks on which we can agree but are forced to produce agreement on everything in order that any action can be taken at all, is one of the factors that contributes the most to determining the character of a planned system.[9]

This fear is not entirely unfounded and, if true, the danger to a free society is obvious. As Roland Pennock points out:

> The existing freedom to choose one's vocation, one's employer, and the way one would manage his savings or spend his income would give way in greater or lesser degree to regimentation in all these areas by governmental fiat. It might provide greater security or more equality, but it could hardly fail to reduce liberty.[10]

(In this connection it is interesting to note that the Labour government of Great Britain found it necessary to forgo its announced policy of attempting a planned economy without the compulsion of labor. In less than two years this government was forced to provide for a limited labor conscription.)

Hayek's argument goes further. A planned economic system presupposes, he claims, the existence of a complete ethical code in which all human values have an assigned place. Only such an arrangement can guide the planner unless he is to rely exclusively on his own judgment as to the common good. Hayek believes that the latter is exactly the situation that would result, since there is no such hierarchical ordering of ethical values on which all can agree. This leads Hayek to fear an excessive reliance on administrative discretion. The mere fact that the planners may be democrati-

---

[8] Hayek, *The Road to Serfdom*, p. 26.

[9] *Ibid.*, p. 62.

[10] J. Roland Pennock, *Liberal Democracy: Its Merits and Prospects* (New York: Holt, 1950), p. 333.

cally chosen is not enough protection. Power can be arbitrary even if the power holders are chosen by democratic procedures, for "it is not the source but the limitation of power which prevents it from being arbitrary."[11] It then follows that great faith must be placed in the planner, but, says Hayek, this faith is not justified. He argues that in a planned society it is inevitable that "the worst get on top." The planner must find a solid basis of mass support for his policies. This support is not likely to be found in the upper strata of a society because, with more education, individual taste becomes more and more differentiated. For more uniformity it is necessary to descend to the level of lower moral and intellectual standards where the most primitive and "common" instincts prevail. A strong leader is able to appeal to this group by a negative program appealing to group hatreds.

The last major point of Hayek's argument is an attack on the moral basis of a planned system. For him such a system is the negation of individualist morals. No act can be moral unless the actor is himself responsible for his action:

Only where we ourselves are responsible for our own interests and are free to sacrifice them has our decision moral value. . . . A movement whose main premise is the relief from responsibility cannot but be antimoral in its effect, however lofty the ideals to which it owes its birth.[12]

In commenting upon Hayek's critique of planned economic systems, I shall begin by quoting Joseph Schumpeter:

In a sense, of course, the present day forms and organs of democratic procedure are as much the outgrowth of the structure and the issues of the bourgeois world as is the fundamental principle of democracy itself. But this is no reason why they should have to disappear along with capitalism.[13]

Following this line of argument, there is no logical contradiction between economic planning and democracy. E. H. Carr's opinion in *The New Society* is noteworthy: "To reconcile democracy

---

[11] Hayek, *The Road to Serfdom*, p. 71.

[12] *Ibid.*, pp. 211–212.

[13] Joseph Schumpeter, *Capitalism, Socialism and Democracy* (New York: Harper, 1942), pp. 300–301.

with planning for socialism is a difficult task. It may have been undertaken too late. But it is the only course which may yet, if war can be avoided, enable democracy to survive." Perhaps the same may be said of planning. The unaided market economy, subject as it is to such defects as have been encountered earlier, apparently is not a sufficiently powerful mechanism for ordering the economic system except in the theoretical speculations of laissez-faire economists. "Planning for socialism" (whatever that may mean) may not be inevitable, but some sort of planning probably is. Therefore, it is necessary to examine the possibilities of maintaining a free society even under a system planned to a greater or lesser extent.

As Hayek points out, the mere existence of democratic procedures and of faith in the intent of the governors to serve in the best interests of the nation is not sufficient protection against arbitrary rule. On the other hand, the tradition of democratic rule in the United States cannot be ignored. Democratic traditions are certainly no automatic guarantee of continued democracy, but surely the existence of a well-established democratic political culture in America is an important factor. Inertia is of some significance in a political system, and the odds are that a nation habituated to democracy will continue along that road. A planned economy may exert great pressures on the niceties of everyday existence in Western democracies—pressures of a kind Americans will certainly want to withstand. However, it is unsafe to assume that these pressures are irresistible and that a planned economy *inevitably* results in tyranny. As Wootton argues, while power always involves risks, it also has its advantages. And unless there is recognition that the latter sometimes outweigh the former, the result is anarchy. The risks must be weighed against the advantages without prejudgment of the issue.[14]

Like many other economists, Hayek tends to argue that if facts do not correspond to theory, then so much the worse for the facts. In this particular case, he is guilty of comparing the competitive system as it exists in the world of economic theory with planned systems as they exist in the world of reality. He is confus-

---

[14] Wootton, *Freedom Under Planning*, p. 28.

ing the useful analytic concepts of theoretical economics with actuality. To quote Miss Wootton again: "The alternatives are not planning on Utopia; they are planning, for better or for worse, and a planless world, to which very serious exception can be taken on good grounds." The comparison, then, is between two imperfect and probably imperfectible human institutions. It borders on nonsense to contend, as does Hayek, that planning *cannot* stop short of serfdom. While control of a complex modern economy involves a considerable extension of governmental power, it is not logically necessary for this extension of power to result in a totalitarian ordering of society. It may be said that logically a continuum extends from the ruins of laissez-faire through a mixed economy such as ours to a totalitarian socialist system.

The critical issue is the problem of knowing where on this continuum to stop. The answer is to be found in such factors as the quality of the planners and the social system, the historical tradition, and the political culture of the particular society in question. The governmental tradition of a nation, its system for restricting state authority, its economic institutions, and the like must be considered before a decision can be made as to the permissible extent of planning. Each case must be decided on its merits. It is of no help to make a blanket condemnation of all planning. And in the end, as Miss Wootton points out, "A wise choice of planners and a watchful eye on plans may well be the price of freedom."

If this is true, then the arguments raised by Hayek as to "why the worst get on top" are of crucial importance. If such is the case, it is quite clear that a planned society is in for trouble. However, once again, Hayek's fears have led him to overstate his case. His arguments are framed in terms of the methods by which a dictator must win support. As Miss Wootton argues, he is assuming the truth of his hypothesis; in other words, he assumes that totalitarian dictatorship is the inevitable result of economic planning. But this result remains to be shown, and Hayek has not done so.

Unless it can be refuted, Hayek's point with regard to the essential immorality of a planned system is the most damaging of his arguments against the planner's case. It is hard to disagree with his contention that no act can be moral without the element of choice being involved. As the man who knows no fear cannot be said to show courage when he advances to meet a dangerous situation for the reason that true courage consists in overcoming fear and acting in spite of it, just so is it true that the man who acts because he has no chance to do otherwise cannot be considered to have acted either morally or immorally. Man must choose before he can claim moral sanction for his actions. Where Hayek goes wrong is in assuming that a real choice exists for everyone in a market economy. In actual practice the area of choice may be so small as to be virtually nonexistent. The worker who is forced by economic circumstance to take a job detestable to him is not exercising free choice and is therefore not acting morally. As even Hayek would admit, freedom of choice is very much more limited for some than for others. This truism does not make the denial of choice which may be a necessary factor in a planned system any more palatable. Perhaps it does point to the classic Niebuhrian dilemma—the attempt by imperfect man to achieve a perfectly moral existence. However, this attempt must be made, and it is not easy to dismiss the feeling that a reduction of the area of choice which *may* be necessary in a planned system is more than made up for in increased opportunity to choose and therefore increased opportunity to act morally in noneconomic spheres of human existence.

The empirical foundations of Hayek's view may also be challenged. As noted, to him—and to Friedman as well—a free economy is the prerequisite of a free society. Two points must be made by way of comment. First, it is by no means clear on the historical evidence that laissez-faire must precede or accompany democracy. After all, the roots of modern Anglo-American democracy antedate the rise of capitalism; these roots are, in fact, medieval in origin. It might also be pointed out, in agreement with Paul Samuelson, that "In our history, the days of most rugged individualism—the Gilded Age and the 1920's—seem to have been the ages least tolerant of dissenting opinion."[15]

---

[15] Paul Samuelson, "Personal Freedoms and Economic Freedom in the Mixed Economy," in Earl F. Cheit, ed., *The Business Establishment* (New York: Wiley, 1964), p. 218.

Second, a look at nations around the world also casts doubt on the libertarian formulations. On their showing for example, both the Scandinavian socialist nations and Great Britain ought to be nearer "serfdom" than the United States. And yet, to use an example noted by Samuelson, both the British Broadcasting Company and the Scandinavian radio (which are government-owned) are more tolerant of dissent than are the radio and television networks in the United States. It would appear at the very least that Hayek's road requires a considerable period of time to travel, since his first formulation of his thesis appeared in 1938, at a time when the Scandinavian welfare states were already well established.[16] Even an avowed conservative like Wallich is forced to admit this point and argue that a nation which has a tradition of democracy and freedom need not court the demon of dictatorship if it decides to institute some form of economic planning. Thus, to Wallich, the argument against planning rests on criteria of economic efficiency rather than on political grounds.

In regard to the compatibility of planning and democracy, it may well be that the conception of democracy needs refining. As Schumpeter notes, the great trouble with the classical theory lies in the idea that the people hold rational ideas on each and every public issue and that they give expression to these rationally determined views by choosing representatives to carry them out. Selection of representatives is made secondary to the primary purpose of democracy, which is to vest the power of deciding issues in the electorate. In this light, it must be said that the critics of planning require a degree of choice which, curiously enough, is radically democratic in its demands and which assumes a level of information about public issues found nowhere in the world. However, the classical formulation could very well be inverted so as to make the deciding of public-policy issues secondary to the selection of representatives. Schumpeter continues: "And we define: the democratic method is that institutional arrangement for arriving at political decisions in which individuals acquire the power to decide by means of a competitive struggle for the people's vote."[17]

---

[16] On this point, see Samuelson, *ibid.*, particularly pp. 225–227.

[17] Schumpeter, *Capitalism, Socialism and Democracy*, p. 269.

It is clear from this definition that there is no necessary *logical* relation between the type of economic system and the presence of truly democratic institutions. Nor is there any necessary incompatibility between democracy and socialism. As Schumpeter points out, "in appropriate states of social environment the socialist engine can be run on democratic principles."[18]

The significant question then becomes: What are the "appropriate states of social enviornment" conducive to democratic success? Recent research has indicated a number of such factors. Democracy seems to depend on a high level of economic development, coupled with a wide distribution of the products of the economy. A wide range of indices correlate with democracy: high per-capita income, an industrial society as opposed to an agricultural society, a high degree of urbanization, and a well-educated citizenry.[19] But economic development in itself is clearly not enough to ensure stable democracy; if it were, then surely Weimar Germany would have been able to preserve its democratic character against the depredations of the Nazis. The political system, as Lipset points out, must also be legitimate and effective. Thus, a democracy must "engender and maintain the belief that the existing political conditions are the most appropriate ones for the society," and it must convince the population at large, as well as the major power groups within it, that its performance satisfies the basic needs of the society.[20]

Schumpeter adds a number of other considerations:

1. The human material of politics must be of sufficiently high quality.

2. The effective range of political decision should not be too great.

3. There must be a well-trained bureaucracy of good standing and tradition.

4. There should be an element of democratic self-control. Legislation not acceptable to important groups in the nation is to be avoided.

---

[18] *Ibid.*, p. 284.

[19] Seymour Martin Lipset, *Political Man* (Garden City, N.Y.: Doubleday, 1960), pp. 45–76; see especially the statistical tables on pp. 51–54.

[20] *Ibid.*, p. 77; for an extensive development, see pp. 77–96.

The last point is of the greatest importance. As Schumpeter says:

In fact the reader need only review our conditions in order to satisfy himself that democratic government will work to full advantage only if all the interests that matter are practically unanimous not only in their allegiance to the country but also in their allegiance to the structural principles of the existing society.[21]

This factor clearly must be considered in any attempt to apply planning to the American economy. As the economist John Maurice Clark has noted, it is possible to conceive of any number of possible systems which might be substituted for the existing one, ranging from thoroughgoing laissez-faire all the way to centralized collectivism. But these are not real alternatives for the United States.[22]

The American consensus is a narrow one. Alternatives which deviate far from the present norms are unlikely to receive a very careful hearing. As Galbraith and many others have noted, this nation has developed an economy whose functioning depends on competing groups. Labor has found it necessary to organize in order to offset the power of manufacturing interests. Farm and professional interests are highly organized. Group organization has become necessary to the common man. It is his "alternative to serfdom." These competing groups cannot be done away with unless the government acts in such a way as to confirm Hayek's worst fears. However, the power of these groups must be controlled and put to good use. As Clark has pointed out, open, unregulated competition may have been a feasible alternative in the simpler economy of past years, although it might have meant the exploitation of the weak by the strong. However, in an economy dominated by the gigantic combines of today, the pursuit of self-interest may have shattering consequences. Methods must be found for balancing economic groups and forcing the responsible exercise of their great powers.

On the other hand, it must not be assumed that because the American economic structure and indeed the whole national herit-

---

[21] Schumpeter, *Capitalism, Socialism and Democracy*, p. 296.

[22] John Maurice Clark, *Alternative to Serfdom* (New York: Random House, Vintage Books, 1956), p. 130, pp. 5–6.

age preclude both a completely socialized economy and classical laissez-faire that the only course lies midway between the extremes. As Wootton has stressed, there is more than one kind of freedom. A limited plan may destroy certain freedoms, while a more comprehensive scheme might leave others untouched. It may well be that the simultaneous enjoyment of economic, civil, political, and cultural freedoms is impossible, at least if these freedoms are sought as absolutes. The point is that each aspect of a plan, each one of the series of well-integrated laws, must be carefully examined for its effect on the delicate balance among these freedoms.

The essential task is to determine the areas of agreement among societal groups, although Hayek is probably correct in assuming that there is no hierarchically ordered system of values on which all may agree. However, in this country at any rate, the substantial agreement between the two major political parties on most public issues is perhaps indicative of the extent of basic agreement throughout society. The tacit agreement of the Eisenhower administration to the reforms of the New Deal has firmly established those actions as a basis for the future. With this evidence in mind it seems that although no mathematical system for determining a schedule of economic preference exists, it is by no means sure that such a schedule cannot be approximated.

Conservatism and the Affluent Society

Most conservative positions on economic and social issues follow from the position outlined and criticized above. The roots of antiegalitarianism and the distrust of centralized government— indeed, of any government—can be clearly seen. Most American conservatives are not opposed to liberal egalitarian measures out of any devotion to the principles of Burke. Rather these stands stem from a commitment to a particular economic order which is, paradoxically, closely related to the individualism and egalitarianism of early nineteenth-century liberalism. It is this order which they desire to conserve, or, in the case of a Friedman, to restore, since he believes that America has already strayed too far from the paths of righteousness.

The policy implications of these beliefs are clear. To the

group of conservatives clustered around the *National Review,* Friedman's list of policies to be avoided is one with which they can agree. Naturally, they view with distaste proposals such as those of John Kenneth Galbraith for a readjustment of the balance between the public and the private sector of the economy. To William Buckley, for example, Galbraith's proposals are a declaration of "total war" against the individual's right to allocate resources as he sees fit. Buckley suggests, in fact, that the argument of *The Affluent Society* might well be reversed: Rather than providing economic nonessentials for the public as the nation grows richer, government can leave more for the people to provide for themselves on their own. Thus, for example, he argues that the case for socialized medicine is a great deal stronger in India than it is in the United States for the simple reason that fewer Indians than Americans can afford to pay doctor bills.

Considerably more moderate conservatives, like Henry Wallich, share this view *in its essentials.* While agreeing with Galbraith that some consumer wants are to be more highly valued than others, Wallich is wary of arguing from this assumption that expenditures for items of lesser importance should be actively discouraged. Moreover, he believes, Galbraith's case is not as strong as it might be. Gadgetry and other trivia account for only a tiny fraction of personal consumption, he argues. However, within less than a page, he hints that a "new puritanism" directed against wasteful consumption might be damaging to the economy; at the very least, it would make no "great contribution." The concession is a damaging one, for if trivia are of little importance, how could a campaign against them harm the economy?

In addition, Wallich questions the need for an increase in the public share of the Gross National Product. The pressures on behalf of private spending are real, he admits, although advertising is overrated as a villain. At the same time, Wallich points out, the pressures, particularly of a political nature, for greater public spending should not be overlooked. No one can say for sure just what the balance between private and public spending is. However, the increasing percentage of GNP accounted for by taxes of all kinds provides no reason "to suspect that the expansive forces lack vigor."

This contention brings up another key point in Wallich's

argument. Meeting consumer needs by public action is held to be a highly inefficient approach—inefficient not in the sense of popular suspicion of bureaucratic incompetence, but rather because Wallich feels the market to be a much more precise instrument for the allocation of resources than any government action could ever be.

Finally, the argument comes full circle as Wallich stresses once more his view of the connection between political and economic freedom. The present allocation of resources is the product of a particular balance of interests. An alteration of the pattern of resource allocation would thus require a political attack on this balance of interests. This exercise of political power is to be avoided, argues Wallich. The dangers of an increasing economic role for government must be considered.

But Wallich's argument is based on virtually the same assumptions made by Hayek, though Wallich is not willing to pursue them quite so far. If Hayek's argument is invalid, then so is Wallich's. Moreover, Wallich's view includes tacit approval of a particular configuration of interests without providing any defense for it other than the fact that it exists. Ethically, this is a dubious approach. If Galbraith fails as a social philosopher because he offers no guidelines for the redistribution of expenditure he seeks, Wallich fails similarly by neglecting to provide an adequate defense of the status quo he wants to preserve.

On the surface, the difference in policy preferences between Galbraith and Wallich seems considerable. Below the surface, however, there is a fundamental similarity. The policies Wallich explicitly endorses are essentially New Deal policies, and although Galbraith expresses a desire to move beyond the New Deal, he offers little that is specific along these lines. These facts are clear-cut illustrations of the triumph of the New Deal and its place at the center of the American consensus. Conservatives of the Friedman type are far removed from this consensus, but their views are those of a minority, not only among economists, but in the general public and even—as shown in the 1964 elections— among many businessmen who are normally loud in their praise of laissez-faire.

The behavior of business groups in the 1964 election raises a significant point which must be taken into account in any discussion of American conservatism. For decades, the ideology of the business community has been opposed to active involvement of the government in economic affairs. Yet 1964 saw a shift of major proportions away from a candidate who openly espoused beliefs which businessmen were supposed to hold. In fact, some business leaders announced for President Johnson even before the nomination of Senator Goldwater. It is too early to say whether this shift is a passing phenomenon or whether it represents a basic change of position.

It should be noted that conservative groups in other advanced industrial societies do not display the attachment to laissez-faire which has for so long been characteristic of their American counterparts. Thus, in Germany, for example, the conservative Bismarck long ago introduced a substantial measure of what would now be called welfare-state ideas. Herbert Spiro notes that to this day there is "no tradition of principled opposition to state interference in the economy." In fact, most German interest groups display a positive desire to be regulated. In Great Britain, Benjamin Disraeli's Tory Democracy stole much of the reformer's thunder in the late nineteenth century, thus functioning in much the same way as Bismarck's policies. Even the Manchesterian liberals so admired by laissez-faire conservatives in this country were, unlike many of their American exponents, quite pragmatic in their approach. To them, laissez-faire was not an eternal law, but rather a doctrine well suited to particular social needs at a particular time and place. As a third example, a recent study by Roy Macridis indicates that French elites desire more regulation than the government now performs, and they fear the decline of economic planning and a revival of laissez-faire.[23]

Whether American business leaders develop beliefs similar to

---

[23] For a discussion of business in the 1964 campaign, see David Bazelon, "Big Business and the Democrats," *Commentary* (May 1965), pp. 38–46. For a discussion of business attitudes, welfare policies, and the like in Germany, see the contribution of Herbert Spiro to Samuel Beer and Adam Ulam, eds., *Patterns of Government* (2nd ed.; New York: Random House, 1962), pp. 569–583, especially pp. 570 and 577. On Great Britain, see Harry Eckstein in *ibid.*, pp. 201–230, especially pp. 205 and 207. For French elite attitudes, see Roy Macridis, Karl Deutsch, *et al.*, *France, Germany, and the Western Alliance* (New York: Scribner's, 1967), p. 53. It should be noted that the

those discussed remains to be seen. If the new political economy wins gradual acceptance, the basis of much of American conservatism will have changed. Certainly, the potential is there, and if realized, the prospect is for a good deal of ideological fluidity and perhaps for a major realignment of political forces.

At present, however, these prospects must remain in the realm of speculation. All it is possible to say now is that the contemporary American conservative ideologist is in a difficult, if not impossible, position. He tacitly accepts a good deal of the liberal program of the twentieth century even while he rejects the ideological foundations on which the program rests. He resists further change in the direction the country has been moving. Therefore, even moderate conservatives like Professor Wallich become tacit, although perhaps unwilling, allies of the forces which have produced the sterility of mass culture. As a result, they find themselves in opposition to the liberals *and* those conservatives—the Galbraiths and the Vierecks—who at least consider a change in the status quo. This is a high price to pay for adherence to the dogma of laissez-faire.

The current division between liberal and conservative economists is not deep, although their differences *could* be accentuated if liberals begin to push seriously for increased governmental intervention in economic affairs. As matters stand now, however, differences tend to be over technical matters rather than over basic beliefs. Most conservatives, though they fear government, are not ready to do away with the New Deal; in fact, they accept it more or less willingly. Most liberals, for their part, might like to see a more positive role for government, but have been unable to win widespread political support for this position. In a sense, then, the basic cleavage of American political history has been papered over, at least for the moment.

This fact gives rise to the belief that ideology is no longer of importance in American politics. If the traditional ideological

remarks of Macridis refer to French elites as a group and do not isolate businessmen alone.

As every schoolboy knows, if American businessmen were to forsake the ideology of laissez-faire, it would really represent a return to an earlier Hamiltonianism.

dividing line has been obscured by a new consensus and if politics is merely a process of bargaining and compromise over technical detail, then surely "the end of ideology" is a serious possibility. In a later chapter, this contention is examined with care. Before doing so, however, it must be noted that in foreign policy and civil rights wholly new sources of conflict seem to be arising. Policy questions—and ideological questions—spawned by these new forces are having an increasing impact on the American political system. There is thus reason to believe that the sources of political conflict are different from those in the past. The next two chapters devote special attention to evolving ideological positions on foreign policy and civil rights.

❧ BIBLIOGRAPHICAL NOTES ❧

A great deal has been written about the problem of economic planning. As indicated in the text, much of the controversy has revolved around Hayek's *The Road to Serfdom* (Chicago: Phoenix Books, 1957; orig. pub. 1944). For all that it is now more than twenty years old, this book is still the best statement of the anti-planning position. Herman Finer's *The Road to Reaction* (Boston: Little, Brown, 1945) is perhaps the most famous critique of Hayek. However, it is by no means the best, because it is often marred by a certain intemperance of argument. Barbara Wootton's *Freedom Under Planning* (Chapel Hill: University of North Carolina Press, 1945) is much superior, and I have been much influenced by it. Joseph Schumpeter's study, *Capitalism, Socialism and Democracy* (New York: Harper, 1942), is one of the great classics of modern social science. The definition of democracy propounded by Schumpeter has been much criticized of late, although it still dominates American political science. See Peter Bachrach, *The Theory of Democratic Elitism: A Critique* (Boston: Little, Brown, 1967). See also E. H. Carr, *The New Society* (London: Macmillan, 1951). A recent volume which assesses "the changing balance of public and private power" is Andrew Schonfield, *Modern Capitalism* (New York: Oxford University Press, 1965). An impressive paper by the distinguished economist Paul Samuelson should be consulted: "Personal Freedoms and Economic Freedoms in the Mixed Economy," in Earl F. Cheit, ed., *Ths Business Establishment* (New York: Wiley, 1964), pp. 193–227.

For present purposes the most important book by William Buckley is *Up From Liberalism* (New York: Hillman Books,

143

1961). See also Buckley's *God and Man at Yale* (Chicago: Regnery, 1951) and *Rumbles Right and Left* (New York: Putnam, 1963). Barry Goldwater's views on domestic policy are spelled out in *The Conscience of a Conservative* (New York: Macfadden, 1960).

The Cost of Freedom (New York: Macmillan, Collier Books, 1962) by Henry C. Wallich is the best statement of more moderate conservative economic views. The similarity of Wallich's work to Galbraith's is argued by Stephen Rousseas in "Fences Against Power," *The Nation* (April 27, 1963), pp. 343–349. Indeed, Rousseas goes further, arguing that these two theorists are "part of the same obsolescent tradition" as Friedman's *Capitalism and Freedom* (Chicago: Phoenix Books, 1963). The argument is provocative but is pushed further than is warranted.

CHAPTER VI

THE
PROBLEM
OF
FOREIGN POLICY

The first of the two major sources of potential ideological change is in the area of international affairs. The world political arena changes with sometimes startling rapidity, and the alterations present numerous challenges to established American ways of dealing with other nations. The fundamental problem is the evident obsolescence of many of the basic ideas which have guided American foreign policy since World War II. In order to understand the current malaise, it is necessary to examine the consensus which emerged from that conflict.

The first factor to be noted is the near-irrelevance of traditional right-left or liberal-conservative categories. These labels are primarily an outgrowth of domestic political conflict and have only a tenuous connection with foreign affairs. It is a convention to refer to writers who sympathize with doctrines of international cooperation, who support the aspirations of the underdeveloped areas, and who stress the importance of ideals as opposed to force in international politics as liberals. There is also a tendency to refer to those holding the opposite positions as conservatives. Nevertheless, a much more meaningful dividing line is that which separated "realists" from "idealists" in the late 1940's and early 1950's. The triumph of the realists in this debate set the basic pattern of American foreign policy for the years since. It is the principles underlying that policy with which this chapter is concerned.[1]

The Basic Doctrines

World War II forced a fundamental reexamination of the root assumptions of the American approach to international politics. Prior to the war, America had been essentially an isolationist nation devoted largely to the creation of an industrial economy and to the enthusiastic pursuit of "manifest destiny." It is true that war was waged on Mexico and Spain; indeed, in the "lovely little War" over Cuba a modest empire was acquired—seemingly almost by accident. These adventures, however, did not constitute significant participation by the United States in world affairs. Although this nation had the potential to make its presence felt, the United States scrupulously followed Washington's injunction to avoid foreign entanglements, and as a result made little or no impact on world politics as conducted by the great powers. The machinations of those nations were regarded with supreme contempt, born of the deep-seated belief that somehow "power politics" was inherently wrong and immoral.

The first really important intervention in world affairs—one that materially affected the balance of power—was participation in World War I. This move did not mean that the earlier antipolitical idealism had been forsaken; on the contrary, the war effort represented the quintescence of that idealism. The war was viewed

---

[1] It should be pointed out that, in much of the realist literature, there is considerable criticism of liberal attitudes toward foreign relations. "Liberal" is normally used in those writings in the same sense as it is used by Reinhold Niebuhr; see the discussion in Chapter II, pp. 18–19, 22–23 especially.

as a great moral crusade, waged for the noble purpose of "making the world safe for democracy" and perhaps even better than that, of ending war itself. After an apparent victory in this crusade, the United States withdrew once again into its isolationist shell, there to remain until World War II forced its emergence once again.

This time, the situation at the war's end was radically different from that which prevailed twenty-five years earlier. Most of the former great powers—Germany, Japan, France, England—were totally spent by their efforts. A dramatically different world emerged—a world polarized between two "superpowers," the United States and the Soviet Union. Moreover, prior to the war's end a definite commitment had been made by this country to the creation of a viable international organization and hence to the acceptance of the responsibilities of a major political power.

Before these responsibilities could be accepted, it was clear that a revolution in the basic attitudes of the United States toward foreign affairs had to occur. This revolution came in the form of a stinging critique of the American diplomatic tradition delivered by such men as George Kennan and Hans Morgenthau. The fundamental problem, Kennan argued, was the "legalistic-moralistic approach to international problems" which "runs like a red skein through our foreign policy of the last fifty years."[2] This approach meant, first of all, "the belief that it should be possible to suppress the chaotic and dangerous aspirations of governments in the international field by the acceptance of some system of legal rules and restraints." This kind of thinking was faulty for a number of reasons. First, argued Kennan, the idea of subordinating nations to a rule of international law assumed that other nations were as well satisfied with their lot as was the United States, and hence that international tension could easily be minimized in a world of law; this was patent nonsense. Second, this rule of law tends toward a one-government/one-vote international order which "glorifies the concept of national sovereignty," thus ignoring the unstable character of the nation-state system. Third, international offenses, such

---

[2] George F. Kennan, *American Diplomacy: 1900–1950* (New York: Mentor Books, 1952; orig. pub. 1951 by the University of Chicago Press), p. 82.

as ideological warfare or subversion, which bypass the legal institutions cannot easily be subjected to control of the sort envisaged by American idealists. Finally, this legalistic approach completely overlooks the difficulties inherent in providing meaningful sanctions against offending nations.[3]

The first great deficiency of American foreign policy—that is, its legalism—was related to another yet more dangerous—its moralism. The second, in fact, is a product of the first, claimed Kennan. "Whoever says there is a law must of course be indignant against the lawbreaker and feel a moral superiority to him." This attitude leads to results totally foreign to the intentions of the advocates of the legalistic approach. Consider the difficulties posed by war fought as a moral crusade. Such a war is hard to conclude short of total domination of the loser by the victor. But total war is a dangerous policy to pursue, and the consequences of the pursuit may be very hard to calculate in advance. Certainly, as Kennan points out, the two total wars fought in this century have ended in disillusionment for the winners. Moreover, it is not merely a question as to the desirability of total war; there is even a question as to its feasibility. "In a sense," Kennan concludes, "there is no total victory short of genocide." Total military victory is thus a quixotic goal.[4]

What Kennan believes, then, is that while it is possible to win victory in a battle, in war there can be only "achievement or nonachievement of your objectives." The concept of total victory is a "dangerous delusion" stemming from the pervasive moralism of American foreign policy. The fact that this illusion and others are deeply rooted in American history does not make them less pernicious. On the contrary, Kennan asserts, "A nation which excuses its own failures by the sacred untouchableness of its own habits can excuse itself into complete disaster."

Thus, in Kennan's view, great changes are required in the American outlook on foreign policy. In place of the deluded pursuit of the ideally moral, Americans must cultivate "an attitude of detachment and soberness and readiness to reserve judgment."

---

[3] For these arguments, see *ibid.*, pp. 83–86.
[4] *Ibid.*, p. 87.

The goal to be sought in the proper conduct of foreign affairs is not morality but the national interest. The new attitudes will include an admission that this interest is all that can be surely known or understood. It then follows, Kennan contends, that if domestic purposes are decent, the pursuit of the national interest "can never fail to be conducive to a better world."[5]

This position was not totally new even in this country. Speaking of the realist school, Kennan has said that Reinhold Niebuhr is "the father of us all."[6] These ideas have definite roots in the Niebuhrian distinction between moral man and immoral society with its insistence that collectivities, by their very nature, must occasionally perform acts which would be rejected by the ethical standards applied to individuals. Thus, there is a clear-cut distinction in the Western political tradition between premeditated murder as the act of an individual and the planned destruction of lives in warfare. However, the acceptance of "the realist position," as it came to be known, raises a number of important issues.

First, what is the national interest? How can idealistic nonsense be distinguished from a realistic appraisal of a given situation? One need not despair of making a reasonable approximation of an answer (as do many modern critics) to accept the fact that an adequate understanding of this seemingly simple goal may be hard to achieve. Just what does the goal mean in terms of public policy? At the highest level of generality, it can be agreed, for example, that national survival is in the "national interest." Conversely, sudden and complete disarmament would probably not be in the "national interest." This is a simple example, and it must be admitted that agreement is harder to find as issues become more concrete. The question as to what policy is in the national interest in Vietnam amply illustrates the extremely slippery nature of the concept.

Second, the terms of the realist argument are somewhat unfair. In a sense, the "realists" appear to have demolished a straw man. Their position is tantamount to announcing, "I take the

---

[5] *Ibid.*, p. 88.

[6] Quoted in Kenneth W. Thompson, *Political Realism and the Crisis of World Politics* (Princeton: Princeton University Press, 1960), p. 23.

realistic position. What position do you take?" This is merely a question-begging way of stacking the deck. After all, what is realism? This question often goes unanswered.

A third problem is more important since it presents a fundamental moral dilemma. The realists are often charged with having adopted a cynically amoral approach. For three leading realists—Kennan, Morgenthau, and Niebuhr—the charge is hard to support, but its source can be readily understood. As Robert Good has pointed out, Kennan is clearly committed to a relativistic ethic.[7] If a nation can know only its own national interest, then clearly it cannot teach morality to other nations far removed in space and habits. Morgenthau's position is more complex. Contrary to popular interpretations of his work, it is clear that he believes in transcendental norms which define just behavior. The trouble is that the tension uniting norms and politics in Morgenthau's work snaps, thus leaving no connection between his ideals and political reality. As a consequence, the ideals are rendered nearly useless as standards of behavior. In other words, the transcendent is so far removed from this world that the rules of interest-oriented politics almost inevitably must dominate. In the end, then, Morgenthau is reduced to a position substantially the same as Kennan's. On the role of normative standards, Niebuhr is closer to Morgenthau than to Kennan. He, too, believes in transcendent moral principles, but he also believes that man is too corrupted by self-interest to determine them. Niebuhr is therefore reduced to his brand of realism and to his Christian faith. But realism, as has been pointed out, is notoriously hard to define, and Christianity is not a faith shared by all.

These three leading realists are thus in a rather uncomfortable position. All are eminently moral men; it would be hard indeed to contend that they are either cynical or amoral; all three, in fact, are moralists in the best sense of the word. Moreover, a large proportion of what they say about the philosophy of international affairs makes the best of sense. The evidence is compelling that America's

---

[7] This discussion of morality and the national interest owes a heavy debt to Robert C. Good, "The National Interest and Political Realism: Niebuhr's 'Debate' With Morgenthau and Kennan," *Journal of Politics*, 22 (November 1960), 597–619.

penchant for moralistic crusades has done serious harm to the national interest. A great power can no longer abdicate a leadership role; to exercise leadership is also to exercise power. All of these points have become truisms in political discourse, and a debt is owed to the realists for this enlightenment.

However, the world has changed since 1945. Nuclear weapons have on at least one occasion brought the world to the brink of destruction. These new weapons systems significantly alter the calculus with which men must work. Virtually everyone agrees that nuclear war would not be in the national interest of any country. On the other hand, a smaller-scaled war might conceivably serve some useful end. The Korean War is an example, albeit a controversial one in some circles. However, when the danger of escalation from a "brush-fire war" to a nuclear holocaust is considered, not only the question of national interest, but also the dictates of morality must be examined very carefully. It is one thing for a nation to deny itself the right to pass judgment on the moral qualities of a particular regime with which it has relations; it is quite another to abdicate moral responsibility in a situation where human survival may well be at stake. It may well be that in the area of the relation of nuclear weapons to foreign policy, the pursuit of morality and the pursuit of the national interest have come to coincide.

It is no longer possible simply to say that nations sometimes have to exercise power in ways which an individual would find abhorrent. The national interest itself can now be said to require a much more finely calculated consideration of moral problems than was necessary in pre-Hiroshima days. This is not to say that the Niebuhrian distinction between man and society is no longer valid. It is to argue, however, that under present conditions, much more caution must be exercised about what policies are justified by an appeal to this distinction.

The Policy of Containment

It was on the basis of such realist doctrines as those discussed above that American policy since 1945 has been built. The basic theme was announced in the Truman Doctrine. Faced in 1947 with the danger of Soviet penetration into the Mediterranean area by way of Greece and Turkey, the President declared it to be the policy of the United States "to support free peoples who are resisting attempted subjugation by armed minorities or by outside pressures." In support of this policy, Congress appropriated money for military and economic aid and authorized the use of American personnel to supervise the use of this aid. Shortly thereafter came the Marshall Plan, the massive transfusion of economic aid to the war-shattered European nations which began the controversial foreign-aid programs.

Soon after the passage of the Marshall Plan, George Kennan wrote an article which explained the rationale of the new American policies and in fact indicated the line along which the implementation of the new realist doctrines would take American policy. This article, entitled "The Sources of Soviet Conduct" and appearing anonymously under the pseudonym "X" in the journal *Foreign Affairs*, is of vital importance since at the time of its appearance Kennan was director of the Policy Planning Staff of the State Department; hence, the document takes on a quasi-official status.

The policy enunciated is summed up in one word—containment. The need for such a policy stemmed from the sources of Soviet behavior. The Russian leaders, Kennan argued, saw their position vis-à-vis the West as one of inherent opposition. Their Marxist ideology told them this, as did their national history. Further, when the intransigent behavior of the regime provoked opposition, this opposition itself was interpreted as indicative of the fundamental hostility of the outside world. No opposition could be admitted to possess any merit. Thus arose an almost paranoid fear of what Stalin called "capitalist encirclement." Still, Kennan goes on,

> there is ample evidence that the stress laid in Moscow on the menace confronting Soviet society from the world outside its border is founded not in the realities of foreign antagonism, but in the necessity of explaining away the existence of dictatorial authority at home.

However, the rulers of the Soviet state could dispense with neither the apparatus of totalitarianism nor "the fiction by which the maintenance of dictatorial power had been defended."

What did this paranoia mean in terms of Russian foreign policy? It meant, first of all, that "there can never be on Moscow's side any sincere assumption of a community of aims between the Soviet Union and powers which are regarded as capitalism." Brief détentes may be expected, but they do not lessen the basic antagonism which exists. This antagonism and the consequences that flow from it will remain, said Kennan, "for the foreseeable future." Thus, for a long time the Soviets will be difficult to deal with. It is impossible to wave a legal or moral wand and have the threat to American security disappear. Moreover, the Russians will be persistent in their demands and in the application of pressure, although—because they feel sure of final victory—they are not likely to take great risks. "Thus the Kremlin has no compunction about retreating in the face of superior force."

Then follows the heart of Kennan's doctrine: "In these circumstances it is clear that the main element of any United States policy toward the Soviet Union must be that of a long-term, patient but firm and vigilant containment of Russian expansive tendencies." There must be a resolute "application of counterforce at a series of constantly shifting geographical and political points."[8]

It is this point of view which has come to dominate American foreign policy. It provides the intellectual foundation for such diverse activities as NATO and the other alliance systems, the extensive foreign-aid program, and American intervention in Korea and Vietnam. It is a hard doctrine. It demands that Americans give up their traditional isolationism, that they cease looking for quick, final solutions to international problems, that they forsake a highly congenial moralism, that they entrench themselves for a long "twilight struggle." In brief, it demands that the United States assume the responsibilities of a great power which it so long avoided. Given the nature of these demands, the acceptance of the containment doctrine has been remarkably widespread—from virtually all decision makers (although on occasion the undertow of a

---

[8] Kennan, *American Diplomacy*, p. 99. Note that "The Sources of Soviet Conduct," originally published July 1947 in *Foreign Affairs*, is reprinted in this volume at pp. 89–106.

lingering idealism still seems to affect policy) and from the general public as well. The intense criticism to which American foreign policy has been subjected has been, for the most part, from within the consensus, on the grounds of a lack of sufficient firmness in pursuit of containment or of bungling on matters of detail. *Not until recently* have the fundamental doctrines been seriously challenged. However, in the past several years important criticisms have been leveled at these ideas, and what is more, these demands for change have won significant political support. It should be profitable to examine three of the major lines of argument.

The Crypto-Imperialists

Crypto-imperialism[9] is for the most part the foreign policy of romantic conservatism. Its motto is the title of Barry Goldwater's book, *Why Not Victory?* "In war there is no substitute for victory," said Douglas MacArthur and from this premise the rest follows. The United States *is* at war (World War III, according to James Burnham's column in *National Review*), and the enemy is communism. Numerous positions flow from these basic assumptions:

1. The goal should not be peace but rather victory.

2. There is positive harm in carrying on negotiations with the communist enemy. Since the West is always on the defensive, "the focal point of negotiations is invariably somewhere in the non-communist world."

3. The United States should withdraw diplomatic recognition of the Soviet Union.

4. The United States should announce to the world that we are against disarmament.

5. The United States should therefore be wary of proposals to cease nuclear testing. "Our government was originally pushed into suspending tests by Communist-induced hysteria on the subject of radio-active fallout. *However one may rate that danger, it simply has no bearing on the problem at hand.*" (Italics added.)

---

[9] This label is William G. Carleton's; see *The Revolution in American Foreign Policy* (New York: Random House, 1964), p. 125.

6. The participation of the United States in the United Nations "may be leading to an unconstitutional surrender of American sovereignty."

7. The United States must be prepared to risk war because "any policy, short of surrender, does that." America must beware the "craven fear of death" which has infected the nation.

8. Finally, the United States must always remember that the conflict with communism is irreconcilable.

These positions are all drawn from Mr. Goldwater's two volumes, *The Conscience of a Conservative* and *Why Not Victory?*[10] They are sufficient to give a sense of the full range of his thinking and the assumptions on which it rests. The Presidential campaign may have clouded his views somewhat, but these are the positions which won him his following. The stands outlined above clearly represent a repudiation of the containment doctrine. They explicitly deny that victory is impossible in modern war. They reject the notion that the struggle with the enemy must of necessity be long, hard, and costly. They reject the idea that such progress as can be made in the highly imperfect arena of international affairs must be made by slow, careful, painstaking negotiation. Most important of all, while rejecting the earlier legalism of American foreign policy, they embrace its traditional moralism with a vengeance. Once again total victory becomes an ethical imperative.

The form of this recrudescent moralism is somewhat different from that which has normally prevailed in this country. Whereas the moralists of an earlier day might well withdraw into isolation on the grounds that international power politics was evil and hence to be shunned, the crypto-imperialists are fervent internationalists—not perhaps in the old sense which signified active cooperation with other nations, but certainly in a new sense characterized by an almost feverish international activity. This new imperialism is really a form of what William Carleton has called

---

[10] *The Conscience of a Conservative* (New York: Macfadden, 1960); *Why Not Victory?* (New York: McGraw-Hill, 1962). Even though Mr. Goldwater's star may have fallen after his unsuccessful bid for the Presidency, his views are still representative of a substantial minority.

"unilateralism"—the belief that America can "go it alone" in world affairs. At its roots this sentiment is not unlike isolationism, however, and can probably best be interpreted as the nationalist analog to the intense individualism also favored by the romantic conservatives.

The last point suggests a key to the proper interpretation of this militant new nationalism. The movement is a product of forces whose roots lie in the previous century. We Americans are unaccustomed to the tensions of participating meaningfully in international politics; still less are we able to face with equanimity a situation in which we do not easily get our way. We are used to easy victory. Our whole history has conditioned us to expect it. As Hans Morgenthau stated the matter some years ago, we are the victims of "the illusion of American omnipotence." Most Americans have managed to escape from the effects of this myth. For the romantic conservatives, however, it is not myth but reality. America is in fact invincible. But the facts of life in a world populated by nuclear powers makes nonsense of this contention. Romanticism, which under other circumstances might be treated as a bizarre eccentricity, becomes a real threat in a thermonuclear age. The fact that the illusion on which this threat is based has deep roots in the American past only makes it more dangerous. It is hard to avoid the suspicion that for many the doctrines of realism and containment are but a thin veneer over the more entrenched illusions of limitless power. As long as Cold-War tensions persist, the dazzling simplifications of this school of thought are likely to persist as well. The tide will ebb and flow, but it will be with us for some time to come. Under these circumstances it would be well to heed George Kennan when he warns that a nation which excuses itself by an appeal to history may very well court disaster.

A Realist Critique of Realism in Action

A second major critique of realism and containment is a criticism from within. As an example there is Hans Morgenthau, a master of the realist approach and in fact one of its progenitors. Morgenthau has not forsaken the doctrines of his earlier years. Instead he objects to the vestigial remnants of idealism in American foreign policy and even more fundamentally to the lack of vision with which containment is pursued.

Americans are victims, Morgenthau argues, "of the perils of political empiricism." In the past the error was to attempt a total withdrawal from world politics. Yet today, Morgenthau contends, we go "to the other extreme of surrendering piecemeal to the facts of foreign policy, of allowing ourselves to be sucked in by them, of thinking and acting as though there were nothing else to foreign policy but this particular set of empirical facts concerning, say, Laos or Cuba."[11] We do this in the name of pragmatism, an approach deeply rooted in the traditional American distrust of "elaborate philosophies and consistent theories." But indiscriminate pragmatism is not a sufficient guide to public policy. Facts have no meaning in themselves; meaning is imposed by the mind of man. If meaning is *not* imposed in the form of some consistent viewpoint, then man is forced back upon "an implicit and untested philosophy which is likely to blur understanding and mislead action." Thus, we Americans now have a respect for hard facts in the conduct of foreign policy which was lacking in the idealist tradition, but we have lost any clear sense of direction and with it the ability to control our national destiny.

More specifically, Morgenthau sees a number of interrelated problems with which America must deal in order to put her foreign policy on a sound basis.[12] Objectively, the United States is the most powerful nation in the world. At the same time, however, we are "incapable of making the actions of even the weakest of foreign governments" conform to the desires of our government. This represents not an isolated failure, but a pattern inherent in a number of factors.

First of all, two objective conditions limit our power: "the availability of nuclear weapons and the moral stigma that attaches to colonialism and to the policies traditionally associated with it." In the past it was much easier than today to consider force as an

---

[11] Hans J. Morgenthau, "The Perils of Political Empiricism," *Commentary*, 34 (July 1962), 60.

[12] The following reconstruction of Morgenthau's thinking is based on his brilliant article, "The Impotence of American Power," *Commentary*, 36 (November 1963), 384–386. All quotations are from this piece.

instrument of policy. In fact, "in a world of sovereign nations it is impossible to support national interests effectively without the ultimate resort to military force." But since nuclear war is a "suicidal absurdity" and conventional war might well escalate into nuclear war, the nuclear powers are badly handicapped and their range of action severely limited. "Thus," to take two examples, "the impotence of American policy toward Cuba is matched by the impotence of Soviet policy with regard to Berlin."

The other important objective condition which acts as a limit on our power is anticolonialism. Consider the case of Cuba. Twenty years ago it would have been quite simple to remove the Castro regime from power. Today, however, this would be very difficult to accomplish, even without the hazard of nuclear war, because of the risk of "moral reprobation" and the consequent loss of American prestige that would flow from such an overthrow.

These objective factors are important, Morgenthau contends, but the United States "has gone further in abstaining from the use of its power than is justified" by them. Part of the paralysis is also due to the twin moral principles of equality and nonintervention. Thus, for example, we are faced with allies who sometimes do not want to accept the demands made by our leadership. We have sufficient power to force acceptance of our desires, but to apply this power would reduce our allies to satellites, thereby defeating the purpose of the alliance. We tend, therefore, to assume equality with our allies even though our interests sometimes do not coincide and in spite of the very palpable fact that our strength greatly exceeds theirs. The result, argues Morgenthau, has been the virtual disintegration of our alliance systems (as in the case of NATO) or the "exploitation" of America by weaker powers.

This difficulty is compounded by our attitude toward intervention in the affairs of other governments. Actually, Morgenthau points out, it is not intervention but only *certain kinds* of intervention that we oppose. Thus we intervened by putting President Diem in power in Vietnam, but hesitated much too long in intervening to remove him when it became apparent that he could not achieve our ends. Ultimately the problem is not moral but intellectual, says Morgenthau. The moral issue so often raised in connection with intervention is really nothing but a rationalization of our hesitation to act. The problem is that we favor safe routine and dread unprecedented actions. It is only when we are faced with a clear *military* challenge that we are willing to innovate. When faced with a complex political problem, we try to escape by redefining it in military terms. For instance, as Morgenthau pointed out earlier in *The Purpose of American Politics*, we could easily meet the threat of Russian military power posed by the postwar situation in Greece and Turkey, but we seem ill-equipped by reason of our distaste for politics to meet a complex political, military, and ideological challenge.[13]

Finally, we are handicapped by "our commitment to anti-communism as the overriding objective of our foreign policy." As a result, we have tended to turn the Cold War into an ideological struggle while our "indiscriminate" anticommunism blinds us to concrete national interests. Thus it is possible, Morgenthau suggests, for our allies to deprive us of our freedom of choice by countering every move they do not like by threatening to "go communist."

In summary, the importance of American power is said to stem only in part from objective circumstances over which we have no control. More important than these conditions in many ways is our defective moral, intellectual, and political judgment.

This, then, is Morgenthau's most recent comprehensive interpretation of the ills of American foreign policy. One point mentioned only briefly in the article discussed here requires further elaboration. For Professor Morgenthau, international politics consists of a struggle for power between autonomous nation-states. This is perhaps the most vital single fact about the arena of world politics. And it is also this fact which has us hovering on the brink of disaster. The sovereign nation-state, argues Morgenthau, is no longer "a viable principle of organization"; it is not even suited for "the elemental task of any political organization: to safeguard the biological survival of its members." Nuclear weapons lodged in the grip of sovereign states only increase the risks which supposedly are minimized by the states. From this, Morgenthau concludes that

---

[13] For an extended discussion of this point, see Morgenthau, *The Purpose of American Politics* (New York: Knopf, 1960), pp. 132–196.

the task of governments is to "make themselves superfluous as the guardians of their respective territorial frontiers by transferring their nuclear weapons to an agency whose powers are commensurate with the world-wide destructive potentialities of these weapons."[14]

Thus, in the end, the supreme realist turns to something approaching world government as the ultimate hope for survival in a nuclear world. He does not minimize the magnitude of the problem, but he does believe that we must beware "designing a house [foreign policy] for the top of a volcano that, barring a miracle, cannot fail to erupt." It is, no doubt, the belief in the necessity of some sort of supranational force for the control of nuclear weapons that gives Morgenthau's voluminous writings a good deal of their underlying pessimism. If Morgenthau's analysis of the forces behind international behavior is correct, then the changes he requires are unlikely to occur and foreign relations becomes the stuff of high tragedy—with men fighting forces over which they have no control. It is also notable that at this key point in his argument Morgenthau offers no constructive solution that might lead to a way out. For such proposals, it is necessary to turn to critics of our foreign policy even more radical than Morgenthau.

The Radical Critique

This section will discuss a group which has been a fertile source of ideas and at the same time a storm center of controversy. The radical critique is centered around such groups as the Committee for a Sane Nuclear Policy (SANE) and such diverse intellectual leaders as C. Wright Mills, William Appleman Williams, David Riesman, Erich Fromm, and H. Stuart Hughes. Moreover, it has received substantial support from a new school of revisionist historians led by Gar Alperovitz.

All of these writers hold two assumptions in common. The first is that in this age of modern weapons the much-touted "realism" of American foreign policy, based as it is on nuclear

14 *Ibid.*, p. 308.

deterrence, is not realism at all but a form of behavior verging on insanity; it is, to use Mills' phrase, "crackpot realism." These writers are certain, as is the much more conservative Morgenthau, that disaster is inevitable if the arms race continues.

The second major assumption, also shared with Morgenthau, is that communism—at least as an economic system—is not the enemy. The real quarrel with communism is with its "tyranny over the mind of man." But even granting the frequent abuses of civil liberty by communist regimes, Hughes argues that "the various aspects of communism are separable and that the system as a whole is capable of evolving in a liberal direction."[15] In the end, Hughes cautions against the assumption that communism is worse than war. To Hughes—and no doubt to the others of this school—war is the primary enemy.

The radical critique then moves on to a stinging indictment of the policy of containment. One element of this indictment involves a reevaluation of the Cold War. George Kennan had suggested in his famous article on "The Sources of Soviet Conduct" that Soviet expansion was inevitable and inexorable unless countered by force. This position has now been disputed on several grounds. It is argued by such historians as Alperovitz that Soviet policy was in fact not inexorably expansionist and further that much of the blame for the origins of the Cold War must be shifted to the United States with its various errors of omission and commission. The prevailing American interpretation has been that the Cold War began in 1947 with the Soviet coups in the East European satellite countries. Alperovitz contends that in fact it began in 1945, when President Truman tried to use the newly created atomic weapons as an instrument to bend the Soviet Union to his will. Moreover, much tension could have been alleviated if the United States had extended economic assistance for the reconstruction of the war-shattered Soviet system. Alperovitz also argues that the usual American interpretation of the origins of the Cold War glides too lightly over the fact that from 1945 to

---

[15] H. Stuart Hughes, *An Approach to Peace* (New York: Atheneum, 1962), p. 50.

1947, the Soviets, for whatever reason, were willing to allow democratic elections in the East European states.[16] Thus, while not exonerating the Soviet Union for its role in precipitating the postwar tension—he accuses the regime of "duplicity, brutality, and intransigence"—Alperovitz does offer an interpretation in which our government, particularly under President Truman, bears a good deal more responsibility than historians have previously suggested.

Other scholars have taken different angles of attack on the containment doctrine. William Appleman Williams, who has been a major source of ideas for the New Left at the University of Wisconsin, has argued that containment was a policy which would inevitably inflame an already suspicious Soviet Union:

Having argued that they [the Soviet Union] had to create imaginary foreign dangers in order to stay in power at home, Kennan concluded with a policy recommendation to create a very serious (and from the Soviet point of view, mortal) outside challenge to their authority.[17]

Williams concludes that it is not possible to maintain seriously that the Soviet Union had no valid fears of attack.

It is not necessary here to evaluate the historical question at issue. The matter is exceedingly complex, and even Alperovitz is quite willing to admit that more than one interpretation of the available evidence is possible. However, there can be no question that the findings of the revisionist historians call into question some of the basic assumptions on which the American response to the Russian challenge has rested and that their findings in turn provide fuel for an ideological critique of our policy.

More comprehensive challenges have also been made. For a spokesman, Stuart Hughes is a useful choice; his book *An Approach to Peace* is highly provocative and much neglected.

---

[16] See Gar Alperovitz, *Atomic Diplomacy: Hiroshima and Potsdam* (New York: Simon and Schuster, 1965) and "How Did the Cold War Begin?" *New York Review of Books* (March 23, 1967), pp. 6–12. This article is an extended review of Martin F. Herz, *Beginnings of the Cold War* (Bloomington: Indiana University Press, 1966).

[17] William Appleman Williams, *The Tragedy of American Diplomacy* (rev. and enlarged ed.; New York: Dell, Delta Books), p. 281.

Hughes' critique is in some ways as radical as that of the crypto-imperialists. We have become the prisoners of our own propaganda, he contends. Our commitment to the containment of communism whenever and wherever it appears has caused us to make all sorts of pledges we simply do not have the power to redeem. In brief, we are "perilously overextended." "We have fallen into the opposite extreme from the isolationist mentality which was once our undoing. Where formerly we did too little in the foreign sphere, we have now been doing too much."[18]

What, then, must be done? Hughes calls for a "frankly radical and unashamedly utopian" viewpoint; as he puts it:

I agree with Mills that "We are at a curious juncture in the history of human insanity; in the name of realism, men are quite mad, and precisely what they call utopian is now the condition of human survival." [19]

Hughes' utopianism consists of two primary elements. The first is the position on nuclear weapons for which he became more or less famous in the popular press. In his estimation the worst thing that can happen is war. And yet our whole armaments policy leads us closer and closer to war. Not only is this true, he contends, but it is also true that this policy has not worked. Our application of the theory of deterrence has not prevented the expansion of Soviet influence in many areas of the world. The way out, then, is to make an "act of faith" and *if necessary* to take steps toward unilateral disarmament. Hughes is careful to point out that this alternative is not his first choice; clearly, multilateral disarmament is far more preferable. But failing this, someone must begin. "The sole means of overcoming distrust is for one of the parties to prove by actions rather than words that it has faith in the other."[20]

Nor does Hughes stop here; he is willing to pursue his argument to the logical conclusion. Asked the classic question "Would you rather be red than dead?" he forthrightly answers "Yes." At the same time, he insists that the question is an unfair formulation of the problem. The ground for his answer is his choice of "life

---

[18] Hughes, *An Approach to Peace*, p. 16.
[19] *Ibid.*, p. 21.
[20] *Ibid.*, p. 70.

over senseless slaughter." The emphasis should be placed on the adjective "senseless." For Hughes, death in a nuclear war is simply not a meaningful way to perish. If he were given the choice of a meaningful alternative, Hughes might choose it. Nuclear destruction in a contest with a misapprehended enemy does not meet this standard.[21]

The risks of such a policy are obviously great, as Hughes freely admits. To some extent these risks can be minimized by pursuing a program of "unilateral initiatives"—disarmament in a series of small and hopefully not dangerous steps which would induce other powers to follow. But in the end, the logic of unilateralism lies in the "complete renunciation of nuclear weapons."

It is this portion of Hughes' work that has attracted the greatest popular attention; he even bears the distinction, rare among professors, of having been attacked by such a mass-circulation weekly as *Life*. However, the second basic element in Hughes' foreign policy is perhaps even more radical, although in a more subtle way. In effect he calls for a reexamination of America's place in the world. Our rise to world leadership came too late, Hughes asserts. It was too late, first, because it came at the beginning of the postimperial period in modern history and, second, because by the time the American people became willing to undertake a leadership role, "they were no longer suited for it." A global policy requires a militant spirit which had been snapped by several decades of rapid social change.[22]

To Hughes the course to be followed under these circumstances is clear. We must desist from the heroic stance of containment; if we are overextended, we must cut back our efforts and content ourselves with being merely a major center of power, "no more, no less." American policy should move toward a new world balance with "each major region taking charge of its own concerns." Thus the major reexamination of our position demanded by Hughes leads to the conclusion that the United States, like Britain before her, must content herself with a considerable diminution in power. He argues that by ceasing to be a world power we

---

[21] *Ibid.*, pp. 72–73.
[22] *Ibid.*, p. 35.

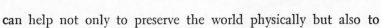

can help not only to preserve the world physically but also to conserve the humane values of Western civilization.

What can be said of this daring proposal? Certainly it has an imaginative sweep which makes the conventional analysis of American foreign policy seem tame indeed. As a stimulus to careful thinking about these problems, it may well be unsurpassed. But is it sound either in part or as a whole? A comparison of Hughes and Morgenthau may shed some light on this question.

Conclusions

The first thing to note is that some of the assumptions of Morgenthau and Hughes are strikingly similar. This in itself is of considerable significance, in view of the belief in "realism" by one and in "utopianism" by the other. They share a belief in the disutility of nuclear weapons. Both would agree that these weapons, simply because of their destructive power, are a handicap rather than a help in the conduct of foreign affairs. Paradoxically, the very use of these weapons is no longer credible even while they pose a real threat to the survival of civilization.

The first major difference between them concerns a course of action. Curiously, Morgenthau's "realistic" answer is a flight of utopian speculation beside which the self-confessed radicalism of Hughes seems rather pallid. To create a supranational power strong enough to control nuclear weapons would mean a revolution in the behavior of states so great as to be nearly beyond comprehension. As Professor Morgenthau well knows, nationalism is one of the more potent ideological forces of today's world. Under these circumstances supranational control of nuclear weapons, while perhaps desirable, is highly unlikely. Hughes does not contribute very much to a solution either. As he admits, the risks of unilateralism are appalling; moreover, the chances of winning adequate political support at home for such a policy are almost nil. Fortunately, however, unilateralism may turn out to be unnecessary for the reason that a measure of disarmament and a general reduction of tension seem to be in the national interest of both major nuclear powers. Both, for example, are deeply worried over what is known in the arms-control literature as the nth country problem—that is, the spread of nuclear weapons to a whole succession of states beyond the handful who now have them. Both the United States and the Soviet Union have a vital interest in limiting the number of nuclear powers—particularly now that China has staged a successful nuclear test. Therefore, there is reason to hope that disarmament may continue to progress without resort to unilateralism or to a supranational control organization. Once more, calculations based primarily on national interest seem to lead to sound conclusions even, it would seem, in the ethical sphere, as long as the new coincidence of the twin pursuits of morality and interest is granted.

A second major point on which Morgenthau and Hughes agree is the fundamental absurdity of simple anticommunism as *the* basic doctrine of American foreign policy. But they diverge sharply thereafter. *Realpolitik* tells Morgenthau that we must define the enemy not in terms of its economic system but in terms of its attitude toward the United States. Thus, although I know of no place where Morgenthau has suggested this, it would not be impossible to imagine a situation in which the United States would once again be aligned with the USSR, this time against Red China. (There is already precedent for this. Both the United States and the Soviet Union went to the aid of India in her border dispute with China. China has since accused the three countries of forming an alliance against her.) There is, however, no sign that Morgenthau wishes a general retreat from our worldwide commitments. Some observers might argue that Morgenthau's well-publicized opposition to the policy of the Johnson administration in Vietnam would shift him over to Hughes' camp. However, Morgenthau does not urge the abandonment of containment altogether. He rejects outright the label of "neo-isolationist," maintaining that he is merely opposed to the indiscriminate extension of American commitments which he refers to as "globalism." Containment and the Truman Doctrine suggest a willingness to combat communist expansion *wherever it appears*. However, as Morgenthau points out, American policy has never before during the Cold War followed official American pronouncements. Only under President Johnson have rhetoric and policy been brought into consonance with each other.[23] Morgenthau does not challenge the basic concept of containment, but only its present application. In fact it is clear that one of his major concerns is the frequent inability of the United States to make the best use of its power. Thus, Morgenthau would like to see a more viable arms-control scheme so that, among other reasons, the United States would be more fully able to wield her power without fear of a nuclear catastrophe.

Hughes, on the other hand, would no doubt shrink from the use of arms-control schemes as a weapon of *Realpolitik*. At the same time, Morgenthau's critique of "globalism" and Hughes' suggestion that the United States should strive to be, at most, the leader of a regional power bloc have remarkable similarities despite their authors' radically differing ideological perspectives. The crisis in Southeast Asia has therefore precipitated a thorough reexamination of the limits of American power and has forged—if only temporarily—a coalition encompassing such diverse figures as the utopian idealist Hughes, the conservative realist Morgenthau, and the traditional liberal Henry Steele Commager.[24]

Certainly, the Vietnamese situation lends credence to the belief that the United States is overextended militarily. Guerrilla warfare halfway around the world presents seemingly insurmountable problems. Even more important perhaps is the apparent depolarization of the international system. Europe, under the leadership of France, is becoming increasingly independent, and the Soviet bloc is clearly approaching a state of total disarray. Under such conditions the wisdom of a remark by George Kennan is clear:

---

[23] Morgenthau, *The United States and Viet Nam* (Washington: Public Affairs Press, 1966), pp. 81–91.

[24] For Commager's views, see his testimony before the Senate Committee on Foreign Relations, *Changing Attitudes Toward American Foreign Policy* (Hearing before the Committee on Foreign Relations, United States Senate, Ninetieth Congress, 1st Session, January 30, 1967). For other liberal views, see John Kenneth Galbraith, "An Agenda for American Liberals," *Commentary* (June 1966), pp. 29–34, and Arthur Schlesinger, Jr., *The Bitter Heritage* (Boston: Houghton Mifflin, 1967).

Many Americans seem unable to recognize the technical difficulties involved in the operation of far-flung lines of power—the difficulty of trying to exert power from any given national center, over areas greatly remote from that center. There are, believe me, limits to the effective radius of political power from any center in the world.[25]

To the extent that this appraisal is true, there seems to be a real chance that the multibloc world envisaged by Hughes may be developing, whether this nation wishes to accept it or not.[26] Probably it will not, since the United States gives every sign of being as reluctant to forgo world responsibility as it was to accept it in the first place.

This point raises the most significant problem in Hughes' approach. Suppose for the moment the existence of a multibloc world with the United States reduced to a position of dominance in the Western hemisphere or even in North America alone. In view of the United States' power, would it really be possible to abdicate a larger role? Would it not be more likely that international tensions would impose such a role again, just as they did in the two world wars? Realism suggests that the answer is yes. There is no reason to think that regional power blocs will provide Professor Hughes with the utopia he seeks. International stability might be temporarily enhanced by the creation of such blocs, but conflicts of interest would no doubt remain and the dominant power in each bloc would be compelled to react to those conflicts. As Morgenthau has argued for so long, politics is permanent, and American foreign policy will be better off when that principle is recognized.

Enough has been said to indicate that thinking about American foreign policy is in a state of ferment. Both right and left contend that the Cold War must be ended—on the one hand because there is no substitute for victory, and on the other because

25 George Kennan, *Russia and the West Under Lenin and Stalin* (Boston: Little, Brown, 1961), p. 276.

26 Roger Masters argues rather persuasively that this is the case. See *The Nation Is Burdened: American Foreign Policy in a Changing World* (New York: Knopf, 1967), pp. 107–113. For a more formal argument, see Masters' article, "A Multi-Bloc Model of the International System," *American Political Science Review* (December 1961), pp. 780–798.

its continued existence is a standing invitation to destruction. Even in the center of this storm, devastating and often sound criticisms are being made, not merely on matters of detail but also on the basic structure of American policy. A fundamental debate is shaping up which cannot—or at least should not—be forestalled indefinitely. The Presidential campaign of 1964 gave promise of providing such a debate but was sidetracked into essentially peripheral matters. But the issues will not die; the imperatives of both domestic and international politics will see to that. Moreover, there is an increasing intrusion of international issues into domestic politics. These are new issues for most Americans, and their intractable nature combined with the national history is bound to breed tension and frustration. The John Birch Society and other such organizations are the product of these frustrations. When the debate comes, it will not be a pleasant one. People burdened with the "illusion of American omnipotence" will not want to see this myth seriously challenged.

As Morgenthau has suggested, the United States is faced with an inversion of the typical relation between domestic and international issues. Because the latter now involve biological survival, they must be granted a paramount place. As a result, the traditional ideological cleavages in the American political system are likely to be replaced, and there will be an increasing prominence of foreign-policy issues in domestic politics. As yet, these new issues have not even been properly defined, but it is not too much to say that upon the success of definitional efforts such as those discussed here rests our national survival.

🦅 BIBLIOGRAPHICAL NOTES 🦅

The best general survey of realist thought is Kenneth Thompson, *Political Realism and the Crisis of World Politics* (Princeton: Princeton University Press, 1960). This is a good guide to the major figures in the movement despite its bias in their favor. The realist-idealist controversy is placed in historical context by Robert E. Osgood, *Ideals and Self-Interest in America's Foreign Relations* (Chicago: University of Chicago Press, 1953).

Niebuhr's most important study in the field of international relations is *The Structure of Nations and Empires* (New York: Scribner's, 1959). The foundation of much of his work is laid in *Moral Man and Immoral Society* (New York: Scribner's, 1932).

Aside from *American Diplomacy: 1900–1950* (New York: Mentor Books, 1952; orig. pub. 1951 by the University of Chicago Press), George Kennan's most important book for our purposes is *Realities of American Foreign Policy* (Princeton: Princeton University Press, 1954). *Russia and the West Under Lenin and Stalin* (Boston: Little, Brown, 1961) is not directed precisely at the topic at hand, but it is filled with interesting asides on the conduct of diplomacy.

A major theoretical work by Hans Morgenthau is *Scientific Man Versus Power Politics* (Chicago: University of Chicago Press, 1946), which lays the basis for much of Morgenthau's work. This volume was followed by his magisterial text, *Politics Among Nations* (4th ed.; New York: Knopf, 1967). See also the three volumes of Morgenthau's collected essays, *Politics in the Twentieth Century* (Chicago: University of Chicago Press, 1962). The distinctions between the views of Professor Morgenthau and such men as H. Stuart Hughes are illustrated in Morgenthau's article

"To Intervene or Not to Intervene," *Foreign Affairs* (April 1967), pp. 425–436. In this contribution Morgenthau makes it quite clear that he would support American intervention in overseas conflicts *if* such interventions are in the "national interest." He thus makes it implicitly clear that his position on Vietnam does not indicate a repudiation of his general theoretical position. A critique of American foreign policy highly praised by Morgenthau is to be found in John Paton Davies, *Foreign and Other Affairs* (New York: Norton, 1964). For a critique of Morgenthau's thought based on the collected essays, see the stimulating article by George Lichtheim, "The Politics of Conservative Realism," *Commentary* (June 1963), pp. 506–516.

Two volumes which shed much light on the theoretical issues under discussion in this chapter are Kenneth Waltz, *Man, the State, and War* (New York: Columbia University Press, 1959), and Arnold Wolfers, *Discord and Collaboration: Essays on International Politics* (Baltimore: Johns Hopkins Press, 1962). The Waltz volume has an extensive bibliography.

In addition to the works of Barry Goldwater, the foreign policy of crypto-imperialists is exemplified in James Burnham, *Suicide of the West* (New York: Day, 1964).

Besides the works of Hughes, Williams, and Alperovitz, two of the leading works of the radical critics are C. Wright Mills, *The Causes of World War III* (New York: Simon and Schuster, 1958), and Erich Fromm, *May Man Prevail* (Garden City, N.Y.: Doubleday, Anchor Books, 1961). David Riesman's views may be found in a number of essays in *Abundance for What?* (Garden City, N.Y.: Doubleday, 1964).

A number of general studies of American foreign policy are of interest in connection with this chapter. John Spanier, *American Foreign Policy Since World War II* (2nd rev. ed.; New York: Praeger, 1966), devotes a chapter to the intellectual sources of American policy. In *Power, Freedom, and Diplomacy* (New York: Random House, 1963), Paul Seabury devotes a good deal of attention to philosophical issues. Roger Masters, *The Nation Is Burdened* (New York: Knopf, 1967), is a very stimulating attempt to analyze American policy in terms of the probable nature of world politics for the next several decades. William G. Carleton,

The Revolution in American Foreign Policy (New York: Random House, 1963), provides a good historical survey of American policy in the postwar period.

A collection of essays on military policy that spans the ideological spectrum from pacifism to a fairly hard-line posture is Robert A. Goldwin, *America Armed* (Chicago: Rand McNally, 1963).

CHAPTER VII

THE
PROBLEM
OF
EQUAL RIGHTS

Do I really want to be integrated into a burning house?—*James Baldwin*

A house divided against itself cannot stand.—*Abraham Lincoln*

In 1944, in his monumental study of the American Negro, the Swedish economist and sociologist Gunnar Myrdal argued that "The American Negro problem is a problem in the heart of the American."[1] Myrdal meant that the conflict is fundamentally a clash between the generally egalitarian tenets of American ideology and a set of lower-order values which sanction the wide range of discriminatory behavior all too familiar to this day.

[1] Gunnar Myrdal, *An American Dilemma* (rev. ed.; New York: Harper, 1962), p. lxxi.

Twenty years later, Charles Silberman, an American student of the same problem, was moved to challenge Myrdal's formulation. In a sense, Myrdal was too optimistic, Silberman contends. It is true that for more than a thousand pages Myrdal meticulously documented the miseries of the Negro in this country, but his basic contention was wrong. The difficulty is that "there is no American Dilemma." Whites in America are not in a state of internal conflict because of the gap between their ideals and their behavior. At most, they are upset because domestic tranquillity has been shattered, rather than because justice is not being done.[2]

Present indications support the belief that for the most part Silberman's pessimistic appraisal is right. It would be pleasant to be able to think that Americans have tormented consciences as a result of the widespread denial of civil rights to Negroes, but almost all the available data analyzed in connection with the "white backlash" indicate that perhaps a majority of white Americans are quite ready to abrogate the rights of Negroes. Nor, on reflection, should this appraisal come as a surprise. The data discussed in connection with Peter Viereck's analysis of the radical right demonstrate with frightening clarity the shaky popular foundations of civil rights and civil liberties in America, even though Viereck's interpretations of these data need not be accepted.

The facts about discrimination also provide no comfort, although they do powerfully suggest the motivating force behind the upsurge of civil-rights agitation. Consider just a few of the well-known facts about housing and economic discrimination. Louis Lomax has pointed out in *The Negro Revolt* that average Negro family income is only 55 per cent of average white family income; that although Negroes comprise 11 per cent of the total population, they live in 4 per cent of the residential area of this country; and that even in the North, since most Negroes live in racial ghettos, they suffer de facto school segregation. Moreover, there is no point in liberals issuing a blanket denial to all the claims of racists to the effect that Negroes are inferior. From the point of

[2] Charles E. Silberman, *Crisis in Black and White* (New York: Random House, 1964), p. 10.

view of middle-class white values, Negroes are inferior; the racist stereotype is partially true. Seen from this perspective, Negroes *are* apathetic and lacking in ambition. Promiscuity and crime rates *are* high, and the Negro family *is* markedly unstable. Negro children *on the average* do poorer work in school than do white children, and they score lower on IQ tests than do whites of a comparable socioeconomic status.[3] The sad fact is that the relative position of the Negro has worsened in recent years. As a study by Herman Miller shows, the proportion of nonwhite families who exist below the poverty line increased from 20 to 23 per cent between 1951 and 1963.

The question, then, is not whether Negroes are somehow "different"; they obviously are and the difference is more than skin-deep. The real question is whether these differences are a racial inheritance so debilitating as to make effective Negro participation in American life impossible or whether they are culturally determined. The best-informed conclusions of responsible biologists and anthropologists unquestionably support the contention that the differences are cultural. Negroes are the victims of what has been called, in another connection, the "culture of poverty." The crime, the disease, the apathy, and the lack of education are characteristics not only of American Negroes, but of the poor everywhere.

It is this fact, among others, which renders the concept of the affluent society so curiously unsatisfying and which flings a challenge at it. Suddenly, Negroes are announcing that they want "in," that they want not only to share in the affluence, but also to assume the dignity of others in our society. America has succeeded in avoiding this challenge for a long time, but it is finding it increasingly difficult to do so. Civil rights has become probably the most important and certainly the most dramatic issue in domestic politics. It is necessary, then, to try to come to grips with the ideology of civil rights in order to understand fully what is happening in the American political system.

In this chapter, I shall devote a great deal of careful attention to the ideas of the Negro novelist and essayist James Baldwin. To

---

[3] *Ibid.*, p. 74.

some, Baldwin may appear to be a somewhat unrepresentative and hence misleading spokesman for Negro aspirations. To be sure, he is a notably complex and ambivalent figure whose main concerns are not political—at least in the narrow sense of the word. On the other hand, he is important partly because of these very character-istics, for the civil-rights movement itself is complex and ambiva-lent and an analysis of Baldwin's views therefore should help considerably in the attempt to understand this critical problem. In particular, there is reason to believe that Baldwin's analysis of the sources of Negro discontent and of Negro attitudes toward the white majority provides not only the most eloquent testimony available on these questions, but also a point of view which a great many Negroes would endorse. Moreover, because Baldwin is a writer of compelling stylistic and moral power, he has won a large audience, not only among Negro intellectuals, but also among white liberals.

The Psychology of Civil Rights

To understand what is happening in civil rights it is necessary to understand some complex psychological problems. The first is the prolonged "identity crisis"—to borrow Erik Erikson's phrase—of the American Negro. This problem is a persistent one in Negro literature. In a brilliant novel, Ralph Ellison makes the paradoxical claim that the Negro is an invisible man—paradoxical in the sense that although the Negro, by reason of his color, stands out in American society, he is still unseen as a person. He is not viewed as an individual human being, but as a thing. To James Baldwin this loss of identity can be symbolized in the title of his collection of essays, *Nobody Knows My Name*. The identity crisis is a product of the period of slavery, when Negroes were uprooted from their African homes and transplanted to an entirely new environment in which every effort was made to impress upon them a sense of distinctness and inferiority. Thus the Negro was doubly alienated—from his past and from his present. Describing his situation, Baldwin writes of the forced recognition that he was an alien in Western civilization because his ancestry could be traced not to Europe, but to Africa. At the same time, Baldwin notes that only this very European heritage could provide him with roots, since the American experience had left him "unfitted for the jungle or the tribe."

In the end, the Negro has come to hate his color and thus to hate himself. Small wonder, for in addition to the cultural estrangement and economic deprivation of the Negro, there is a pervasive symbolism—by no means limited to Europe and the United States—which stresses the virtues of white and the vileness of black. As Silberman points out, blackness is associated with evil, corruption, death, and despair, while white indicates purity, goodness, and hope. Such symbolism leaves its mark. For instance, psychological studies discussed by Silberman have shown that as early as the first grade, 80 per cent of Negro children make unfavorable comparisons of themselves with others, compared with 30 per cent of white children of the same age and economic background who manifest similar reactions.

Slavery and segregation have left their marks on whites as well as blacks. The white man, too, has problems which affect his status and his identity. But he can displace his hostility toward himself onto the Negro because, no matter how low the white man's fortunes, in our culture the white is reasonably sure that the Negro is somewhere below him. This psychological phenomenon is one of the factors at the heart of the civil-rights crisis. The Negro has begun to insist that he is not a thing, that he must be treated as a man, and that something is dreadfully wrong with a society that refuses to understand these simple imperatives. The impact on the white consciousness of these assertions is immense. "Try to imagine," Baldwin asks, "how you would feel if you woke up one morning to find the sun shining and the stars aflame." Such an aberration would breed terror because it would attack one's sense of reality. As Baldwin sees it, the Negro revolution has brought an analogous situation, for to the white man the Negro has functioned as a "fixed star" so that his new activities have a profoundly unsettling effect. This recent threat to stability is what underlies the white-backlash phenomenon. There is, among many whites, a deep-seated insecurity born of the pressures of life in a presumably egalitarian society—a society in which many are unsure of how they fit into the scheme of things. All too often the inferior social status of the Negro fills the white's need for a compensating sense of position.

But the attitude of the Negro is changing, or at least the attitude of the Negro intellectual is changing. He is beginning to come to terms with America. In Baldwin's words, he has come to accept the fact that he is a political and cultural "hybrid." He is forging an identity out of the extremity of his situation. For Baldwin, the discovery of himself was made during his long European exile. To his surprise, he discovered that white Americans seemed no more at home in Europe than he, for the simple reason that both were Americans and therefore set apart from Europe by a common background. At the same time, he came to see that the question of color "operates to hide the graver questions of the self." And having seen through the problem of color and the problem of finding a viable tradition for sustenance, Baldwin came to a decision: "The world was enormous and I could go anywhere in it—including America: I decided to return here because I was afraid to."

Just as white Americans are not identical with one another, Baldwin has come to realize that black Americans are in fact different from other Americans—and that this difference should be a source of pride rather of shame. In this realization lies another key to the drive for civil rights, for once again Baldwin typifies the growing mood of his race. The rise of independence and influence of the African nations has contributed greatly to this upsurge of racial pride. "The world is white no longer," Baldwin writes; "black has *become* a beautiful color—not because it is loved but because it is feared." And along with this newfound pride has come a new interest in African history, art, and poetry.

As attitudes toward blackness change, new attitudes (or at least newly expressed attitudes) toward whites begin to appear. Baldwin has said that in coming to an understanding of himself, he was forced to face another deeply submerged problem, one that he, like most Negroes, had always hidden from himself—the fact that he "hated and feared white people."[4] This theme occurs again and again in Baldwin's writing. More than any other single feature of his work, it is this blunt honesty that has so moved and so

---

[4] Baldwin, *Notes of a Native Son* (Boston: Beacon Press, 1957), p. 7.

agitated white intellectuals. They—perhaps I should say *we*—are surprised to be told these things. But there is really no reason for surprise; as Silberman points out, Richard Wright had been saying the same thing for twenty-five or thirty years before Baldwin. It is the peculiar genius of Baldwin that he has been able to get people to listen to these old grievances and, what is more, to believe him.

The Ambivalence of the Equal-Rights Movement

The tensions discussed here—the ambiguous attitude toward color, whether white or black, and the peculiar sense in which the Negro is alienated from both his own world and the white world at the same time that he is inextricably linked to both—are reflected in the proliferation of organizations concerned with advancing the Negro cause.

At one pole there is the Negro student movement. This movement, I believe, will prove to be the very last attempt made by American Negroes to achieve acceptance in the republic, to force the country to honor its own ideals.

At the other pole are the Black Muslims.[5]

The student movement makes fantastic demands on its followers. Led by such men as Martin Luther King and steeped in the theories of nonviolence of Thoreau, Tolstoy, and Gandhi, these young people are asked not only to abstain from physical retaliation against the enemy but even to refuse to hate him. As Baldwin says:

The student movement depends, at bottom, on an act of faith, an ability to see, beneath the cruelty and hysteria and apathy of white people, their bafflement and pain and essential decency. This is superbly difficult. It demands a perpetually cultivated spiritual resilience, for the bulk of the evidence contradicts the vision.[6]

Baldwin's point is compelling and it penetrates to the heart of the violence in the summer of 1964 and since, as well as to the

---

[5] Baldwin, *Nobody Knows My Name* (New York: Delta Books, 1962), p. 75.

[6] *Ibid.*, p. 76. On Dr. King and his work, see Louis Lomax, *The Negro Revolt* (New York: New American Library, 1963), pp. 92–111.

sources of the demand for Black Power. King and his followers have all the good will in the world, but it is a bitter fact, as Baldwin is careful to point out, that the Muslims have the evidence on their side. The condition of the Negro remains wretched, and such victories as have been won have been for the most part more symbolic than real. (For example, in Montgomery, Negroes have resumed riding in the back of the bus.) In brief, progress in the area of civil rights has been neither great enough nor fast enough. Thus the more moderate Negro leaders and organizations find themselves under increasing pressure from the rank and file to step up the tempo of demands. Some observers have gone so far as to suggest that Dr. King has lost his constituency, as the center of the civil-rights struggle has moved from the rural South to the urban North. According to this view, King is simply not militant enough and not sufficiently in touch with the Negro masses in the Northern slums to have the sort of impact he had in his native South.

America must therefore face the other pole of the dilemma posed by Baldwin. The Black Muslims, the advocates of Black Power, and the nationalist groups represent the negative side of the newfound pride in blackness. To the Muslims, for instance, the white man is a devil and this devil is doomed; his allotted span as ruler of the earth is nearly over. Conversely, the black man is by nature divine. The traditional symbolic values of white and black are reversed, and the Muslims can be classified as racists, and, in fact, as segregationists. This racial glorification is, as Baldwin says, a recipe for murder, but white racists must expect counterparts on the other side of the gulf they so assiduously cultivate.

All the same, it must be noted that the Muslims have made some positive contributions within the Negro community, particularly in the rehabilitation of criminals and in other forms of social work. Muslims neither smoke nor drink, they are not promiscuous, they do not use dope, and former criminals among them rarely lapse back into crime. As Baldwin has pointed out, Elijah Muhammad has succeeded where generations of social workers and other moderates have failed.[7]

[7] Baldwin, *The Fire Next Time* (New York: Dial, 1963), pp. 64–65. See also Lomax, *The Negro Revolt*, pp. 190–191.

One further thing about the Black Muslims must be re-marked, for I think it tells something important about the peculiar position of the Negro in America. As noted above, the Muslims are black supremacists and want to be as completely separated from the white devil as possible. One of the conditions which particularly irritates residents of Negro ghettos is that most of the businesses are owned by whites. Muslims feel that this situation reinforces Negro economic servitude and hence they not only recommend that Negroes "buy black" but also preach an ethic of thrift and hard work which culminates in a great deal of Muslim-owned business property. But the values described here are not the values of traditional Muslim countries. They are, on the contrary, the values of white Protestant America, particularly in its nine-teenth-century incarnation. All that remains is for the Muslims to espouse the tenets of Social Darwinism. But since the Protestant ethic is not universal, the Muslims derive it from their immersion in American culture. This fact, as well as any other, strikingly illustrates the problems of the Negro separatist. As Baldwin dis-covered, there is no escaping America. The hope for Negroes must be to change *this* country, not to create another, for this is the only country they have.

What, then, is to be done? On a course of action, Baldwin is eloquent but not very precise. There is a peculiar twist to his argument. The *white* man is not free, Baldwin contends, and what must be understood is that the white man is not free because the Negro is not free. The price the white man must pay to win *his* liberty is clear: "The price of the liberation of white people is the liberation of the blacks—the total liberation, in the cities, in the towns, before the law, and in the mind."[8]

But from what must the white man be liberated? From the perspective of the Negro, he certainly must appear almost godlike in his freedom to do as he pleases. The key to the answer has already been given: To Baldwin, it is in his mind that the white man is not free. Baldwin continues with some rather murky psy-chologizing. America, he says, is a country afflicted by Puritan-ism—a country that is Anglo-Teutonic and antisexual. As a result,

---

[8] Baldwin, *The Fire Next Time*, p. 111.

Americans have never learned to love each other. The resulting tensions have particularly dire results in the South, where white-Negro sexual rivalries are the root of much racial violence.[9]

For the Northerner, the problem is somewhat different. He never really sees Negroes; they are, to use Ellison's term once again, "invisible men." As a result the white man tends to ignore them. But whether invisible or ignored, the Negro is not seen as a man. He is, Baldwin contends, either a ward or a victim, but never a real person. "These are two sides of the same coin and the South will not change—*cannot* change—until the North changes." And change can come only when the nation as a whole discovers freedom. No man can enslave another, Baldwin points out, without becoming a slave himself.

Scattered through Baldwin's work is another line of argument closely related to the one sketched above. It is essentially a critique of America as a mass society. "The American ideal," Baldwin writes, "after all, is that everyone should be as much alike as possible." Americans cannot stand for people to be different—not culturally, not sexually, not morally, not in dress, nor in the daily routine of life. We have mass-produced a human product as cold and featureless as the standardized products of our industrial system. We have tried to make the Negro less than a man, but our "dehumanization of the Negro then is indivisible from our dehumanization of ourselves: the loss of our own identity is the price we pay for the annulment of his." What is more, in the effort to free ourselves, we have much to learn from the Negro. In fact, the only way for the white man to really free himself is "to become black himself, to become a part of that suffering dancing country."

The Ambiguities of James Baldwin

Few writers in recent years have enjoyed the vogue accorded James Baldwin. His books are best sellers, and his recent play, *Blues for Mr. Charlie*, ran for some months on Broadway. In American terms—which are precisely the terms he would like to reject—he is a success. In a sense this is surprising, for he is one of

---

[9] Baldwin, *Nobody Knows My Name*, p. 70.

our more severe cultural critics. On the other hand, his very success reveals something about the culture he attacks and the way it tends to absorb even the dissenters. Only a system which is very self-confident and more than a little smug feels it can afford to be so tolerant of deviations from the norm. But the crisis in civil rights has breeched this wall of self-satisfaction and, of late, Baldwin and others who write in the same vein have been under severe attack.

It is not only American society which has changed; Baldwin has also changed and therein lies the reason for some of the widespread discontent with his latest works. This change is illustrative of the dynamics of the civil-rights movement generally. The early Baldwin who published *Notes of a Native Son* was a very private man. The essays in that volume are quiet, introspective, brooding. As Dan Jacobson has pointed out, in Baldwin's second collection of articles, *Nobody Knows My Name*, the writing loses some of these qualities. Baldwin's sights are no longer turned inward; he tends rather to focus on public events—the riots in the United Nations following the shooting of Patrice Lamumba, a study of the only Negro boy in an "integrated" school, an intensely political meeting of African writers and artists. The essays are still deeply felt and deeply moving, but Baldwin the public figure, as opposed to Baldwin the solitary writer, is beginning to emerge. He is, in these pieces, becoming a spokesman for his race rather than a lonely and immensely talented young man in search of his identity. The transformation was completed with the appearance of *The Fire Next Time*. Virtually overnight Baldwin became a national celebrity and a semipolitical figure of some consequence.

In becoming a political figure, Baldwin has paid a large price. The younger Baldwin could write, "I don't like people who like me because I'm a Negro; neither do I like people who find in the same accident grounds for contempt. . . . I want to be an honest man and a good writer." A change has taken place in recent years, however. Someone has remarked that whereas once Baldwin wanted to be seen merely as a man, he today requires that he be seen first of all as a black man. And to him the black man has become a very special creature indeed. He has acquired through his trauma in America a tragic sense of life which the white American has missed and withal has managed to maintain a healthy respect for life's sensual pleasures—to resist, in other words, the dessication of mass society. In the children who braved the taunts of white mobs simply in order to go to school, Baldwin sees the only genuine aristocrats produced by this country.

But not all of Baldwin's new perceptions are so positive. The young Baldwin resisted the crude stereotype of the Negro so prevalent in America; today's Baldwin seems almost to relish it. In *Blues for Mr. Charlie,* the stereotype is flaunted before the eyes of the audience. In the play the Negroes are strong, brave, heroic, sexually superior, and even seem endowed with natural rhythm, while the whites are weak, spineless, and cowardly. In this morass of clichés the subtlety has gone out of Baldwin's work. The Black Muslim ideology he attacked in *The Fire Next Time* has now won top billing and upset the delicately calibrated balance of his thought. The early Baldwin knew that the racial crisis could be solved only by transcending race through the recognition of a common humanity. Today's Baldwin wants equality, but he wants it on the Negroes' own terms and those terms are apparently high. (I can only say "apparently" because the terms are no longer as clear as they once were.)

Not all facets of this attitude are new to Baldwin. There has been a deeply felt strain of racial pride in his work for years. Nor is his attitude toward whites wholly new either; as noted above, an important step in Baldwin's development came when he forced himself to admit that he "hated and feared" whites. No one can claim that hatred and fear were not justified. However, in *Notes of a Native Son,* these feelings were set against a sense of compassion for the oppressor that is fading from his current work. The man who wrote the early essays was willing to make distinctions, to admit ambiguity, to see complex problems in shades of gray. The author of *Blues for Mr. Charlie* blurs distinctions, rejects ambiguity, and seems to see things quite literally in black and white. If Baldwin continues along his present path of simplified preachment and propaganda, a great moral force will have been lost.

The dilemma of James Baldwin illustrates a vital point. There can be little doubt that he has exposed many of the roots of our contemporary tensions. It is true that other Negro intellectuals may be more "moderate" or tolerant. Ralph Ellison, for example, is equally sensitive to social injustice, but he also emphasizes the variety and richness of Negro life and seems to feel that the unrelenting protest of a Baldwin or a Richard Wright results in a distortion of values ultimately detrimental to the life of the mind. Moreover, a study of the attitude of Negro leaders conducted by Louis Harris indicates that these men are much more sympathetic to whites than is Baldwin, although even among them there is a noteworthy undercurrent of distrust. However, the same study reveals that roughly 60 per cent of the Negro rank and file feel that the whites desire to "keep them down" or simply don't care what happens to them.[10] Thus, Baldwin seems to have sensed correctly the attitudes of Negro Americans, even though his psychologically oriented explanations of the source of these attitudes may be off the mark.

Baldwin's thinking on this point has a clear similarity to that of the proponents of Black Power. This group, led by Stokely Carmichael, former head of the Student Non-Violent Coordinating Committee, and his successor H. Rap Brown, wish to convert the civil-rights movement into an all-black crusade even at the risk of alienating white supporters. This distrust of whites leads to a disavowal of the politics of coalition which is the typical form of resolving political conflict in America. Moreover, the movement risks not only the loss of possible allies but also the stimulation of the white-backlash phenomenon. The latter failed to materialize in the election campaign of 1964, but there is every reason to suspect that under other circumstances than were provided by the Goldwater-Johnson contest there would be a sharp increase in white opposition to the civil-rights movement. Certainly, the widespread rioting in a number of large Northern cities during recent summers and the sharp Congressional reaction to these conditions provide ample, if impressionistic, evidence to support this point. A survey taken by Louis Harris for *Newsweek* confirms this judgment. The evidence is clear that a good-sized majority of whites feel that the Negro revolution is "moving too fast." For example,

---

[10] William Brink and Louis Harris, *The Negro Revolution in America* (New York: Simon and Schuster, 1964), p. 126.

64 per cent of the whites in Harris' sample feel that Negroes "were asking for more than they were ready for." In addition, the evidence confirms the widely held belief that antagonism to the civil-rights movement is much stronger among low-income, low-status whites than it is among high-income, high-status whites.[11] Since it is the former group with whom Negroes are likely to come into conflict, it is quite clear that the potential for further violence and disorder is great. This potential will be increased if the militant faction of the movement wins widespread mass support. At present, the Harris survey shows that a broad base is lacking, but even a minority of 10–15 per cent can do great damage to the cause of civil rights.

It would appear, then, that the civil-rights movement may have reached a significant turning point as it hovers between "protest and politics." The dynamics of American politics are such that moralizing must give way to concerted political action if the ferment of the past decade is to be converted into significant social change. If this line of argument is valid, then the theory of Black Power is dysfunctional to the movement its advocates seek to advance. Politics is an arena of bargaining and compromise; and while ideals are vital as a spur to action and a standard of judgment, there is real political danger in uncompromising fanaticism. The aggressive militancy which stirred the conscience of so many now seems strident and out of place. In the end the Black Power movement rests on a dangerous gamble—namely, that white leadership will respond to this dramatic new ideology with substantial social and economic change rather than with a negative reflex which will seriously undermine the already weak position of the Negro. At this writing, the evidence suggests an outcome closer to the second alternative than to the first.

In any case, it is clear that the movement of Baldwin's ideas parallels in a rough way the development of the civil-rights movement. He has been quoted as saying that he feels it necessary to "keep up with the kids," and it must be said that the "kids" are moving rapidly indeed. In a sense, then, Baldwin's recent work

---

[11] "Crisis of Color '66," *Newsweek* (August 22, 1966), pp. 20–59. For a more detailed analysis of this survey, see William Brink and Louis Harris, *Black and White* (New York: Simon and Schuster, 1967).

may reflect a more general trend of thought—not formalized to be sure, but a genuine change in the climate of opinion. The new militancy displayed, starting with the spring and summer of 1964, may well prove to have been only the beginning. This is the way with revolutions; they develop a momentum which is hard to stop; one concession tends to whet the appetite for another. Therein lies the danger—and the opportunity—of the struggle for civil rights in America. The stepped-up drive of the past years must be channeled into our political institutions without stifling the demand for change or disrupting those institutions.

Liberals and the Negro

In the nature of things, the civil-rights revolution cannot be led by conservatives. Not that American conservatives are by any means all opposed to the mélange of aspirations associated with the civil-rights movement. Few people indeed are opposed to "civil rights" as such, but many people *are* opposed to the really fundamental changes in the structure of American society which the achievement of Negro aspirations may well require. Consequently, conservatives, with occasional exceptions like Peter Viereck, must inevitably oppose the movement or at least try to slow its pace. And in the future the conservative opposition will not have to rely on racist propaganda. There are signs that it is becoming intellectually respectable to argue against Negro demands for reform. Consider two brief examples, both by well-known political scientists, published in a recent symposium. Walter Berns argues not against the justice of the demands being made, but against the processes by which some of these demands are being met. In particular, he objects to the role played in recent years by the Supreme Court. The Court, says Berns, has been making "unprincipled" decisions on civil-rights cases—unprincipled not because the end sought is wrong, but because the Court, in its zeal to secure and protect civil rights, is distorting the meaning of the Constitution (a price which Berns is not willing to pay). It is quite possible, Berns claims, "that there are some unjust acts that are not, by that fact alone, unconstitutional." There are limits to what law can do to combat discrimination, and in transgressing those limits (as Berns feels the Court has done), serious threats are posed to the American system of government; particularly there is danger that the law itself will come to be held in contempt.[12] While Berns' interpretation need not be adopted (indeed, I do not), it cannot simply be dismissed as racist nonsense.

In the same collection of essays, Herbert J. Storing's article points to another reasoned approach conservatives may well adopt on the question of civil rights. According to Storing, "The hardships and injustices faced by the Negro in America are not tragic or even exceptional." The fate of the Negro, Storing contends, has been the fate of every race which has had to climb the ladder of civilization. Negroes should have their civil rights, but only when they are ready for them. They must be prepared to accept gradual progress toward their goal. Once again it is not necessary to agree with the argument. I have said that Storing's view is reasoned and that we can expect to hear more of similar viewpoints; it must be emphasized, however, that not all reason is good reason. If we are concerned with justice at all—as Storing apparently is—then the question of whether the injustice is tragic or exceptional is as irrelevant as is talk about Negroes *earning* their civil rights. In the end, then, Storing's position is damaged by a serious logical flaw; moreover, the practical problems inherent in his injunction to go slow are immense, as the following discussion will make clear.[13]

I have mentioned the essays by such responsible conservatives as Storing and Berns merely to indicate that America is only now moving into serious ideological and philosophical debate over equal rights and to demonstrate that the burden of positive action will fall to liberals. This last point raises certain political difficulties because a few Negro leaders—James Baldwin and Stokely Carmichael being leading examples—display a profound mistrust of white liberals. To Baldwin, for instance, the white liberal is an "affliction" who cannot or will not understand the radical imperatives of the civil-rights situation. It is safe to say that Baldwin's

---

[12] See Walter Berns, "Racial Discrimination and the Limits of Judicial Remedy," in Robert A. Goldwin, ed., *100 Years of Emancipation* (Chicago: Rand McNally, 1964), pp. 182–217.

[13] Herbert J. Storing, "The School of Slavery: A Reconsideration of Booker T. Washington," in *ibid.*, pp. 47–79.

view does not represent that of all civil-rights groups. Both the NAACP and CORE have substantial white memberships. But the NAACP and CORE are middle-class organizations, and as the civil-rights drive moves to the "left," more and more "rank and file" Negroes will be taking to the streets. Already CORE has adopted a decidedly more militant stance under the leadership of Floyd McKissick. If Baldwin is right about the undercurrent of distrust for the whites, then this country is in for an increasingly stormy period in which political and ideological conflict may be expected to increase substantially. Such conflict is inevitable unless rapid progress is made toward meeting the demands of the civil-rights movement.

Another factor must be considered, however. Many Negro leaders have reached the conclusion that real gains must come through concerted political action rather than by isolated demonstrations of discontent. But the strategy of a protest movement is quite different from the strategy of a political movement. Politicians must compromise; they must make advances in small steps. It is impossible, in the nature of politics, to have everything now. Thus, a main theme of the demonstrations of past years may have to be dropped. This is the significance of Bayard Rustin's appeal to disillusioned adherents of the Mississippi Freedom Democratic Party at the 1964 Democratic Convention. Rustin, who directed the march on Washington in the summer of 1963, argued, in what can only be called a paradoxically passionate plea for moderation, that while Negroes might be unhappy with the decisions of the convention, they had no real choice but to throw their political support behind Lyndon Johnson. By and large, this position was adopted. Rustin has gone further and, with the help of men like socialist intellectual Michael Harrington, is hard at work trying to forge a coalition of Negroes, the poor, and organized labor. The difficulties of such a task can hardly be overemphasized, for the poor are unorganized, labor is—with a few notable exceptions— hardly enthusiastic about the demands of the civil-rights movement, and Negro leadership is badly split over such questions as coalition politics and the relation of the movement to white liberals.

Nevertheless, such a coalition could bring American liberalism to a significant turning point. For example, the persistent problem of unemployment is particularly acute among Negroes, most notably in the large Northern cities where Negroes comprise an ever larger proportion of the population. This high unemployment rate can be traced to discrimination in a number of settings: in vocational and academic training, in apprenticeship programs, in labor organizations, by state employment offices, in the training opportunities offered by the armed services, and by individual employers.[14]

Unemployment among Negroes is likely to get worse before it gets better. Our economy increasingly requires highly trained people; and if groups of citizens are systematically denied access to the sort of training that makes employment possible, they are not going to be able to improve their position. This difficulty is compounded by the growing use of automated devices in industry. The economic plight of untrained Negroes is likely to grow steadily worse under these conditions. It is facts like these which lead Whitney Young of the Urban League to demand a Marshall Plan for Negroes. Young demands that special compensation be given the Negro for the indignities he has suffered. What the Marshall Plan involves is the designation of Negroes as an underdeveloped people who need to be given special treatment if they are to catch up. A policy of preferment must be undertaken even at the risk of angering Negroes who resent any implication of inferiority. But, as Lomax points out, "The background of the Negro masses is inferior, for whatever reason, and Young is saying that to overcome this the current Negro generation must be moved forward en masse and at a swifter pace than the current white generation."[15] Harlem, Lomax goes on, is the New World's Congo. If the whites left, the Negroes could not run it—not for lack of inherent talent, but for lack of training.

These facts, combined with the persistent unemployment unrelated to race, as well as other economic problems such as

---

[14] Lomax, *The Negro Revolt*, pp. 79–80. Lomax draws on the United States Civil Rights Commission Report Number Three, *Employment*, published in 1961.

[15] *Ibid.*, p. 228.

inflation and industrial concentration, should have a great impact on contemporary liberal thought. Even without the pressure of a militant civil-rights movement, there has already emerged a tendency among liberal thinkers to consider an increasing role for government in promoting economic welfare. Moreover, the pressures of a modern economy tend toward this direction. Walter Lippmann has predicted that "it will prove impossible to approach the equality of opportunity for the Negroes without reviving and renewing the progressive movement in American politics, which has been quiescent for some ten years." In this assessment, Lippmann is undoubtedly right. As mentioned above, there has already been a call for a coalition between organized labor and the civil-rights groups which will work for fundamental structural changes in the economic system.

Hans Morgenthau even goes so far as to argue that unless such changes occur, the conjunction of the issues of unemployment and civil rights may lead to a disruption of the consensus on which American politics rests. The riots in Harlem and elsewhere, which occurred *after Morgenthau's prediction*, are eloquent testimony to the grim nature of the problem.[16] Moreover, the changing structure of American politics situates the Negro in a position where he is beginning to exercise real power. The heavy concentration of Negro voters in large urban centers, coupled with the Supreme Court decisions attacking rural overrepresentation in our legislative bodies and demanding reapportionment in favor of the cities, gives Negroes a great deal of political leverage. Thus, *in the long run*, the nature of the situation is such that street demonstrations will probably decline and political action rise as the vehicle for Negro protest.

But before there can be a move toward a solution, whether by political or other means, there must be a considerable clarification of the goals of the civil-rights movement. To conclude this chapter I would like to consider just a few of the points at issue.

---

[16] On this matter, see Morgenthau, "The Coming Test of American Democracy," *Commentary*, 37 (January 1964), 61–63, and Lippmann, "Change of Course," *Newsweek*, 62 (July 8, 1963), 15.

Some Unresolved Questions

The civil-rights movement is underdeveloped theoretically. Its goals have by no means been fully worked out. Much of the thinking is devoted to tactical considerations. There are extended discussions over the position of whites in the movement, over whether and when to press forward with more demonstrations, over the type of demonstration to be employed, over the question of coalition politics, and so on, while more fundamental questions are slighted.

To begin with, there is a great deal of talk about equality. But what, after all, is equality? Clearly, no two people can ever be equal in all things; inevitably there are differences of intelligence, strength, appearance, and a host of other factors. Should the struggle be for equality of opportunity? Undoubtedly, yes; in principle at least, no feature of the American value system is so widely accepted. But this commitment must be translated into concrete form. Some people contend that equality of opportunity requires a radical reconstruction of the entire system of education, including, quite possibly, the destruction of the neighborhood-school system. Is this a price that must be paid? Is this a price that should be paid? What is the hierarchy of values involved here?[17]

Consider another situation. It is often contended that equality of opportunity requires substantial equality of economic condition; this contention, in effect, is the basis of Whitney Young's plea for a domestic Marshall Plan. Moreover, there is certainly a close connection between the poverty-stricken status of the Negro and his lack of opportunity. It may therefore be necessary to effect radical changes in the structure of the economy if equality of opportunity is to be realized. But, as noted, these changes will meet serious opposition. It is thus at least conceivable that the civil-rights movement may contribute to a rupture of the present consensus on economic policy, and with this rupture could come fundamental political realignments. The point is that the civil-

---

[17] For a critical view of the idea of equality of opportunity, see John H. Schaar, "Some Ways of Thinking About Equality," *Journal of Politics*, 26 (November 1964), 867–895.

rights question does not exist in a vacuum; it presents issues that cut across numerous aspects of American life. Only on the basis of a careful consideration of the whole character of our society can there be any meaningful attack on the problem. James Baldwin is quite right on this point, even though he may present an excessively pessimistic and somewhat distorted view of the matter.

For another example, take the question of integration. What does integration really mean, and is it the goal Negroes want to achieve? Under many circumstances it seems a most elusive target. Is it really possible, for instance, to "integrate" the public schools of New York City where 75 per cent of the students in the system are already Negro or Puerto Rican? Clearly, such a goal is utopian if by "integration" is meant a one-to-one racial correspondence in each school; as Charles Silberman puts it, there simply are not enough whites to go around. It is quite possible that the great symbolic value of school integration may have deluded Negroes into wasting time, effort, and more than a little good will in a quest for the unattainable.

Other questions also arise. Does integration mean the disappearance of the Negro community? Is a Negro neighborhood *necessarily* inferior? Certainly, the answer to the second question is "No," and there is good reason to think that the answer to the first ought be "No" also. We Americans tend to expect the dissolution of minorities in the great mythical melting pot whose image pervades our egalitarian doctrines. "But the crucial thing about the melting pot was that it did not happen: American politics and American social life are still dominated by the existence of sharply-defined ethnic groups."[18] Integration into the mainstream of American life need not depend on complete assimilation, and indeed Silberman insists that it cannot. The peculiar difficulty of the civil-rights movement is that the Negro is harder to integrate than any other minority group—even in a relatively limited sense—simply because of the obvious fact of color. Facts—especially obvious facts—cannot be overlooked in the quest for the

---

[18] Silberman, *Crisis in Black and White*, p. 165. Silberman relies here on Nathan Glazer and Daniel P. Moynihan, *Beyond the Melting Pot* (Cambridge: MIT and Harvard, 1963).

ideal. Moreover, there seems to be no good reason why the new-found racial pride of American Negroes should be overwhelmed by total assimilation. Other minorities maintain a certain distinctiveness and yet would be classified as "integrated." Why should the same not be true of the Negroes?

Finally, a few words must be said about the pace of social change. One need not be opposed to all change to recognize that some changes can be disruptive of social order if they occur too quickly. We Americans have resisted any change at all for so long that now massive change is necessary and urgent. It would stretch the point to argue that the current situation is analogous to that of the *ancien régime* in 1789, but it is not altogether absurd. Certainly, like the French, we face the problem of rapid social change and we find it very painful. Our situation may not be revolutionary but certainly the consensus shows signs of strain. In some areas the veneer of American civilization has already worn very thin. It will be very hard to channel the pent-up forces of hundreds of years into constructive reforms. It will be particularly difficult to find a blend of protest and political action that will maintain the basic structure of our institutions and yet at the same time keep alive the impetus necessary for reforms which must inevitably come. This balance will call for political skill of a high order and for a brand of sophistication not deeply ingrained in the American tradition. James Baldwin once wrote that Americans "have yet to be corrupted by the notion that society is never anything less than a perfect labyrinth of limitations." Some of the more militant civil-rights leaders—Baldwin included—have forgotten this injunction, while white segregationists apparently have never learned it.

In 1964 the signs were hopeful. A surprising number of Southerners seemed to accept responsibility for a reasonable degree of enforcement of the various civil-rights acts. Almost simultaneously, some civil-rights leaders began an attempt to convert militant street protests into political action. However, this détente proved to be brief, and the level of tension has since risen sharply. Professor Morgenthau exaggerates but little when he suggests that the consensual foundation of American politics may ultimately be endangered. The merging of the issues of civil rights with those of unemployment and technological change poses a challenge not only for American liberal thought, but also for the political order itself. The elements of a genuinely explosive situation are present. The nation is faced, quite literally, with the question of whether it can govern itself.

All of these practical and theoretical difficulties require political thought of a high order for their solution. We live in a period which tends to discourage such thought. We are told that the great tradition of political philosophy is nothing but high-flown metaphysics and that the clash of ideologies has been replaced by a much more down-to-earth system of bargaining and compromise among pragmatic specialists in the art of government. In a sense these are pernicious notions and they must be carefully examined. The chapter which follows attempts to do so.

🦅 BIBLIOGRAPHICAL NOTES 🦅

Gunnar Myrdal's *An American Dilemma* (rev. ed.; New York: Harper, 1962; orig. pub. 1944) is still, after twenty-five years, perhaps the best study of the American Negro. Of the recent general books, I have found the somewhat journalistic *Crisis in Black and White* (New York: Random House, 1964) by Charles Silberman to be most helpful. For Herman Miller's data on poverty, see "Changes in the Number and Composition of the Poor," in Margaret Gordon, ed., *Poverty in America* (San Francisco: Chandler, 1965), pp. 91–92. Much material on the social condition of the Negro may be found in the famous Moynihan report on the Negro family. The text of the report is contained in Lee Rainwater and William Yancy, *The Moynihan Report and the Politics of Controversy* (Cambridge: MIT Press, 1967). This report fully illustrates the sensitivity of the issues involved in any discussion of Negro behavior patterns. It deals with the furor that arose over the report and contains extended excerpts from the controversial literature.

Fiction by Negro writers can give important insights into Negro attitudes. The interested reader should explore such novels as Ralph Ellison's *Invisible Man* (New York: Random House, 1952), James Baldwin's *Go Tell It on the Mountain* (New York: Dial, 1963) and *Another Country* (New York: Dial, 1962), and Richard Wright's *Black Boy* (New York: World Pub., 1950) and *Native Son* (New York: New American Library, 1962). A fascinating debate on the Negro writer was touched off by Irving Howe in "Black Boys and Native Sons," *Dissent* (Autumn 1963), pp. 353–368. Howe is answered at length by Ralph Ellison in an essay entitled "The World and the Jug," in *Shadow and Act* (New

York: Random House, 1964). This essay stresses the variety of Negro existence as opposed to the stereotyped sameness.

Baldwin's principal essays are collected in three volumes: *Notes of a Native Son* (Boston: Beacon Press, 1957), *Nobody Knows My Name* (New York: Delta Books, 1962), and *The Fire Next Time* (New York: Dial, 1963). Dan Jacobson's essay on Baldwin is entitled "James Baldwin as Spokesman," *Commentary* (December 1961), pp. 497–502.

Martin Luther King's primary works are *Stride Toward Freedom* (New York: Ballentine Books, 1960), which deals with the Montgomery bus boycott, and *Why We Can't Wait* (New York: Signet Books, 1964), which contains the famous "Letter from a Birmingham Jail." A new volume, *Where Do We Go From Here?* (New York: Harper, 1967), appeared too late to be used here. Sections of the book have also appeared in periodicals. These publications give King's assessment of the strengths and weaknesses of the Black Power movement. See "A New Kind of Power," *The Progressive* (June 1967), pp. 13–17, and "Martin Luther King Defines 'Black Power,'" *New York Times Magazine* (June 11, 1967), pp. 26ff. Andrew Kopkind is among those who have argued that King has lost his influence and is now simply irrelevant to the future of the civil-rights movement; see "Soul Power," *New York Review of Books* (August 24, 1967), pp. 3–6. Good collections of readings on the theory of nonviolent resistance are Mulford Q. Sibley, ed., *The Quiet Battle* (Garden City, N.Y.: Doubleday, Anchor Books, 1963), and Staughton Lynd, ed., *Nonviolence in America: A Documentary History* (Indianapolis: Bobbs-Merrill, 1966).

The Black Muslims have been discussed in two first-rate books: C. Eric Lincoln, *The Black Muslims in America* (Boston: Beacon Press, 1961), and E. U. Essien-Udom, *Black Nationalism* (New York: Dell, 1964). Baldwin's *The Fire Next Time* also has much interesting material on this group.

Black Power is a very confusing concept whose meaning is by no means clear. Perhaps the best statement is Stokely Carmichael's "What We Want," *New York Review of Books* (September 22, 1966), pp. 5–8. For a critique, see Bayard Rustin, " 'Black Power' and Coalition Politics," *Commentary* (September 1966), pp.

35–46. See also Gene Roberts, "From 'Freedom High' to 'Black Power,'" *New York Times Magazine* (September 25, 1966), pp. 27ff, and the articles by Martin Luther King cited above. The impact of the emergence of Africa on Negro thinking is discussed in Harold Isaacs, *The New World of Negro Americans* (New York: Viking, Compass Books, 1963).

The tension between liberalism and the Negro is well illustrated in "Liberalism and the Negro," *Commentary* (March 1964), pp. 25–42. This is the transcript of a panel discussion featuring James Baldwin, Nathan Glazer, Sidney Hook, and Gunnar Myrdal. In "From Protest to Politics," *Commentary* (February 1965), pp. 25–31, Bayard Rustin analyzes the need for coalition politics.

Two good collections of essays present a wide range of ideological opinion on civil rights. The first is Robert A. Goldwin, ed., *100 Years of Emancipation* (Chicago: Rand McNally, 1964), which contains views ranging from Baldwin's through those of Southern segregationist James Jackson Kilpatrick. The second is Francis L. Broderick and August Meier, *Negro Protest Thought in the Twentieth Century* (Indianapolis: Bobbs-Merrill, 1965).

A number of general, interpretive works should be mentioned. Oscar Handlin, *Fire Bell in the Night* (Boston: Little, Brown, 1964), offers a standard liberal view of the civil-rights problem. Nat Hentoff observes the same issues from the point of view of one sympathetic to the New Left in *The New Equality* (New York: Viking, Compass Books, 1965). In *White and Black* (New York: Harper, Colophon Books, 1966), Samuel Lubell reports on extensive, if rather unsystematic, interviews. Robert Penn Warren's *Who Speaks for the Negro?* (New York: Random House, 1965) presents fascinating interviews with a wide range of Negro leaders. Warren's comments, which are those of a liberal white Southerner living in the North, are also of considerable value. This is an indispensable book. A massive collection of scholarly studies has been edited by Talcott Parsons and Kenneth Clark: *The Negro American* (Boston: Houghton Mifflin, 1966). In *The Second American Revolution* (New York: Bantam Books, 1965), Anthony Lewis has collected *New York Times* dispatches covering developments on civil rights. It is a very useful volume. See also C.

Vann Woodward, "What Happened to the Civil Rights Movement?" *Harper Magazine* (January 1967), pp. 29–37.

Finally, it should be noted that a number of Negro leaders are now associating themselves with the peace movement. This development may have great significance not only for the civil-rights movement but for left-liberal politics in general. See Martin Luther King, "Declaration of Independence from the War in Viet Nam," *Ramparts* (May 1967), pp. 32–37.

CHAPTER VIII

THE
RETREAT
FROM
IDEOLOGY

Much of the preceding discussion casts into sharp relief the inadequacies of what is perhaps the most characteristic and certainly the most fashionable development in recent American political thought: the belief that we have seen the last of ideology in the Western world. The primary exponents of this point of view are Seymour Martin Lipset and Daniel Bell. The widespread acceptance of the thesis makes it worthy of careful examination.

The term *ideology* has been the subject of a great variety of conflicting definitions. Unfortunately, Bell's most straightforward attempt is not particularly clear, so that the implications of his usage must be relied on for an understanding of his approach to the problem. He writes, "Ideology is the conversion of ideas into social levers." He continues by arguing that what gives ideology its power is its passion and that "the most important latent function of ideology is to tap emotion." A social movement can accomplish this function when it can do three things: "simplify ideas, establish a claim to truth, and, in the union of the two, demand a commitment to action." He argues that the radical ideologies of the nineteenth century were successful in reaching these goals. However, in the Western world of today, these ideologies have lost their former potency. The reasons are not hard to find. The Moscow trials, the Nazi-Soviet Pact, the concentration camps, the failure of the Hungarian rebellion, and other such events make the sort of chiliastic optimism which Bell associates with ideology difficult, if not impossible. Moreover, the transformation of the predatory capitalism of the nineteenth century into the welfare state of the twentieth has lessened the zeal of reformers.[1]

Among the old radicals, Bell claims, politics is no longer viewed as a moral crusade. This shift in the attitudes of politically minded intellectuals is particularly evident in the generation of American radicals which was active during the 1930's. Representatives of this generation include Lionel Trilling and Reinhold Niebuhr, who are viewed by Bell as returned prodigals now repenting their radicalism. By understanding their fate, it is possible to understand the loss of innocence which Bell feels is the key American experience of the 1930's. That generation failed because it tasted power for the first time, and in so doing became corrupt. The form of this corruption was a dogmatic singlemindedness of vision. The end of ideology represents a reaction to this sort of messianism.[2]

As a result, Bell says, American politics in the 1940's and 1950's has tended to be antiideological. There is a skepticism toward the rationalistic claims of socialists that an alteration of the economic base would solve all of our pressing social problems. There is, in fact, a kind of antirationalism which appears to be closely linked to the vogue of Freudianism and Niebuhrian neo-orthodoxy. No longer does the liberal intellectual feel compelled to make the world over; instead, the feeling seems to be that the

---

[1] Daniel Bell, *The End of Ideology* (Glencoe: The Free Press, 1960), p. 373.

[2] *Ibid.*, pp. 291–292.

task is too great even to contemplate. Revolution has been replaced by acquiescence.

As has already been indicated, Bell is not alone in his analysis.
Perhaps the first to note "the end of ideology" was the French
sociologist Raymond Aron, writing in 1955. In this country Seymour Martin Lipset has also argued the position with considerable
force. Lipset's starting point is the lament of Friedrich Hayek at
the 1955 meeting of the Congress for Cultural Freedom that the
traditional issues which used to divide right and left have seemingly declined to relative insignificance. The operative word here is
probably "traditional," although it is not clear that Lipset and
Hayek recognize this fact. Certainly, it can be agreed—with J.
Kenneth Galbraith—that, as far as the United States is concerned,
reputations for liberalism or radicalism continue to depend on the
desire to continue and expand the work of the New Deal. To a
large extent, liberals—and indeed many conservatives—are still
living on the ideas of this period. There have been few, if any,
major new ideas injected into the mainstream of American politics
for a number of years. However, the fact that a mixed economy
and a halfway welfare state have been generally accepted by all
segments of the political spectrum does not necessarily mean that
the period of ideological thinking is at an end. Moreover, it surely
does not mean that such a development, to the extent that it has
actually taken place, is necessarily to be welcomed. Let us consider
some of the evidence.

A Critique of the Bell-Lipset Thesis

Has the end of ideology in fact come? If the contention is
limited to the United States, are Bell and Lipset correct in their
empirical analysis? If the extremely narrow definition of *ideology*
which their context suggests is accepted, the answer is "Yes." By
ideology, they clearly mean messianic, Marxist socialism. Such
doctrines *are* virtually extinct in the United States today. But this
is the extinction of a rare species indeed. Certainly, Bell exaggerates the extent to which radicalism permeated the political atmos-
phere in the 1930's. In view of the conditions prevailing during the

Depression, it is really startling that there was not a good deal more ideological fanaticism than there was. The United States need only be compared with Weimar Germany to emphasize this point: while Germany produced Hitler and the Third Reich, America produced F. D. R. and the New Deal. The American consensus has remained remarkably stable through time and, viewed in this context, the ideological fervor of the 1930's assumes much more realistic proportions than in Bell's work.

Still, it must be admitted that there has been widespread satisfaction with the performance of the economic system, particularly since the start of World War II. This satisfaction has persisted even in the face of the chronic difficulties with which our economy has been faced. The assumption of affluence has been widespread, and the already narrow spectrum of economic conflict has tended to become still narrower. The result is that what once were ideological disputes have now become mere technical administrative difficulties suited to the problem-solving skills of managerial elites. In addition, the rapprochement between President Johnson and many leading business interests may further this trend.

But the Marxists to the contrary notwithstanding, there is more to ideology than economics. In the late 1950's, new issues began to make an impact on our politics, the following of Ayn Rand became something of a cult, the works of C. Wright Mills progressively shifted in emphasis from sociology to ideology, and the radical right has grown apace. More important have been the growing critique of the basic assumptions of American foreign policy emanating from both right and left and the veritable revolution in civil rights. As H. Stuart Hughes concludes, it has been the misfortune of Bell and his followers to have advanced their thesis at the end rather than the beginning of a nonideological period in our history. What seems to be happening is that the bases of ideological conflict are being altered. Where once economic affairs were the primary divisive forces in American politics, the evidence of the last two chapters indicates that foreign relations and civil rights will in the future dominate our political struggles. In these areas the old ideological battle cries, whether derived from Marx or not, are likely to be of little importance.

There are, however, more serious objections to the end-of-ideology thesis as formulated by Bell and Lipset. These objections are essentially normative rather than empirical. There is a reasonable doubt whether the situation depicted should be welcomed so nearly without qualification as it is in the work of these analysts. All sensible people want to avoid ideological fanaticism. Few indeed are the political thinkers who favor the reign of either terror or virtue. But is the choice really between ideologically motivated extremism or piecemeal adjustment of social problems in the absence of over-all vision?

As Rousseas and Farganis have pointed out, "Ideology need not be . . . equated with chiliastic fanaticism. Its major function is to apply intelligence—the fusion of passion and critical reason—to the problems of the modern world."[3] In other words, there is a very important distinction to be made between ideology defined as "a system of ideas concerning the existing social order, and at the same time concerning actions to be taken regarding it" and a totalitarian ideology defined as "a total rejection of an existent society and a program of total reconstruction."[4] It is easy to sympathize with a rejection of the latter, but the former presents quite a different problem. An absence of ideology in this sense may well doom a society to frustrating stagnation. A healthy political system must have some set of values, some long-range goals which can function as a guide to both short-run and long-run policy formulation. The system must operate with some conception of the public interest, some general idea of welfare; it is this which ideologies seek to provide. The fact that they are not always successful is no reason to damn *all* ideology.

Bell would deny that stagnation is the logical result of his conception of ideology. In reply to criticism leveled against him by Dennis Wrong, he has explicitly stated that "the end of ideology must not mean the end of utopia as well."[5] The intellectual is still

---

[3] Stephen W. Rousseas and James Farganis, "American Politics and the End of Ideology," in Irving Louis Horowitz, ed., *The New Sociology* (New York: Oxford University Press, 1964), p. 274.

[4] Carl J. Friedrich, "Political Philosophy and the Science of Politics," in Roland Young, ed., *Approaches to the Study of Politics* (Evanston, Ill.: Northwestern University Press, 1958), p. 186.

[5] Daniel Bell, "Ideology and the Beau Geste," *Dissent*, VIII (Winter 1961), 75.

seen as having a major role to play even in a world devoid of ideology. Taking note of the fear of the masses or indeed the fear of almost any social action which characterizes so much of the new conservatism, Bell maintains that while sharing some of these fears, one must maintain a detached and even alienated position so as to avoid the acceptance of "any particular embodiment of the community as final."[6]

The very idea of alienation suggests that a member of society has judged his surroundings by some outside standard and found it wanting. But how can detached criticism be provided in the absence of some set of beliefs which are somehow on a higher level of generality than those found in the day-to-day battles which form the stuff of politics?

Henry David Aiken argues that "what Bell appears to be calling for is, among other things, an end to *moral* discourse and a beginning of consistent 'pragmatic discourse' in every sphere of political life."[7] This position makes social criticism very difficult, if not altogether impossible. For example, Aiken contends:

> On such a view one would be permitted to say, "I don't like segregation and I will try—without, however, upsetting the apple cart—to do what I can to limit segregationist practices," but not, "Segregation is an affront to the humanity of the Negro people," or, "Those who practice segregation are unfair and unjust." [8]

As Aiken points out, democratic politics means more than bargaining and compromise among conflicting social groups. It also connotes "a form of politics in which men are governed by, and hence with reference to, principles and ideals—in a word, to morals and to ideology." If this argument is sound, then it follows that a revival of ideological or utopian thought is an important intellectual task. Certainly, as Riesman has pointed out, it is far easier to develop programs which allow the choice of the lesser evil from a variety of policy alternatives. On the other hand, "without

---

[6] Bell, *The End of Ideology*, p. 16.

[7] Henry David Aiken, "The Revolt Against Ideology," *Commentary*, 37 (April 1964), 36. See also the stimulating exchange between Bell and Aiken, "The End of Ideology: A Debate," *Commentary*, 38 (October 1964), 69–76.

[8] Aiken, "The Revolt Against Ideology," p. 36.

great plans, it is hard, and often self-defeating, to make little ones."[9]

This sort of faith in man's rational powers is often lacking today—not only among conservatives, where it is to be expected, but among liberals as well. Both are fond of pointing out the dangers of ideological or utopian excess. Up to a point they are correct in doing so; virtually any set of ideas can be dangerous in the wrong setting. However, a great deal more about the effects of ideology needs to be known, and investigation is not likely to be advanced so long as a pejorative definition of the concept of *ideology* persists.[10] As Bell and Lipset use the term, it is difficult *not* to share their sentiments. But if *ideology* is defined so that its creator is not automatically a fool or a fanatic, then the gains of ideological politics may well outweigh the possible losses. Certainly, this position can be argued of today's America. An intellectually stagnant social system is doomed to stagnation in other areas as well. It will be well to remember the words of Karl Mannheim, one of the most profound analysts of the social role of ideas:

The disappearance of utopia brings about a static state of affairs in which man himself becomes no more than a thing. We would be faced then with the greatest paradox imaginable, namely, that man, who has achieved the highest degree of rational mastery of existence, left without any ideals, becomes a mere creature of impulses. Thus, after a long, tortuous but heroic development, just at the highest stage of awareness, when history is ceasing to be blind fate, and is becoming more and more man's own creation, with the relinquishment of utopias, man would lose his will to shape history and therewith his ability to understand it.[11]

This statement clearly can be assimilated to the framework of traditional liberalism. It suggests that in the free marketplace of ideas, the truth will emerge. Much ideological conflict serves to stimulate discussion and clarify issues. Even so wayward a move-

---

[9] David Riesman, *Individualism Reconsidered* (Glencoe: The Free Press, 1954), p. 70.

[10] For a brilliant discussion of this point, see Clifford Geertz, "Ideology as a Cultural System," in David Apter, ed., *Ideology and Discontent* (New York: The Free Press, 1964), pp. 47–76.

[11] Karl Mannheim, *Ideology and Utopia* (New York: Harcourt, Harvest Books, n.d.), pp. 262–263.

ment as Black Power has helped to pose the issues involved in the civil-rights struggle more sharply, even though it may ultimately do damage to the civil-rights movement.

In summary, then, it is true that the political pursuit of ideological goals may be dysfunctional to the system as a whole. However, to argue that this is true of all ideological politics is to assume a uselessly pejorative definition of the central concept. If this is true, then it follows that some ideological conflict may have positive utility. I do not call for a politics based on fierce ideological struggle. Bargaining and compromise are essential to a democratic system, and these may be incompatible with a completely ideologized politics. However, some ideology has the function of acting as a leavening agent which can help to clarify goals and the means appropriate to the attainment of those goals. In the concluding chapter, this theme will be explored further.

❧ BIBLIOGRAPHICAL NOTES ❧

Karl Mannheim's *Ideology and Utopia* (New York: Harcourt, Harvest Books, n.d.; orig. pub. 1936) is probably the most important modern study of ideology. David Apter, ed., *Ideology and Discontent* (New York: The Free Press, 1964), also has much useful material. In addition to the contribution by Clifford Geertz cited in the text, the Introduction by Apter and the article by Reinhard Bendix (which places the concept of ideology in the context of the history of ideas) are of special value; see pp. 15–46 and 294–327. The volume also has a valuable bibliography. Further bibliographical data and a stimulating essay by Norman Birnbaum may be found in *Current Sociology*, Vol. IX, No. 2, 1960. Carl Friedrich's views on ideology are expounded at greater length in *Man and His Government* (New York: McGraw-Hill, 1963), pp. 83–93. Finally, see a brilliant article by Joseph La Palombara, "Decline of Ideology: A Dissent and an Interpretation," *American Political Science Review* (March 1966), pp. 5–16.

Aron's seminal work on ideology is *The Opium of the Intellectuals* (New York: Norton, 1962; orig. pub. 1955 in French, 1957 in English). It is worth noting that in the preface (pp. ix–xvi) to this new edition of his study, Aron shies away from some of his earlier views, at least insofar as they imply political quietism. The antiideological tone of much of American liberalism pervades the works of Arthur Schlesinger, Jr., discussed in earlier chapters. See also John Kenneth Galbraith, *Economics and the Art of Controversy* (New York: Random House, Vintage Books, 1959).

H. Stuart Hughes' critique of Bell may be found in "End of an Epoch," *Partisan Review* (Summer 1960), pp. 564–568. Dennis

Wrong's views are set forth in "Reflections on the End of Ideology," *Dissent* (Summer 1960), pp. 286–291.

A new quarterly entitled *The Public Interest* and edited by Daniel Bell is devoted explicitly to the nonideological analysis of social issues.

CHAPTER IX

🦅🦅🦅🦅🦅🦅🦅🦅🦅🦅🦅🦅🦅🦅🦅🦅

SUMMARY
AND
CONCLUSIONS

> The dogmas of the quiet past are inadequate to the
> stormy present. The occasion is piled high with diffi-
> culty, and we must rise with the occasion. As our case
> is new, so we must think anew, and act anew. We
> must disenthrall ourselves, and then we shall save
> our country.—*Abraham Lincoln*

It is now possible to tie together the analysis of the preceding
chapters. It need hardly be added that any conclusions are necessarily tentative and that projections of future trends are even more
so. In a real sense, this last chapter is an exercise in speculation.

The first factor that strikes the observer of recent American
political thought is the relative unanimity that prevails with respect to the major questions which have provided sources of conflict within our political culture since the Civil War. As noted at
the outset, these conflicts have been largely economic. In other
words, American politics since the Civil War has been largely
concerned with the distribution of economic benefits and with the

211

role of government in that process—all within the framework of democratic capitalism. The spectrum of conflict has always been rather narrow; in recent years it has grown more narrow still, for the policies of the mixed economy introduced by the New Deal have been absorbed into the consensus. This fact is amply illustrated by the unexpected victory of President Truman in 1948, the tacit ratification of President Roosevelt's program during the Eisenhower administration, and most recently by the overwhelming defeat of Barry Goldwater for the Presidency in the election of 1964.

This widespread acceptance of a positive role for government vis-à-vis the economy, coupled with a profound and quite understandable reaction to the enormous upheavals of twentieth-century politics, has produced a lull in political activity which has come to be known as the "end of ideology." But if the argument pursued in this book is sound, this lull is really no more than a temporary interlude. It is true that on the question of the mixed economy a high level of consensus has been reached. Even this accord may very well disappear if pressure for real economic planning should be generated. But in other areas the thesis of an end of ideology began to disintegrate almost as soon as it was pronounced. This disruption has its pathological aspects, but it may make positive contributions to American political life as well.

On the pathological side, there has been the eruption of a severe case of what Richard Hofstadter calls the "paranoid style in American politics." This style, which in the past was often manifested on the left, has appeared recently in the form of the various ideas and organizations of the radical right. As noted above, the ideologies of these groups hardly repay serious study of their intellectual content. At the same time, they are of considerable sociological interest because they indicate an undercurrent of dissent from the consensus that has dominated American politics since the end of World War II. This dissent finds expression not only with respect to domestic affairs, but also, and perhaps even more importantly, with respect to foreign relations. Whatever its intellectual merits, this current of thought cannot be dismissed as trivial. It is sufficiently strong, well organized, and well financed to have had a significant impact on the Republican Party since 1964. At the very least, it must be said that the candidate most favored by the extreme right won that party's last Presidential nomination. Thus, simply to dismiss the Birch Society and similar groups on the grounds of their intellectual shortcomings is dangerous and delusive.

The radical right is only one illustration of the seamy side of ideological politics. A few words should also be said about the politics of some groups of the so-called New Left. All of these groups are very small and poorly financed, and for these reasons have less organizational significance than do their counterparts on the right. However, note must be taken of the existence of such groups as Students for a Democratic Society, the Maoist Progressive Labor Party and a variety of black-nationalist racial groups.

By and large, while groups on the left may shatter the confines of the prevailing consensus on policy, they are at the same time notable for their emphasis on the more generalized aspects of the consensus, such as the democratic rules of the game. In fact their major complaint has been directed toward what they feel to be the insufficiently democratic character of the policy-making process, notably in foreign policy and civil rights. In these policy areas the consensus shows signs of severe strain. A dual attack has been mounted: On the one hand, the decision-making process is said to be in the hands of a manipulative elite; while on the other, substantive policies are attacked on the ground that their content is not consonant with the egalitarian tenets of democratic theory.

Fundamental challenges have thus been hurled at the structure of public policy in these areas. Moreover, they have already had their impact, as attested by the nuclear test-ban treaty and the various civil-rights acts. Perhaps still more significant than these concrete policy changes is the intellectual ferment generated by the American involvement in Vietnam and the continuing revolution in civil rights, particularly as the latter spreads to the Northern cities. If the challenges posed by these upheavals are squarely met, there should be still more changes in policy to correspond. Moreover, it is likely that ideological responses to these situations will increase in volume and intensity.

In general, it is safe to say that American political thought is passing through a transitional period. The period of ideological quiescence appears to be ending; at the same time, the traditional analytical categories are hard put to be of help in analyzing the change. Even groups near the center of the ideological spectrum are revising traditional beliefs. On many issues, liberals and conservatives have switched roles. Thus, conservatives now complain about the sacrifice of liberty in exchange for security, where once they attached a high value to security as one of the products of order. Liberals, on the other hand, once stressed the values of science but now often bemoan the role which science has played in creating an era of "engineered complacency."[1]

Each of these illustrations displays a genuine concern for the *quality* of American life. This fact symbolizes a new development in our thinking about politics. As the social theorist Peter Drucker has put it, our primary concerns now seem to be political, constitutional, moral, and aesthetic, rather than economic.[2] On the evidence of this book, this assessment is no doubt true. The works of such men as Galbraith, Riesman, and Schlesinger on the liberal side, of such founders of the New Conservative movement as Viereck and Kirk, and of more radical ideologies of both right and left attest to this fact.

With such cross-sectional concern for quality, serious questions arise as to the applicability of a liberal-conservative continuum to the analysis of contemporary American politics. The old issues which dominated our politics since 1865 are dying off, and with them perhaps will die the ideological framework used to describe them. To repeat, our politics has hitherto been largely concerned with distributing the relatively scarce benefits of industrialization. In an age of affluence this problem is no longer so acute. It is true that the existence of substantial poverty belies the prevailing assumption of affluence. I do not wish to suggest that

---

[1] For a discussion of these points, see Charles Frankel, *The Democratic Prospect* (New York: Harper, 1962), p. 6.

[2] Peter F. Drucker, "Notes on the New Politics," *The Public Interest* (Summer 1966), p. 16. This whole article, while somewhat sketchy, is of considerable relevance to the subject matter of this book. In much the same vein is another recent article, which appeared after the bulk of my work had been completed: Arnold S. Kaufman, "A Call to Radicalism: Where Shall Liberals Go?" *Dissent* (September–October 1966), pp. 555–624.

poverty will not be one of the key domestic issues for some time to come. However, the problem of poverty is cast into such sharp relief precisely because the nation as a whole is wealthy. Thus, while the politics of distribution cannot be divorced from the rest of our affairs, it must be seen in a new light—within a framework that is politically and intellectually new. The problems of an advanced industrial society cannot be solved by manipulating the ideological stereotypes of the 1930's.

There is much to be said for Organski's brilliant speculations about a move into a dramatically new stage of political development. Organski argues that nations may be expected to pass through a number of developmental phases, only three of which have yet been experienced by even the most politically advanced societies. These stages are the periods of primitive unification, industrialization, and national welfare. He suggests that America is now moving into a fourth stage, whose defining characteristic is economic abundance and whose onset is signaled by the growing importance of automation. Some of the possible political consequences of this development have already been discussed. It remains only to point out here the improbability that any such fundamental socioeconomic change could occur without corresponding changes in the way society is perceived and interpreted.

The gropings of American political thought in the period since World War II must be seen as an attempt to come to grips with the new social realities. If a comprehensive theory is the goal, then these efforts have clearly not been crowned by success. On the other hand, the more limited attempts at the reformulation of our understanding of man and society by some of the writers discussed in earlier chapters have been highly suggestive. At least, a beginning has been made toward an understanding of the intellectual dimensions of our problems. To expect more at this point would be to deny one of the main themes of this book; namely, that American political thought is entering a transitional period of potentially great significance.

In this connection the stirrings in the areas of foreign policy and civil rights are of special interest. As questions of the distribution of wealth decline in importance, these problems increasingly become the dominant issues of our politics. At the same time, it is also probable that these issues will lead to a more ideological politics. In contrast to the merely technical questions raised with respect to the relation of government to the economy now that the New Deal has been absorbed into the consensus, these issues suggest questions which, to repeat Drucker's words, are constitutional, moral, and aesthetic. These questions are almost without number. In a pluralistic society, what does equality mean? What consequences does it entail? Might the pursuit of equality impede the achievement of other highly valued social goals? Does racial equality require the dissolution of racial and other ethnic groupings, and hence a fundamental alteration in American social structure? These questions are only now being seriously discussed; answers are as yet almost nonexistent.

The questions raised by the international situation today are perhaps even more complex. What is the relation of international morality to the pursuit of the national interest? What is the place of the United States in a world capable of self-destruction? Indeed, is the nation-state system a viable form of international organization under present conditions? The search for answers to questions such as these will compel a reexamination of much of our thinking about international politics, just as the revolution in civil rights will force a rethinking of our domestic politics. These factors, coupled with rapid technological change, should have a great impact on our social thought.

Hints of the directions such a reexamination might take may perhaps best be found on the fringes of the ideological spectrum, particularly in the ideas of the New Left. This school has as yet produced little in the way of substantial theoretical analysis. In fact, like many more moderate groups, the New Left fears falling captive to a rigid ideological framework and has therefore consciously eschewed theory. Consequently, the movement is still of more interest to the political sociologist than to the political theorist. However, many of the liberal themes explored in this book—and interestingly some of the conservative themes too—have been casually pieced together to form a patchwork of ideas which might be called a protoideology. This body of ideas is ideological to the extent that it is critical of existing conditions in the light of certain largely implicit values. In this system of values a rather ill-defined commitment to equality is predominant. The nonideological aspect of the New Left may be observed in its failure to articulate and systematize these values or to develop a coherent program designed to implement them.

Nevertheless, the *materials* for a full-blown ideology are there: the critique of bureaucratic conformity, the antagonism to the centralization of political and economic power in the institutions of big government and big industry, an attack on the *quality* of life produced by a welfare-capitalist system, a denunciation of the hypocrisy of a presumably egalitarian nation which in fact denies meaningful equality to its most significant racial minority, criticism of the prevalence of poverty amid affluence, and militant discontent with a foreign policy regarded as unnecessarily dominated by considerations of the Cold War. These ideas are often inchoate, but they do encompass most of the real issues of contemporary politics. With the exception of the concern over poverty, it should also be clear that these ideas are notable for their emphasis on moral and aesthetic standards of judgment. In fact, even the attack on poverty clearly has strong moral overtones. Thus, essentially "qualitative" considerations may be said to predominate in the ideology of the New Left.

It is the prevalence of such moral concerns which suggests a new efflorescence of ideological politics.[3] This need not necessarily be a disturbing speculation, although it must be conceded that ideological politics may be dangerous to the stability of a political system either because conceptual oversimplification may lead to a serious misperception of social reality or because it may generate the fanaticism which often characterizes the "true believer." On the other hand, such unfortunate consequences are not necessary unless a needlessly pejorative definition of *ideology* is assumed. Indeed, ideologies may have certain positive functions, and failure to perform them can lead to a period marked by political sterility.

---

[3] It should be emphasized that the reference here is to elite behavior. At the mass level, political behavior is still shaped largely by nonideological concerns. See Robert E. Lane, "The Politics of Consensus in an Age of Affluence," *American Political Science Review* (December 1965), pp. 874–895, and Angus Campbell, *et al.*, *The American Voter* (New York: Wiley, 1960), pp. 188–215.

I have argued that, at least to an extent, American politics since 1945 can be evaluated in terms of these functions. If this is so, the renewal of ideological perspectives may help to forge anew a conception of the national purpose, or, to use another much-abused term, a vision of the public interest.

The process I am suggesting operates somewhat as follows. An ideology involves three things: a set of goals, an analysis of the contemporary scene in the light of these goals, and a program designed to achieve the posited ends within the limits imposed by the particular status quo. One major reef on which attempts to define the content of the public interest often founders is that the definitions advanced tend to be excessively abstract. In this context, the virtue of *ideology* as defined is that it has an empirical referent. It is thus not necessarily a form of airy speculation. Because it has empirical referents, an ideology can be subjected to a confrontation with fact. It is in this way that the conflict of ideologies may be of considerable social utility. Such conflict can help to clarify the nature of existing conditions and the likely consequences of the pursuit of certain values or the adoption of certain policies. Thus, for example, ideological conflict over civil rights may well force a clarification of values at the same time that it stimulates efforts to understand the realities of the present. Such debate will not solve the ultimate questions of political philosophy, but it should help in the formulation of viable public policy.

The essence of the position outlined here is clearly liberal in the classical sense of the word. It is based on the ultimate belief that "the truth will out" and that in the long run error will not triumph.[4] This argument may be excessively optimistic, but it is hard to conceive any other arrangements compatible with the demands of democratic theory.

It is necessary to discuss briefly one other question suggested by the foregoing analysis, although a full-scale treatment is beyond the scope of the present undertaking. This question is the suitability of the institutional framework of American politics for channeling the sort of conflict envisioned. Will a realignment of our party

---

[4] The classic statements of this position are John Milton's *Areopagitica* and John Stuart Mills' *On Liberty*.

system be required, to bring about a more sharply defined division between Democrats and Republicans? A large controversial literature has been devoted to this problem. The prevailing opinion is that such a realignment is unlikely to occur and that, if it did, the effects would be so profoundly divisive as to be a threat to political stability. In this view, our party system is what Herbert Agar has called *The Price of Union*. The proposition that such an event is unlikely is undoubtedly sound, and while there may be less confidence on the subject of potential divisiveness, here, too, the standard analysis has substantial support.

There is certainly no evidence to indicate that ideologically militant mass parties of the European variety are about to take root in American soil. However, this does not mean that the cleavage between the two parties may not become more pronounced. V. O. Key has suggested that the party system is subject to a cyclical dynamic; that is, one party introduces substantial new policy innovations which tend to polarize the system but which gradually are accepted by the opposition and thus absorbed into the consensus, so that the ideological gulf once again narrows. This cycle can be clearly seen in the movement of Republican thinking on the New Deal from outraged horror in the 1930's to more or less complete acceptance in the 1950's. It may be that programs of the New Frontier, the Great Society, the civil-rights movement, and the freedom movement will set this cycle in motion once again.

However, it must be noted that this process takes place within a fairly narrow consensus. Even at their most divided, the parties are likely to remain relatively close to the ideological center of the system. Really sharp ideological cleavage is most likely to occur outside the parties on the fringes of the consensus, or perhaps even beyond the limits of the consensus. Such controversy may in turn feed back into the party system, so that ideological or policy positions of the parties themselves are altered. This certainly is what happened as one consequence of the activities of the civil-rights movement.

A second possibility would be the creation of third-party movements upon a fairly narrow ideological base, also in the hope that such efforts would force changes in major-party positions. Such a development is not without precedent in American political history as the example of the Populist Party indicates. However, third parties have traditionally had a rather hard time of it in this country, and the road for a really extreme third-party movement would in all probability be very bumpy.[5]

It must also be emphasized that the amount of ideological polarization which a political system can successfully endure is not unlimited. While a number of recent studies tend to deprecate the necessity for a high level of consensus, there is little doubt that too sharp a division may be dysfunctional to the stability of the system. Thus, Lipset writes that while normally just the reverse is true, *under some circumstances* "a two-party system is *less* conducive to the preservation of a democratic order than is a multi-party system." A two-party system works best when class, race, political, social, and all other cleavages cut across one another, so that groups may be opposed on one issue but allied on another. This situation minimizes the possibility of a permanently disruptive polarization. In particular, it is necessary for each actor in a two-party system to accord legitimacy to the other. In other words, "each party must be willing to view the other as an acceptable alternative government."[6] In the present context, it is clear that if the American political system were to be polarized by the issue of race relations, for example, an extremely explosive situation could result. Thus, Bell and Lipset are certainly correct when they argue that the pursuit of chiliastic, ideologically determined ends can be disruptive of political and social stability.

The difficulty of the Bell-Lipset position does not lie here, but rather in the assumption that ideological conflict can take only this form. This conclusion seems unwarranted and thus, while overly sharp ideological cleavage may be disastrous, an overly rigid consensual structure may also lead to severe stress by penalizing dissenters and inducing the stagnation that stems from shutting off the flow of ideas.

---

[5] A possible exception to this generalization might be the fate of a candidate whose ideology included a commitment to racism coupled with support for social-welfare measures. For this suggestion I am indebted to a lecture by Seymour Martin Lipset.

[6] Seymour Martin Lipset, *The First New Nation* (New York: Basic Books, 1963), pp. 308–309.

With this point, I return to the main theme. American political thought has been living off its capital; the dominant ideas today are all too often merely extensions of those expressed thirty years ago. This is not to say that there have not been attempts to break through the "conventional wisdom." A number of such attempts have been discussed in this book. However, these attempts have been fragmentary and unsystematic. What is needed is the revival of *programmatic* thinking about American society and politics aimed at a reconstruction of the American consensus.

Two difficulties stand in the way of such a reconstruction. Paradoxically, one is the absence of a genuinely viable American conservatism. As writers since de Tocqueville have remarked, Americans live in an egalitarian democracy. Thus, the reformist-liberal ideology that has dominated much of the politics of the past thirty-five years is very much in tune with one of the dominant themes in American history.

However, at the same time that American liberals have come to dominate the making of public policy, they have begun to absorb a number of essentially conservative ideas. This phenomenon can be observed in the widespread liberal concern over the quality of life in a mass, egalitarian, industrial society as well as in the skepticism displayed with respect to proposals for substantial change. It is probably no accident that the rise of qualitative liberalism following World War II coincided with the appearance of the New Conservatism. This coincidence illustrates a deep-rooted need for the conservative values of order, stability, deference—particularly in the face of high cultural achievement—and, above all, the ability to resist pressures to conform to mass desires, particularly in the areas of civil rights and civil liberties.

Regrettably, the fate of the New Conservative movement indicates that these are difficult values to cultivate in an egalitarian society. The attempt to implant Burkean conservatism in American society has been an apparent failure, as indicated by the increasing domination of American conservatism by what is really a form of libertarian individualism. The failure to create an intellectually and politically viable traditionalist conservatism is a real loss, for the necessary dialogue about the future of our society would be greatly enhanced by a meaningful contribution from this corner. The halfhearted use by liberals of conservative ideas is a poor substitute at best.

The second major obstacle to the much-needed revivification of American political thought is the prevailing conception of the role of the intellectual. It is this role which is the basic issue in the end-of-ideology controversy. Bell, Lipset, and the others of this school have perceptively analyzed half of the problem. They have shown the dangers which may flow from the irresponsibility of intellectuals detached from power and unconcerned with the possible effects of their ideas. The emphasis is on a form of intellectual corruption which stems from political irresponsibility derived in turn from a failure to understand the practical and moral limitations of power. But the intellectual can also be irresponsible by refusing to act as a social critic and by failing to advance new programs for needed social change. Thus, there may be corruption in acquiescence as well as in revolt. Professors Bell and Lipset have tried heroically to avoid this pitfall. However, by assuming that the good society already exists in America and that only the solutions of certain essentially technical problems remain to be found, they leave the way open for lesser thinkers to fall into what C. Wright Mills has called the "celebration of the status quo."

The intellectual is by nature a critic. While it behooves him to criticize responsibly, he must at the same time avoid the temptation not to criticize at all. He must navigate between two extremes—between sloganeering and irresponsible criticism on the one hand, and the failure to attack that which deserves attack on the other. Too much contemporary social science has foundered on this second shoal.

Avoiding these pitfalls is important because there is much for the social scientist as intellectual to do. We live in a society that is doubly affluent; we are rich not only in material wealth but in destructive power. Vital groups within our society, as well as whole nations without, demand to share this affluence. The problems posed by these demands are immense. They cannot be solved by the ideas of thirty years ago. We need to reconsider the soundness of our basic values as we move into a new era in American history, to weigh our public policies in the light of those values, and to suggest programs that can help us to achieve our ends. As noted at the outset, the discipline of political science is peculiarly suited to this task. Such a role may generate no little controversy, but this should not bother us, for controversy is the lifeblood of a free society.

❦ BIBLIOGRAPHICAL NOTES ❦

In a real sense everything cited previously has contributed to this chapter. Hence only a few items are necessary. Richard Hofstadter, *The Paranoid Style in American Politics* (New York: Knopf, 1966), offers many insights into extremist politics in the United States, as does Daniel Bell, *The Radical Right* (Garden City, N.Y.: Doubleday, 1963).

The literature by and on the New Left is growing rapidly, although virtually nothing of a really scholarly nature has been done. For an introduction, see Jack Newfield, *A Prophetic Minority* (New York: Signet Books, 1967), and Paul Jacobs and Saul Landau, *The New Radicals* (New York: Random House, Vintage Books, 1966). See also Irving Howe, "New Styles in 'Leftism,'" *Dissent* (Summer 1965), pp. 295–323. This article is of interest in that it is a biting critique of the New Left by a writer who is sympathetic to many of its goals and who classifies himself as a "radical." In general, much may be found on the New Left in such magazines as *Dissent, Studies on the Left, New Politics*, and *Liberation*.

The literature on the American party system is vast. The classic case for more programmatic parties may be found in E. E. Schattschneider, *Party Government* (New York: Rinehart, 1942). The classic defense of American parties as they exist is E. Pendleton Herring, *The Politics of Democracy* (New York: Norton, 1940). See also Herbert Agar, *The Price of Union* (Boston: Houghton Mifflin, 1950). V. O. Key's analysis of the cyclical dynamics of the party system is in *Politics, Parties, and Pressure Groups* (5th ed.; New York: Crowell, 1964), pp. 222–227.

❧ INDEX ❧

225